XML
DATABASES
AND THE
SEMANTIC WEB

XML
DATABASES
AND THE
SEMANTIC WEB

BHAVANI
THURAISINGHAM

CRC Press
Taylor & Francis Group
Boca Raton London New York

CRC Press is an imprint of the
Taylor & Francis Group, an **informa** business

CRC Press
Taylor & Francis Group
6000 Broken Sound Parkway NW, Suite 300
Boca Raton, FL 33487-2742

First issued in paperback 2019

ISBN-13: 978-0-8493-1031-7 (hbk)
ISBN-13: 978-0-367-39624-4 (pbk)

Library of Congress Cataloging-in-Publication Data

Thuraisingham, Bhavani M.
    XML databases and the semantic web / Bhavani Thuraisingham.
      p. cm.
    Includes bibliographical references and index.
    ISBN 0-8493-1031-8 (alk. paper)
    1. Databases management. 2. XML (Document markup language) 3. Web site development. I. Title.

QA76.9.D3 T4583 2002
005.75′8—dc21

2002017488

Library of Congress Card Number 2002017488

Dedication

To my mentors:
Mr. Henry Bayard,
The MITRE Corporation;

Professor C. V. Ramamoorthy,
University of California, Berkeley;

and

Dr. Rick Steinheiser
Central Intelligence Agency;

and to all those who have helped me
in my work and career.

Preface

Developments in information systems technologies have resulted in computerizing many applications in various business areas. Data are critical resources in many organizations; therefore, efficiently accessing and sharing the data, extracting information from the data, and making use of the information have become urgent. As a result, many efforts on integrating the various data sources scattered across several sites and extracting information from these databases in the form of patterns and trends also have become important. These data sources may be databases managed by database management systems, or they could be data warehoused in a repository from multiple data sources.

The advent of the World Wide Web (WWW) in the mid-1990s has resulted in even greater demand for effectively managing data, information, and knowledge. So much data are now available on the Web that managing the information with conventional tools is becoming almost impossible. New tools and techniques are needed to handle these data. Therefore, to provide the interoperability as well as warehousing between the multiple data sources and systems, and to extract information from the databases and warehouses on the Web, various tools are being developed.

The focus of one of my previous books, *Web Data Management and Electronic Commerce,* was on managing the large quantities of data on the Web as well as on applying various data management techniques to a specific application: electronic commerce (e-commerce). That book was devoted to the emerging technology area called Web data management with special emphasis on e-commerce. In general, data management includes managing the databases, interoperability, migration, warehousing, and mining. For example, data on the Web have to be managed and mined to extract information, patterns, and trends. Data could be in files, relational databases, or other types such as multimedia databases. Data may be structured or unstructured.

Although, *Web Data Management and Electronic Commerce,* addressed numerous topics on Web data management at a high level, some critical technologies have emerged for Web data management. These are Extensible Markup Language (XML), semistructured databases, and the semantic Web. All these critical technologies now have a huge impact on electronic business (e-business), which is much more than e-commerce. Whereas my previous book covered many topics at a high level to give the reader an understanding of what the Web is about, this book focuses on some of the critical technologies needed for organizations to conduct transactions, and to exchange complex documents on the Web.

This book is divided into three parts. Part I describes supporting technologies for XML. XML is the language used to represent various documents on the Web. It essentially supports the uniform representation of documents. Without the WWW, it is highly unlikely that XML would have taken its current form. Therefore, I start with a discussion of the Web followed by an examination of managing data on the Web. Then I cover information retrieval. Note that XML evolved from the Hypertext Markup Language (HTML) as well as Standard Generalized Markup Language (SGML). An overview of both HTML and SGML are provided in Part I. I also provide some details on Web data management because the development of XML has been influenced by the developments on managing databases on the Web. Next I describe information technologies as well as information retrieval that are connected to XML in some way. These connections will be the subject of Part III. Part I also provides an overview of e-commerce and e-business. XML is a key technology for e-business whereas e-business has driven the advancement of XML. Finally, I briefly introduce XML and end Part I with a description of the issues on metadata and ontologies that are closely related to XML.

Part II describes XML, one of the most significant developments in information technology for the late 1990s. Is XML a data model, a metadata model, or something else? Although different views have been given about XML, it can be viewed as all these. Essentially, it specifies a format you can use to represent documents that can be universally understood. These could be documents of text, multimedia, relational data, and financial data. Finally, XML gives the means to specify features in a common way. Because the Web has millions of users, we need XML for document representations.

XML is a specification by the World Wide Web Consortium (W3C) for document representations. It initially was developed to represent text documents. Text documents could be memos, letters, and papers. XML is a semistructured format for data with interesting tags. Tags are defined by tagsets called document type definitions (DTDs). DTDs can be used to specify memos, letters, and other documents. XML is used only for specification. Its counterpart, Extensible Style Language (XSL) is used for presenting a document. Various application programming interfaces (APIs) are used for accessing XML content. Links between documents are provided by XML Link Language (Xlink), a form of hyperlinking. XML Pointer Language (Xpointer) is used to point within an XML document. XML evolved from HTML and SGML. SGML was developed before the Web and had too many unnecessary details. HTML was developed for the Web and had limitations. For example, HTML has a fixed set of markup tags, and these tags do not help in understanding the content. These tags are designed to help a browser know how to display the document. Consequently, the best search engines can index HTML documents based on items such as frequency of words. HTML cannot do one-to-many linking, extract pieces of text out of a document, and link to arbitrary portions of Web pages. These are just some of the deficiencies of HTML. XML attempts to overcome these deficiencies.

XML provides the facility for creating one's own set of markup tags. That is, a document can be defined the way you want it. As long the receiver's machine can understand XML tags, then the receiver can look at the document the way it was intended. One can think of XML as a metalanguage, or a language describing how to create one's markup language. By changing the tags, an XML document can take a completely different shape. XSL is used for creating one's own set of presentation rules; Xlink enables one-to-many linking and also enables bidirectional linking; and Xpointer enables one to point into a document without putting any anchor tags into it. Thus, XML, XSL, Xlink, and Xpointer are the essential components for document representation on the Web.

Various groups are proposing XML for representing documents such as financial securities, chemical structures, e-commerce information, and multimedia data. One specific area of interest to the data management community is a query language for XML (such as XMLQL). XMLQL is a declarative and relationally complete query language. A simple XMLQL query extracts data from an XML document. For example, a query could be to extract the author and title from an XML document. A more complex query can perform joins on contents in XML documents as well as other complex operations. Queries can also be nested. An XMLQL has associated with it a data model, which is usually a graphical model. Various proposals such as XMLQL have been submitted to W3C for query languages for XML, and W3C is standardizing a language called XML Query Language (Xquery).

One of the current limitations of XML is its inability to specify semantics. Some argue that it is not up to XML to specify semantics. Others argue that ontology work has to be integrated into XML. We can expect some resolution in the next few years. Ontology, which is an important aspect of metadata, is closely tied to XML. XML specifications are continually evolving like many standards. Therefore, I urge the reader to keep track of the developments in www.w3c.org. XML implementations may not conform entirely to the standards. Thus, users need to be aware of such issues before using an XML product.

A closely related topic to XML is the semantic Web. One often asks what the difference is between the Web and the semantic Web. Languages such as XML enable one to focus on the syntax of the documents. The Web has objects with complicated relationships. We need a way to specify all these relationships. Furthermore, the Web pages currently are for human consumption and manipulation. One needs the Web pages to be understood by machines. This is the idea behind the semantic Web. A semantic Web is not a single entity, but instead a collection of XML documents, semistructured databases, and millions of objects on the Web for which rich semantics need to be described. Furthermore, based on information on the Web, the machines and agents need to conduct actions and make decisions. Work on the semantic Web is just beginning, but we need to master this technology to conduct effective e-business.

Part II also describes semistructured databases that use XML to represent the documents. Since Codd [CODD70] published his article on the relational data model, considerable work has been conducted on developing various data models. These models mainly represent structured data. By structured data we mean data having a well-defined structure such as data represented by tables. In this example, each element belongs to a data type such as integer, string, real, or Boolean; however, with multimedia data, there is very little structure. Text data could be many characters with no structure. Images could be a collection of pixels. Video and audio data also have no structure, with no organized way to represent such multimedia data. This type of data has come to be known as unstructured data. It is nearly impossible to represent unstructured data. Therefore, to better represent such data, one introduces some structure. For example, text data could be represented as title, author, affiliation, and paragraphs. Such data are called semistructured data, which are not fully structured like relational structures but instead have partial structure.

During the past 5 years researchers have focused on developing models to represent semistructured data. Some of the early models were object based. Object-relational models were also being proposed for semistructured data. With the advent of the Web and W3C, however, there is much interest in developing models for text data. One of the most popular representation schemes is XML. Note that XML is not a data model, but instead it is a metamodel to represent various documents, such as memos, letters, books, and journal articles. In other words, XML defines the structure to represent such textual documents.

The approach taken to represent text data with XML is adopted to represent various types of data such as video, chemical structures, biological structures, financial securities information, and medical imagery. XML extensions are also being proposed for e-commerce. In a way, all these representations can be regarded as representations for semistructured data. Essentially, semistructured data models can be used as the global data models in the integration of structured data with, for example, text data or to directly represent semistructured databases. Some extensive research on semistructured databases has been conducted at Stanford University in the Lore project. Various other research efforts on semistructured databases have also been reported. With the advent of XML, we can expect research and practice of semistructured databases to grow tremendously. Part II ends with a discussion of semistructured databases.

Whereas Part I focuses on supporting technologies for XML, Part II discusses semistructured data, XML, and the semantic Web. Part III focuses on the implications of the critical technologies discussed in the previous parts to various applications including e-business and related areas. E-business is about conducting business on the Web such as buying and selling products as well as advertising products. XML may be used to specify e-business documents. Semistructured databases hold data for e-business activities. The semantic Web lays the foundations for e-business because millions of objects have to interact with each other to conduct effective e-business. As we make more progress on XML and related technologies, e-business will continue to expand and explode. Part III also discusses some other applications of XML including XML and databases; and XML and information technologies such as agents, multimedia, and wireless information management. Part III also examines some of the emerging standards and products. Part III ends with a discussion of building the semantic Web.

It should be noted that no method to build the semantic Web has yet been developed. Different groups claim that they have built some sort of semantic Web. I discuss some of the ideas on this topic. Although Part III mainly deals with XML applications, I include a discussion of building the semantic Web because it makes more sense to discuss it at the end of the book after describing the various technologies for XML, XML constructs and applications, and some concepts about the semantic Web.

This book also includes two appendices. Appendix A provides an overview of data management and a framework for data management. This shows where Web data management and XML fit into this framework. Appendix A also gives an overview of my previous books in data management and how they relate to each other. Because data management is key to many of the topics discussed in this book, Appendix B provides an overview of database systems and related technologies such as objects and security. An understanding of object models, in particular, helps with the understanding of XML.

Although my first four books, *Data Management Systems Evolution and Interoperation, Data Mining: Technologies, Techniques, Tools, and Trends, Web Data Management and Electronic Commerce,* and *Managing and Mining Multimedia Databases,* serve as excellent sources of reference to this book, this book is fairly self-contained. I have provided a reasonably comprehensive overview of the various background materials necessary to understand XML and the Web both in Part I and in the Appendices; however, some of the details on this background information, especially on data management and mining, and e-commerce and multimedia systems, can be found in my previous texts.

I have tried to obtain information on products and standards that are current. As repeatedly stressed in my other books, however, vendors and researchers are continually updating their systems so that the information valid today may not be accurate tomorrow. I urge the reader to contact the vendors and get up-to-date information. Many of the products are trademarks of various corporations. If I know or have heard of such trademarks, I have used italic letters for the product when first introduced in this publication. Again due to the rapidly changing nature of the computer industry, I encourage the reader to contact the vendors to obtain up-to-date information on trademarks and ownership of the various products.

I have tried my best to obtain references from books, journals, magazines, and conference and workshop proceedings. Although I tried not to give uniform resources locator (URLs) as references, I found that it was almost impossible to write a text about the Web without giving a few. URLs contain excellent reference material, but some of them may not be available even when this book goes into print. Therefore, I also encourage the reader to check the Web from time to time for current information on XML developments, prototypes, and products. A series, called the XML conference, is devoted to this topic and is held annually around the world. The W3C consortium also has been formed to develop various standards for the Web including XML. So much information exists and is changing so rapidly that I found it quite challenging to write this book.

I would like to stress to managers and executives that to be competitive one needs to maintain a Web site for an organization. This is an excellent way to create information sharing, however, managers should not rush into developing Web sites. They should think about the audience, what information to post, security issues, and ways that the organization would benefit the most before embarking on such a project. A Web site has to be maintained continually, requiring both manpower and funds. That is why understanding technologies such as XML, semistructured databases, and the semantic Web is critical for these managers.

I repeatedly use the terms *data, data management,* and *database systems* and *database management systems* in this text, with elaboration on these terms appearing in one of the appendices. I define data management systems as those that manage the data, extract meaningful information from the data, and make use of the resulting information. Therefore, data management systems include databases, data warehouses, and data mining. Data could be structured data such as those found in relational databases, or unstructured such as in text, voice, imagery, and video. Numerous discussions in the past distinguish between data, information, and knowledge. In my previous books on data management and mining, I did not attempt to clarify these terms. I simply stated that data could be just bits and bytes or could convey some meaningful information to the user.

However, with the Web and also with increasing interest in data, information, and knowledge management as separate areas, in this book I take a different approach to data, information, and knowledge by differentiating between these terms as much as possible. Data are some values such as numbers, integers, and strings. Information is obtained when some meaning or semantics is associated with the data such as "John's salary is $20K." Knowledge is something that you acquire through reading and learning. That is, data and information can be transferred into knowledge when uncertainty about the data and information is removed from someone's mind. It is rather difficult to give strict definitions of data, information, and knowledge. Sometimes, I use these terms interchangeably also. My framework for data management helps clarify some of the differences. Although I have chosen to use the term *Web data management* instead of *Web information management* or *Web knowledge management,* I discuss information and knowledge management technologies for the Web. To be consistent with the terminology in my previous books, I also distinguish between database systems and database management systems. A database management system is a component that manages the database containing persistent data. A database system consists of both the database and the database management system.

This book provides a fairly broad overview of XML and the semantic Web with an emphasis on data management. It is written mainly for technical managers and executives as well as for technologists interested in learning about the subject. The goal of this book is not to make the reader proficient in XML, but instead to provide the big picture about Web data management, XML, and their applications to e-commerce. Various people have approached me and asked questions about XML. Because of the complex way XML is presented in books, it is difficult to explain the concepts in a less complex way. Therefore, I decided to express the complicated ideas in a simplified manner and yet provide much of the information needed. This was also the reason for writing my previous books on data management, data mining, Web data management, and multimedia data management and mining. Like many areas in data management, unless someone has practical experience in conducting experiments and working with the various tools, it is difficult to have an appreciation of what is available and to go about developing Web sites. Therefore, I encourage readers, especially those who are interested in developing e-business solutions, to read the information in this book, to take advantage of the references mentioned, and to work with the XML and Web database products.

I have especially emphasized databases because effective management of data is critical for the Web. Again, the databases on the Web have to be integrated and users need timely access to the data. Therefore, representation, query, and integration schemas are needed for these databases. XML provides a solution for the common representation of documents. XML initially influenced the development of semi-structured databases and now is applied to numerous other databases. That is, XML and data management are closely related topics. Data management is also critical for the semantic Web. For the agents to understand the Web pages, we need to first provide good data.

The semantic Web, XML, and semistructured databases are still relatively new technologies and include many other technologies. Therefore, as the various technologies and integration of these technologies mature, we can expect to see progress in the semantic Web and consequently in e-business. We can anticipate access to relational databases and can also manage multimedia databases, warehouses, and mining tools on the Web. We also can expect rapid developments with respect to many of the ideas, concepts, and techniques discussed in this publication. The reader is urged to keep up with all the developments in this emerging and useful area of technology. This book is intended to provide a comprehensive view of the critical emerging technologies for the Web, in general, and XML, in particular. It is important to master these technologies to conduct effective e-business.

Acknowledgments

The views and conclusions expressed in this book are those of the author and do not reflect the views, policies, or procedures of the author's institution or sponsors. I thank my management for providing an environment where it is exciting and challenging to work; my professors and teachers for giving me the foundations upon which to build my skills; my sponsors, colleagues, and all others for supporting my education and my work, and especially those reviewing various portions of this book. I thank my late parents for supporting me in my early years. Finally, I thank the two most important people in my life: my husband Thevendra and my son Breman for giving me so much encouragement and inspiration.

Bhavani Thuraisingham, Ph.D.
Bedford, Massachusetts

The Author

Bhavani Thuraisingham, Ph.D., recipient of the Institute of Electrical and Electronics Engineers (IEEE) Computer Society prestigious 1997 Technical Achievement Award for her outstanding and innovative work in secure data management, is the Director of the Information and Data Management (IDM) program at the National Science Foundation (NSF). Since October 2001, she has been on Intergovernmental Personnel Act (IPA) from the MITRE Corporation to NSF. In this position she is responsible for funding research in information and data management technology and developing strategies for the advancement of this technology in the United States. She also collaborates with other major research funding organizations both in the United States and abroad to provide technical directions in information and data management. She is also involved in the NSF-EU semantic Web initiative and is providing research directions in this area.

Prior to her current position at NSF, she worked for MITRE Corporation, joining the firm in January 1989. Between May 1999 and October 2001, she was a chief scientist in data management at the MITRE Corporation Information Technology Directorate in Bedford, Massachusetts. In this position she provided technology directions in data, information, and knowledge management for the Information Technology Directorate of the MITRE Air Force Center. In addition, she was also an expert consultant in computer software to the MITRE work for the Internal Revenue Service. Her recent work focused on data mining as it relates to multimedia databases and database security, distributed object management with emphasis on real-time data management, and Web data management applications in e-commerce. She also served as adjunct professor of computer science at Boston University for 2 years and taught a course in advanced data management and data mining. As part of her IPA agreement with NSF, she works a day each week at MITRE, conducting research in data management.

Between June 1995 and May 1999, she was the department head in data management and object technology in the MITRE Information Technology Division in the Intelligence Center. In this position, she was responsible for the management of about 30 technical staff in four key areas: distributed databases, multimedia data management, data mining and knowledge management, and distributed objects and quality of service. Prior to that, she held various technical positions including lead, principal, and senior principal engineer; and was head of the MITRE research in Evolvable Interoperable Information Systems and Data Management, and co-director of the MITRE Database Specialty Group. She managed 15 research projects under the Massive Digital Data Systems effort for the intelligence community and was also a team member of the Advanced Warning and Control System (AWACS) modernization research project between 1993 and 1999. Before that, she led team efforts on the designs and prototypes of various secure database systems for government sponsors between 1989 and 1993.

Prior to joining MITRE, Dr. Thuraisingham worked in the computer industry between 1983 and 1989. She was first a senior programmer/analyst with Control Data Corporation for over 2 years, working on the design and development of the CDCNET product and later she was a principal research scientist with Honeywell Inc. for over 3 years, conducting research, development, and technology transfer activities. She was also an adjunct professor of computer science and a member of the graduate faculty at the University of Minnesota between 1984 and 1988. Prior to starting her industrial experience and after completing her Ph.D., she was a visiting faculty member first in the department of computer science, at the New Mexico Institute of Technology, and then at the department of mathematics at the University of Minnesota between 1980 and 1983. Dr. Thuraisingham has a B.Sc., M.Sc., M.S., and also received her Ph.D. degree from the United Kingdom at the age of 24. She is a senior member of the IEEE; and a member of the Association for Computing Machinery (ACM), British Computer Society, International Federation for Information Processing (IFIP) 11.3, and Armed Forces Communications Electronics Association (AFCEA). She has a certification in Java programming and has also completed a management development program. She is the recipient of the 2001 National Woman of Color Technology Research Leadership Award.

Dr. Thuraisingham has published over 400 technical papers and reports, including over 50 journal articles, and is the inventor of three U.S. patents for MITRE on database inference control. She has also served on the editorial boards of various journals, including *IEEE Transactions on Knowledge and Data Engineering, Journal of Computer Security,* and *Computer Standards and Interfaces Journal*; and currently serves on the technical committee in data management for IASTED. She gives tutorials in data management, including data mining, object databases, and Web databases; and has taught courses at both the MITRE Institute and the AFCEA Educational Foundation for several years.

She has chaired or co-chaired several conferences and workshops including the IFIP 1992 Database Security Conference, ACM 1993 Object Security Workshop, ACM 1994 Objects in Healthcare Information Systems Workshop, IEEE 1995 Multimedia Database Systems Workshop, IEEE 1996 Metadata Conference, AFCEA 1997 Federal Data Mining Symposium, IEEE 1998 COMPSAC Conference, IEEE 1999 WORDS Workshop, IFIP 2000 Database Security Conference, and IEEE 2001 ISADS Conference. She is a member of the Object Management Group (OMG) real-time special interest group, founded the Command Control Communications Computers Intelligence (C4I) special interest group, and has served on panels in data management and mining. She has edited several books and special journal issues and was the consulting editor of the *Data Management Handbook* series by CRC's Auerbach Publications for 1996 and 1997. She is the author of the books *Data Management Systems Evolution and Interoperation*; *Data Mining: Technologies, Techniques, Tools and Trends; Web Data Management and Electronic Commerce;* and *Managing and Mining Multimedia Databases* published by CRC Press.

Dr. Thuraisingham has given invited presentations at conferences including keynote addresses at the Second Pacific Asia Data Mining Conference 1998, the SAS Institute Data Mining Technology Conference 1999, IEEE Artificial Neural Networks Conference 1999, IEEE Tools in AI Conference 1999, and IFIP Integrity and Control Conference 2001. She has also delivered the featured addresses at the AFCEA Federal Database Colloquium from 1994 through 2001, and has also been a featured speaker at several object world conferences as well as the client–server world and data warehousing conferences. Her presentations are worldwide including in the United States, Canada, United Kingdom, France, Germany, Italy, Spain, Switzerland, Austria, Belgium, Sweden, Finland, Denmark, Norway, the Netherlands, Greece, Ireland, Egypt, South Africa, India, Hong Kong, Taiwan, Japan, Singapore, New Zealand, and Australia. She also gives seminars and lectures at various universities around the world including at the University of Cambridge in England and the Massachusetts Institute of Technology; and participates in panels at the NSF, the National Academy of Sciences, and the Air Force Scientific Advisory Board.

Table of Contents

Chapter 1   Introduction 1

1.1   Trends 1
1.2   Supporting Technologies for XML 2
1.3   XML Technologies 2
1.4   XML Applications 3
1.5   Organization of This Book 4
1.6   How to Proceed 7

Part I
Supporting Technologies for XML 9

Chapter 2   The World Wide Web and XML 11

2.1   Overview 11
2.2   Evolution of the Web 12
2.3   Corporate Information Infrastructures 14
2.4   Some Supporting Technologies for the Web 15
      2.4.1   Overview 15
      2.4.2   Role of Java for the Web and Data Management 15
      2.4.3   Digital Libraries 17
      2.4.4   Hypermedia Systems 21
      2.4.5   Review of HTML 23
2.5   Word Wide Web Consortium and XML 23
2.6   Summary 24

Chapter 3   Web Database Management and XML 25

3,1   Overview 25
3.2   Web Databases 26
      3.2.1   Overview 26
      3.2.2   Data Representation and Data Modeling 27
      3.2.3   Web Database Management Functions 27
      3.2.4   Semistructured Databases 30
3.3   Data Mining and the Web 30
      3.3.1   Overview 30
      3.3.2   Mining Data on the Web 32
      3.3.3   Mining Usage Patterns 36
      3.3.4   Applications and Directions 37

3.3.5 Security and Privacy Concerns 38
3.4 Architectural Aspects 40
    3.4.1 Overview 40
    3.4.2 Database Access 41
    3.4.3 Three-Tier Computing 42
    3.4.4 Interoperability 42
    3.4.5 Note on Migration..45
    3.4.6 Models of Communication 47
    3.4.7 Note on Federated Computing..50
3.5 Relationship to XML 50
3.6 Summary 52

Chapter 4   Information Retrieval Systems and XML 53

4.1 Overview 53
4.2 Text Retrieval 53
4.3 Image Retrieval 58
4.4 Video Retrieval 59
4.5 Audio Retrieval 64
4.6 Multimedia Data Types..67
4.7 Markup Languages and SGML 68
4.8 Relationship to XML 70
4.8 Summary 70

Chapter 5   Information Management Technologies and XML 71

5.1 Overview 71
5.2 Collaboration and Data Management 71
5.3 Multimedia Data Management 74
5.4 Knowledge Management 75
5.5 Decision Support..78
5.6 Agents for the Web 80
5.7 Some Other Information Technologies...85
    5.7.1 Overview 85
    5.7.2 Training and Distance Learning 86
    5.7.3 Visualization..87
    5.7.4 Quality-of-Service Aspects 89
    5.7.5 Wireless Information Management...89
    5.7.6 Some Directions...90
5.8 Relationship to XML 91
5.9 Summary 91

Chapter 6   E-Commerce and XML 93

6.1 Overview 93
6.2 E-Business and E-Commerce 93

6.3 Models for E-Commerce 97
6.4 Architectures or E-Commerce 99
6.5 E-Commerce Functions..103
6.6 Information Technologies for E-Commerce.................................104
6.7 Relationship to XML 105
6.8 Summary 106

Chapter 7 Metadata, Ontologies, and XML 109

7.1 Overview 109
7.2 Background on Metadata..109
7.3 Metadata for the Web...111
7.4 Mining and Metadata...111
7.5 Note on Ontologies 115
7.6 Relationship to XML 117
7.7 Summary 119

Conclusion to Part I 121

Part II
XML and the Semantic Web..123

Chapter 8 Basic Concepts in XML 125

8.1 Overview 125
8.2 Components of an XML Document...125
8.3 Containers, Elements, and Attributes 127
8.4 Namespaces..128
8.5 Data Types...129
8.6 Other Aspects 130
8.7 Summary 131

Chapter 9 Advanced Concepts in XML 133

9.1 Overview 133
9.2 Semantic Issues 133
9.3 Revisiting DTDs...135
9.4 Xlink and Other Constructs 136
9.5 XML Schemas...137
9.6 XMLQL..138
9.7 Data Integration Issues..139
9.8 Internationalization..140
9.9 Other Aspects 140
9.10 Summary 141

Chapter 10 The Semantic Web 143

10.1   Overview 143
10.2   Semantic Web Concepts.. 144
10.3   RDF.. 145
10.4   Revisiting Ontologies... 148
10.5   Agents and the DAML Program... 148
10.6   Semantic Web as a Database 149
10.7   XML, RDF, and Interoperability 150
10.8   Web vs. the Semantic Web 152
10.9   Summary 152

Chapter 11 Semistructured Databases 155

11.1   Overview 155
11.2   Architectures for Semistructured Databases.............................. 156
11.3   Data Models for Semistructured Databases 157
11.4   Functions of Semistructured Databases.................................... 161
        11.4.1   Overview 161
        11.4.2   Data Manipulation and Query Processing.................. 162
        11.4.3   Transaction Management 164
        11.4.4   Metadata Management... 164
        11.4.5   Storage Management... 164
        11.4.6   Data Distribution... 164
        11.4.7   Quality of Service 165
        11.4.8   Real-Time Processing 166
        11.4.9   User Interface... 166
        11.4.10 Maintaining Data Integrity and Security 166
11.5   Interoperability and Migration of Semistructured Databases 167
11.6   Revisiting XML 167
11.7   Some Developments... 167
11.8   Summary 169

Conclusion to Part II... 171

Part III
Applications of XML 173

Chapter 12 XML Applications to E-Commerce.. 175

12.1   Overview 175
12.2   Discussion of Applications 175
12.3   Some Related Efforts 178
        12.3.1   Overview 178

		12.3.2	ebXML	178
		12.3.3	RosettaNet	180
		12.3.4	Commerce One.Net	181
	12.4	Summary		181

Chapter 13 Applications of XML to Data Management 183

13.1	Overview	183
13.2	Metadata	183
13.3	Semistructured Databases	185
13.4	XML and Query Processing	186
13.5	Transaction Processing	187
13.6	Storage Management	187
13.7	Security, Integrity, and Fault Tolerance	188
13.8	Data Distribution	189
13.9	Interoperability and Migration	189
13.10	Data Warehousing and Mining	190
13.11	Architectures	191
13.12	Object Technology	193
13.13	Summary	193

Chapter 14 Applications of XML to Information Management 195

14.1	Overview	195
14.2	Multimedia and XML	195
14.3	Collaborative Computing and XML	196
14.4	Knowledge Management and XML	198
14.5	Decision Support and XML	199
14.6	Agents and XML	199
14.7	Wireless Computing	200
14.8	Other Information Technologies and XML	201
14.9	Summary	202

Chapter 15 XML-Related Data and Information Management Tools
for the Web 203

15.1	Overview	203
15.2	Web Database System Tools	204
15.3	Web Mining Tools	206
15.4	Web Application Server Tools	207
15.5	Web Knowledge Management Tools	207
15.6	Web Metadata and XML Tools	208
15.7	Other Web Information Management Tools	209
15.8	Breakthrough Standards, Tools, and Services	210
	15.8.1 Overview	210
	15.8.2 SOAP	210

15.8.3 WSDL...210
15.8.4 UDDI..211
15.8.5 DOTNET 211
15.8.6 J2EE 211
15.9   Summary 212

Chapter 16 Building the Semantic Web 213

16.1   Overview 213
16.2   Revisiting Web vs. the Semantic Web.................................213
16.3   Incremental Evolution and Architectural Aspects...............214
16.4   Data and Information Management Aspects 216
16.5   Interoperability Issues, XML, and RDF...............................217
16.6   Web Services...219
16.7   Putting It Together 220
16.8   Summary 221

Conclusion to Part III 223

Chapter 17 Summary and Directions 225

17.1   About This Chapter...225
17.2   Summary of This Book...225
17.3   Challenges and Directions for XML, Databases, and the
        Semantic Web..229
        17.3.1 Overview 229
        17.3.2 Challenges and Directions for Web Data Management.............229
        17.3.3 Challenges and Directions for E-Commerce..............231
        17.3.4 Challenges and Directions for XML and the Semantic Web 232
17.4   Where to Go from Here..232

References 235

Appendix A Data Management Systems: Developments and Trends 239

A.1   Overview 239
A.2   Developments in Database Systems 240
A.3   Status, Vision, and Issues..245
A.4   Data Management Systems Framework 245
A.5   Building Information Systems from the Framework 248
A.6   Relationship between the Texts 250
A.7   Summary 251
A.8   References 252

Appendix B Database Systems and Related Technologies 255

B.1   Overview 255
B.2   Relational and Entity-Relationship Data Models 256
    B.2.1   Overview 256
    B.2.2   Relational Data Model 256
    B.2.3   Entity-Relationship Data Model 257
B.3   Architectural Issues 258
B.4   Database Design 259
B.5   Database Administration 260
B.6   Database Management System Functions 261
    B.6.1   Overview 261
    B.6.2   Query Processing 262
    B.6.3   Transaction Management 262
    B.6.4   Storage Management 263
    B.6.5   Metadata Management 265
    B.6.6   Database Integrity 265
    B.6.7   Database Security 266
    B.6.8   Fault Tolerance 267
B.7   Distributed Databases 267
B.8   Heterogeneous Database Integration 269
B.9   Federated Databases 270
B.10 Client–Server Databases 272
B.11 Migrating Legacy Databases and Applications 274
B.12 Data Warehousing 275
B.13 Data Mining 277
    B.13.1 Overview 277
    B.13.2 Data Mining Technologies 278
    B.13.3 Concepts and Techniques for Data Mining 279
    B.13.4 Directions and Trends for Data Mining 281
B.14 Object Technology 282
    B.14.1 Overview 282
    B.14.2 Object Data Model 282
    B.14.3 Other Object Technologies 285
B.15 Summary 286
B.16 References 287

Index 291

1 Introduction

1.1 TRENDS

Developments in information systems technologies have resulted in computerizing many applications in various business areas. Data are critical resources in many organizations; and therefore, efficiently accessing and sharing the data, extracting information from the data, and making use of the information have become urgent. As a result, many efforts on integrating the various data sources scattered across several sites and extracting information from these databases in the form of patterns and trends also have become important. These data sources may be databases managed by database management systems, or they could be data warehoused in a repository from multiple data sources.

The advent of the World Wide Web (WWW) in the mid-1990s has resulted in even greater demand for effectively managing data, information, and knowledge. So much data are now available on the Web that managing the information with conventional tools is becoming almost impossible. New tools and techniques are needed to handle these data. Therefore, to provide the interoperability as well as warehousing between the multiple data sources and systems, and to extract information from the databases and warehouses on the Web, various tools are being developed.

The focus of one of my previous books was on managing the large quantities of data on the Web as well as on applying various data management techniques to a specific application: electronic commerce (e-commerce). That book was devoted to the emerging technology area called Web data management with special emphasis on e-commerce. In general, data management includes managing the databases, interoperability, migration, warehousing, and mining. For example, data on the Web have to be managed and mined to extract information, patterns, and trends. Data could be in files, relational databases, or other types such as multimedia databases. Data may be structured or unstructured.

Although my previous book addressed numerous topics on Web data management at a high level, some critical technologies have emerged for Web data management. These are Extensible Markup Language (XML), semistructured databases, and the semantic Web. All these critical technologies now have a huge impact on electronic business (e-business), which is much more than e-commerce. Whereas my previous book covered many topics at a high level to give the reader an understanding of what the Web is about, this book focuses on some of the critical technologies needed for organizations to conduct transactions, to understand effective use, and to exchange complex documents on the Web.

The organization of this chapter is as follows: I discuss supporting technologies for Extensible Markup Language (XML) in Section 1.2. Key points on XML and the semantic Web are the topics of Section 1.3. Applications of XML to data management, e-business, and other areas are covered in Section 1.4. (Topics in Sections 1.2 to 1.4, are further examined in the remaining chapters of Part I and in Parts II and III of this book.) The organization of this publication is the subject of Section 1.5. Put all together, I describe a framework for XML and applications that gives some context to the various XML and related data management technologies. Parts 1, II, and III deal with layers 1, 2, and 3 of the framework, respectively. Finally, this chapter is summarized in Section 1.6, which also includes a discussion of directions.

1.2 SUPPORTING TECHNOLOGIES FOR XML

Various supporting technologies exist for the Web, some of which I discuss. First, one needs an understanding of the Web. It is very likely that without the Web we would not have XML. Therefore, Web technologies, in general, are supporting technologies for XML. Another key supporting technology is that of database systems. The Web has considerable data, some stored in files and some in databases. These data have to be managed effectively. Therefore, query processing, transaction management, storage management, and metadata management all play key roles in Web data management.

Another technology that is becoming critical for XML is information retrieval. Information retrieval systems are essentially document management systems. In addition to text retrieval, we also need to provide support for managing images audio and video databases. Metadata and ontologies also play a role in XML. Essentially, metadata descriptions as well as ontologies, which are critical for information management, can be encoded in XML.

Information management includes multimedia data management, knowledge management, collaboration, and agents, all of which are supporting technologies for XML. XML has an impact on multimedia databases as well as collaborative technologies and knowledge management. Finally, e-commerce is key to XML. That is, e-commerce documents are encoded in XML and are gaining much popularity for business-to-business (B-to-B) transactions.

Figure 1.1 illustrates these supporting XML technologies, called the basic technologies. One can build on them to develop the XML technologies. The other chapters in Part I discuss the supporting technologies in more detail. XML technologies are given more detailed considerations in Part II, although I introduce them in Section 1.3. Applications of XML technologies are introduced in Section 1.4 and Part III elaborates on these technologies.

1.3 XML TECHNOLOGIES

The previous section discussed supporting technologies, in general, for XML. In particular, the Web, Web database systems, and information retrieval systems are discussed. This section elaborates on the various XML technologies, which are at the heart of this book. Essentially, XML specifies a format you can use to represent

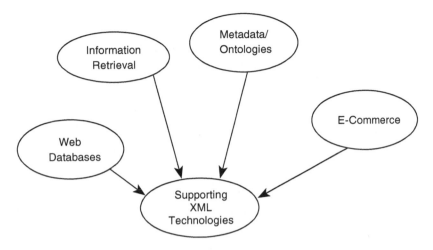

FIGURE 1.1 Supporting XML technologies.

documents that can be universally understood. These could be documents of text, multimedia, relational data, and financial data. Finally, XML give the means to specify features in a common way. Because the Web has millions of users, we need XML for document representations.

Part II elaborates on XML. I first start with a discussion of basic concepts in XML including what XML is about, namespaces, and some syntax. Next I discuss advanced XML concepts such as XML and schemas, and then the semantic Web. I end Part II with a discussion of semistructured databases. By XML technologies, I mean the key information to understand XML. The other sections of this book provide the big picture and set Web data management, XML, and other technologies in place. It is not my goal to make the reader prolific in XML, but to explain the complex ideas in a simple manner.

The semantic Web was a term coined by Tim Berners Lee, the father of the Web. Others like James Hendler have advanced this concept through programs such as Defense Advanced Research Projects Agency (DARPA) Agents Markup Language (DAML). Perhaps one of the best articles on this topic is by Berners Lee [LEE01].

Semistructured data management deals with data models, query strategies, and storage methods for managing data that are partially structured. Initially, XML began as a document representation scheme for semistructured databases. Therefore, I include a discussion of such databases in this book. Contents of Part II are illustrated in Figure 1.2.

1.4 XML APPLICATIONS

Now that I have briefly described the various technologies for the XML, the main concerns are the applications that benefit from XML. The Web has been the single most important development for XML. We hear about training and collaboration on the Web, entertainment on the Web, and lookup service on the Web. These amount to e-commerce, perhaps the single most important activity that has resulted from

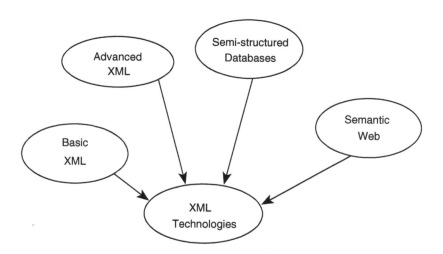

FIGURE 1.2 XML technologies.

the Web. Therefore, with the relationships between XML and the Web and between the Web and e-commerce, a significant application for XML is e-commerce.

E-commerce generally is an activity that is used to conduct business on the Web. Once we had electronic mail (e-mail) and electronic communication facilities, one of the important developments was electronic data interchange (EDI). However, with the advent of the Web, e-commerce is overtaking EDI. Almost any business can be conducted on the Web. The Web can be used to set up Web pages that give out information about you and your company. The Web can also be used to purchase and market your products, and to provide entertainment and training. In many cases one distinguishes between e-commerce and e-business. Whereas e-commerce is conducting transactions, e-business is conducting any business on the Web.

Other key application areas for XML include database systems and information management. Various prototypes and products are also emerging for XML. Therefore, in Part III of this book I discuss various applications relating to XML, including e-commerce and e-business; database management; information management; and prototypes, products, and standards (Figure 1.3).

1.5 ORGANIZATION OF THIS BOOK

This book covers the essential topics in XML in three parts: supporting technologies such as Web data management and information technologies, key XML technologies such as the semantic Web, and XML applications in areas such as data management and e-business. To explain my ideas more clearly, I illustrate an XML framework in Figure 1.4. This framework has three layers: (1) the supporting XML technologies layer, describing the various supporting technologies that contribute to XML (including the Web, Web data management, information retrieval, metadata, information management, and e-commerce); (2) the XML technologies layer, describing the various

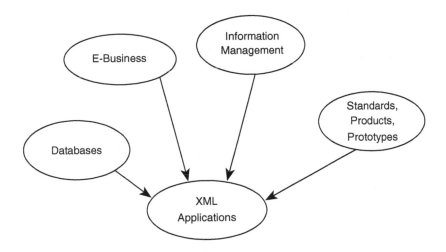

FIGURE 1.3 XML applications.

concepts in XML and the semantic Web; and (3) the XML applications layer, describing XML applications in databases, e-business, agents, multimedia, and other information management technologies. Each layer is described in a part of this book. Part I, consisting of six chapters, describes the various supporting technologies. Chapter 2 describes the Web. Chapter 3 covers Web data management. Chapter 4 discusses information retrieval technologies. Chapter 5 focuses on information management technologies. Chapter 6 discusses e-commerce. Finally, Chapter 7 bridges the gap between Parts I and II and discusses metadata and ontologies. It also introduces the key concepts in XML. Each of these chapters ends with the relevant relationship to XML, because XML is my main focus.

Part II, consisting of four chapters, addresses XML technologies. Chapter 8 is on basic XML concepts. Chapter 9 describes advanced XML concepts. Chapter 10 examines the semantic Web. One type of database system that has pushed the development of XML is semistructured databases. Therefore, Chapter 11 addresses semistructured databases. Chapters 8 to 11 explain at a high level what XML is. I give numerous references that a reader can obtain for a more detailed discussion of XML and related technologies.

Whereas Parts I and II address XML and supporting technologies, Part III addresses the applications of XML. It consists of five chapters. XML and e-business are the subjects of Chapter 12. Chapter 13 provides an overview of XML for databases. XML for other information technologies is the subject of Chapter 14. XML standards and products are discussed in Chapter 15. Finally, Chapter 16 provides some directions for building the semantic Web. The concept of the semantic Web is vague. One cannot say what constitutes the Web and what constitutes the semantic Web. In fact, some argue that there should be no difference between the two. The semantic Web today may not be the semantic Web tomorrow. In any case, I distinguish between what a Web and a semantic Web are today and discuss some issues

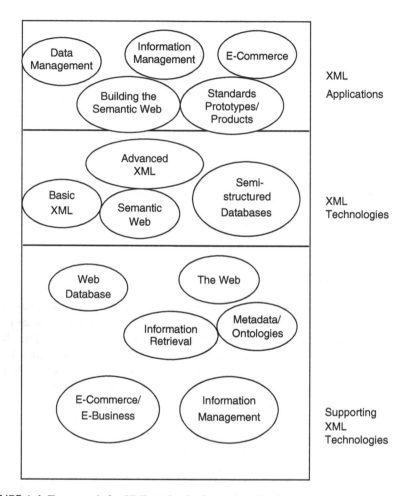

FIGURE 1.4 Framework for XML technologies and applications.

for building the latter. Although this does not fit entirely within the theme of Part III, the applications of XML, I revisit semantic Web issues after I describe concepts, technologies, and applications of XML.

Figure 1.5 illustrates the chapters in which the components of the framework in Figure 1.4 are addressed in this book. I summarize the book and provide a discussion of challenges and directions in Chapter 17. Chapters 2 through 16 start with an overview and end with a summary. Each part begins with an introduction and the last chapter in each part gives a conclusion. Finally, I give two appendices that provide useful background information. Appendix A provides an overview of trends in data management technology, and Appendix B provides an overview of the developments and trends in database systems. We can expect to hear a lot about XML in the future. This text includes a fairly comprehensive list of references in the section on references, obtained from various journals, conference and workshop proceedings, and magazines. In addition, each appendix has its own set of references.

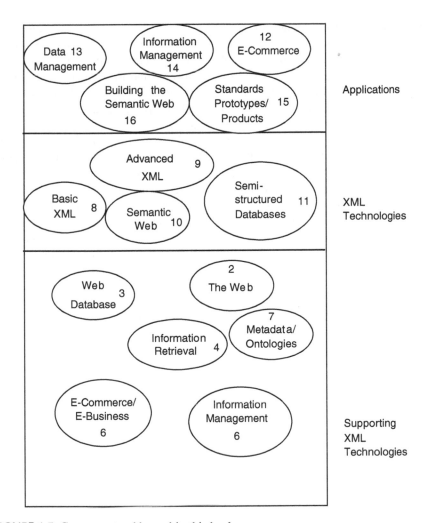

FIGURE 1.5 Components addressed in this book.

1.6 HOW TO PROCEED

This chapter provides an introduction to XML, including a brief overview of the supporting technologies for XML. XML technologies are described next. Finally, applications of XML are discussed. Parts I, II, and III of this book elaborate on Sections 1.2, 1.3, and 1.4, respectively. The organization of this book, as detailed in Section 1.5, also includes a framework for organization purposes. The framework has three layers with each layer addressed.

The text provides information for a reader to become familiar with XML. The purpose is not to give a tutorial on XML but some idea of what Web data management is. For an in-depth understanding of the various topics covered, the reader should consult various references given in this book. Numerous papers and articles have appeared on Web data management and related areas. Many of these are referenced throughout this publication. Some of the interesting discussions have been published in the proceedings of the World Wide Web (WWW) conference series. The World Wide Web consortium (W3C) has also been responsible for tremendous advances on the Web and in XML. The uniform resources locator (URL) for this consortium is www.w3c.org. Major programs such as DAML [DAML] are also developing technologies to make the goals of the semantic Web a reality.

Although I have tried to provide as much information a possible in this text, there is much more to write about XML. Daily, we hear about XML in various magazines and on the Web. It is not my intention to educate the reader of all the details about XML, but instead to provide the big picture and to explain, especially to technical managers, where XML stands in the larger scheme of things. I do provide several references that can help the reader in understanding the details of XML. My advice to the reader is to keep up with the developments, discern what is important and what is not, and be knowledgeable about this subject. This information helps people not only in their business lives but also in their personal lives such as with personal investments and other activities.

Various XML-related conferences and workshops are held. For further details, refer to [VLDB], [ICDE], [WWW], [KDD], and [SIGM]. For background information, refer to my previous books, for example, [THUR97], [THUR98], [THUR00], and [THUR01].

Part I

Supporting Technologies for XML

Part I, consisting of six chapters, describes supporting technologies for XML and the semantic Web. Chapter 2 describes the Web and its evolution. Topics such as Hypertext Markup Language (HTML) are also included. Chapter 3 provides an overview of Web database systems technology and discusses various aspects such as architectures, models, and functions. Chapter 4 discusses information retrieval systems including text, image, and video. Chapter 5 gives an overview of information management technologies such as collaboration, multimedia, and training. Chapter 6 provides an overview of electronic business (e-business) and electronic commerce (e-commerce). XML exploded for two major reasons: Web data management and e-commerce. Chapter 7 describes metadata and ontologies and lays the foundations for Part II, in which essential XML concepts are the focus.

Although Chapters 2 through 7 focus on supporting technologies for the Web, such as data and information management, keep the relationship to XML in mind in examining these technologies. (See Part III for further elaboration on the relationship.) The technology discussed in each chapter is related to XML.

Supporting Technologies
for XML

2 The World Wide Web and XML

2.1 OVERVIEW

The World Wide Web (WWW) is one of the major forces behind the development of XML. Therefore, it is reasonable to start this book with a discussion of the evolution of the Web and the origins of XML.

The developments of the Internet have been key to the development of the WWW. The Internet started as a research project funded by the U.S. Department of Defense. Much of the work was conducted in the 1970s. At that time, numerous developments with networking occurred. We began to see various networking protocols and products emerge. In addition, standards groups such as International Standards Organization (ISO) proposed a layered stack of protocols for networking. The Internet research resulted in Transmission Control Protocol and Internet Protocol (TCP/IP) for transport communication.

While networking concepts were advancing rapidly, data management technology emerged in the 1970s. Then in the 1980s, the early ideas of Bush [Bush 45] for organizing and structuring information in the 1940s started getting computerized. These ideas led to the development of hypermedia technologies. In the 1980s, researchers thought that these hypermedia technologies would result in efficient access to large quantities of information such as library systems. It was not until the early 1990s that researchers at Couseil Européan pour la Recherche Nucléaire, or the European Organization for Nuclear Research (CERN), in Switzerland combined Internet and hypermedia technologies, which resulted in the WWW. The idea is for the various Web servers scattered within and across corporations to be connected through intranets and the Internet so that people from all over the world could have access to the right information at the right time. The advancement of various data and information management technologies contributed to the rapid growth of the WWW. This text comprehensively covers various data and information management technologies for the Web and the application of these technologies such as electronic commerce (e-commerce).

This chapter describes the WWW, because without the Web, I believe that XML would probably not have been conceived. Section 2.2 provides an overview of the evolution of the Web. Section 2.3 discusses how corporations are taking advantage of the Web. Some fundamental technologies for the Web are the subject of Section 2.4. In particular, the role of Java, hypermedia technologies, and an overview of Hypertext Markup Language (HTML) are discussed. XML evolved from HTML and Standard Generalized Markup Language (SGML) (see Chapter 4). A note on the WWW consortium as well as origins of XML is the subject of Section 2.5. The chapter is summarized in Section 2.6.

2.2 EVOLUTION OF THE WEB

Although different people have been credited as the "Father of the Web," one of its early pioneers was Timothy Berners Lee who was with CERN at the inception of the WWW. He now heads the World Wide Web consortium (W3C). This consortium specifies standards for the Web including data models, query languages, and security.

Soon after the WWW emerged, in about 1993 or 1994 a group of graduate students at the University of Illinois developed a browser, which was called Mosaic. A company called Netscape Communications then marketed Mosaic. Since then, various browsers as well as search engines have appeared. These search engines, the browsers, and the servers all now constitute the WWW. The Internet has become the transport medium for communication.

Various protocols for communication, such as Hypertext Transfer Protocol (HTTP), and languages for creating Web pages, such as HTML, also emerged. Perhaps one of the significant developments is the Java programming language by Sun Microsystems. The work is now being continued by Javasoft, a subsidiary of Sun. Java is a language that is very much like C++ but avoids all the disadvantages of C++ such as pointers. Java was developed as a programming language to be run platform independent. It was soon found that this was an ideal language for the Web. Now various Java applications are used as well as what is known as Java applets. Applets are Java programs residing in a machine and can be called by a Web page running on a separate machine. Therefore, applets can be embedded into Web pages to perform all kinds of features. Of course, additional security restrictions exist because applets could come from untrusted machines. Another concept is a servlet. Servlets run on Web servers and perform specific functions such as delivering Web pages for a user request. Applets and servlets are elaborated on later in this chapter.

Middleware for the Web is continuing to evolve. If the entire environment is Java, that is, connecting Java clients to Java servers, then one can use Remote Method Invocation (RMI) by Javasoft. If the platform consists of heterogeneous clients and servers, then one can use the Object Management Group (OMG) Common Object Request Broker Architecture (CORBA) for interoperability. Some argue that client–server technology will be dead because of the Web. That is, one may need different computing paradigms such as the federated computing model for the Web (see Part II).

Other developments for the Web are components and frameworks. We discuss some of them in the chapter on objects (see Chapter 5). Technology such as Enterprise Java Beans (EJBs) is becoming very popular for componentizing various Web applications. These applications are managed by what is now known as application servers. These servers (such as the BEA's Web Logic) communicate with database management systems through data servers, which may be developed by database vendors such as Object Design Inc. Finally, one of the latest technologies for integrating various applications and systems possibly heterogeneous through the Web is Jini. It essentially encompasses Java and Remote Method Invocation (RMI) as its basic elements. (Some of these technologies are also addressed in Part II.)

The Web is continuing to expand and explode. So much data, information, and knowledge are on the Web that managing all these is becoming critical. Web information

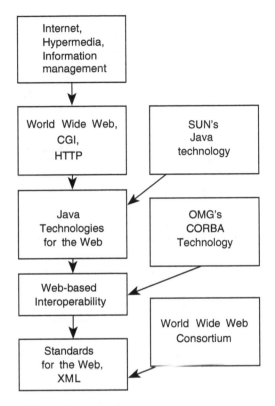

FIGURE 2.1 World Wide Web.

management is all about developing technologies for managing this information. One particular type of information system is the database system. (For some details on Web database management, technologies, and information management, see Part II; for an overview of e-commerce, the new way of doing business on the Web, and a discussion of the applications of Web information management to e-commerce see Part III. Figure 2.1 illustrates some of the Web concepts discussed in this chapter.

One of the major problems with the Internet is information overload. Because humans can now access large amounts of information very rapidly, they can quickly become overloaded with information and, in some cases, the information may not be useful to them. In certain other cases, the information may even be harmful to the humans. The current search engines, although improving steadily, still give the users too much information. When a user types in an index word, many irrelevant Web pages are also retrieved. What we need is intelligent search engines. The technologies that are discussed in this chapter, if implemented successfully, would prevent this information overload problem. For example, agents may filter out information so that users get only the relevant information. Data mining technology could extract meaningful information from the data sources. Security technology could prevent users from getting information that they are not authorized to know.

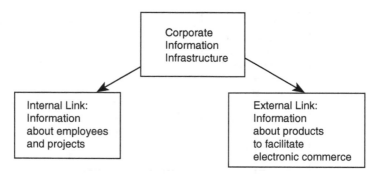

FIGURE 2.2 Corporate information infrastructure.

In addition to computer scientists, researchers in psychology, sociology, and other disciplines are also involved in examining various aspects of Internet database management. We need people in multiple disciplines to collaboratively work together to make the Internet a useful tool for human beings. One of the emerging goals of Web technology is to provide appropriate support for data dissemination. This deals with getting the right data or information at the right time to the analyst or user (directly to the desktop if possible) to assist in conducting various functions.

2.3 CORPORATE INFORMATION INFRASTRUCTURES

After the advent of the Web, there was a national initiative called the National Information Infrastructure (NII) to develop technologies for the Web. Subsequently, organizations such as the United States Department of Defense started initiatives including the Defense Information Infrastructure (DII). Corporations soon began developing their own information infrastructures.

The various corporate information infrastructures usually have two main components. One is for internal use and built on intranets, and the other is for external use and built usually on the Internet. Major security differences exist between internal infrastructures and external infrastructures for a corporation. The external infrastructures have to go beyond the corporation firewall (i.e., the security perimeter). Figure 2.2 illustrates both types of infrastructures for a corporation. The internal infrastructure may contain information about the employees, the projects, and other pertinent information such as corporate news. The external infrastructure has information that a corporation wants to make public. This includes product announcements, links to other organizations, and any information that would facilitate e-commerce.

These corporate information infrastructures are key to the development and prominence of an organization. Over the past 3 to 4 years, almost every major corporation in the world, especially in the developed countries, has its information infrastructure. We can expect more corporations to go online in the future.

2.4 SOME SUPPORTING TECHNOLOGIES FOR THE WEB

2.4.1 OVERVIEW

This section provides some supporting technologies for the Web. Although some aspects of data management are covered, many of the details on Web data management are the subject of Chapter 3. The information presented in this chapter is not directly related to Web data management and XML, but it is useful for understanding the concepts before examining Web data management. The reason for focusing on Web data management is that the developments of XML have been influenced quite a bit by Web data management.

Section 2.4.2 discusses the role of Java for the Web as well as for Web data management. Digital library technologies are described in Section 2.4.3. Digital libraries have been used interchangeably with Web data management; however, digital libraries encompass not only Web data management but also technologies for managing the information effectively on the Web. Finally, Section 2.4.4 covers hypermedia technologies. These technologies are an essential part of Web browsers. HTML is reviewed in Section 2.4.5.

2.4.2 ROLE OF JAVA FOR THE WEB AND DATA MANAGEMENT

Various aspects of Java technology are discussed in the previous section. I elaborate on them again because Java and the Web go hand in hand. Javasoft, a subsidiary of Sun Microsystems Inc., has developed a breakthrough product called Java.* Java is a programming language that was designed to overcome some of the limitations and problems with C++ such as dealing with pointers. Java was originally intended for embedded computing. This language has become one of the breakthrough products in computer science. Although systems can be coded in Java, it was soon found that Internet-based programming is facilitated a great deal with Java. Various programs can be written in Java and are called Java applets. These Java applets are incorporated into HTML programs.** When the HTML programs are executed in an Internet browser environment, the embedded applets are executed. One could then download various Java applets and embed them into HTML programs. These applets, when executed, may solve specific problems. Several such applets are now available on the Internet. Executing applets on the Internet is illustrated in Figure 2.3.

As discussed earlier, other developments with Java technology include the notion of servlets. Servlets are similar to applets except that they execute in the server environment and the results are brought to the client. This way, the client does not have to be concerned with applets coming from untrusted sources. EJBs that are

---

* Information on Java can be found in various Web pages and text. An excellent reference is [JAVA].
** Note that HTML is the language used for Internet programming. That is, Web pages are written in HTML. These programs are executed through various browsers. Not all browsers can handle Java applets. However, we expect an increase in the number of browsers that handle Java applets.

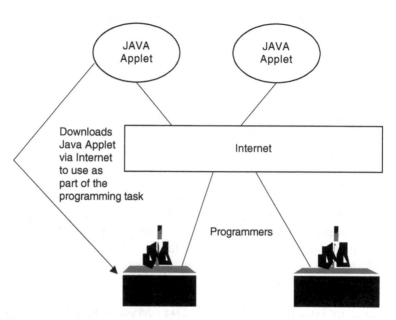

FIGURE 2.3 Java programming over the Internet.

components based on Java, RMI for communication between Java clients and servers, and finally JINI technology for integrating various heterogeneous embedded systems and applications are also emerging Java technologies. Many articles and books have been published about various aspects of Java technology (see, e.g., [CACM99]).

Of interest to the data management community is accessing various database management systems from Java applications. Because more applications are now being written in Java, we need to embed Structured Query Language (SQL) calls into Java programs to access relational database management systems. In the same way, to access object-oriented database management systems, we need to embed SQL calls into Java programs. A standard called Java Database Connectivity (JDBC) has been developed for database access for Java programs. Clients and database servers build interfaces compliant with JDBC. An example approach to communication through JDBC is illustrated in Figure 2.4. In many cases JDBC code may be implemented on top of Open Database Connectivity (ODBC; see, e.g., [ODBC]). That is, ODBC server drivers may lie between the JDBC server code and the actual servers. A high-level view of such a scenario is illustrated in Figure 2.5.

The role of Java in Internet database management has been briefly discussed. Standards such as JDBC have been proposed just recently. We can expect to see major advances in this area in the near future. Although we can expect the number of Java-based application programs to increase by a significant amount, we can also expect more database management systems (i.e., the servers) to be programmed in Java. For a discussion of JDBC, refer to [JDBC].

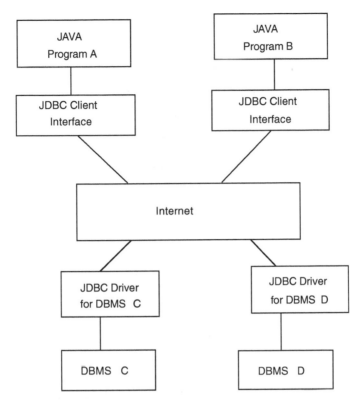

FIGURE 2.4 DBMS access through JDBC.

2.4.3 DIGITAL LIBRARIES

Digital libraries are essentially digitized information distributed across several sites. The goal is for users to access this information in a transparent manner. The information could contain multimedia data such as voice, text, video, and images. The information could also be stored in structured databases such as relational and object-oriented databases. Sometimes digital libraries have also been called Web databases or Internet databases. Closely related to Web data management are digital libraries and Internet database management.*

Major national initiatives are under way to develop digital library technologies. The agencies funding digital library work include the National Science Foundation (NSF), the Defense Advanced Research Projects Agency (DARPA), and the National Aeronautical and Space Administration (NASA) [NSF95]. In addition, numerous

---

* Note that the terms *digital libraries* as well as *Internet* and *Web database management* are used interchangeably. Many of the issues for digital libraries are present for Internet database management. The Internet began as a research effort funded by the U.S. Government. It is now the most widely used network in the world.

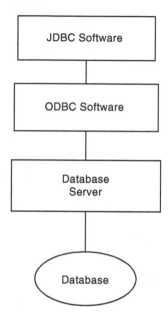

FIGURE 2.5 ODBC and JDBC connection.

projects are funded by organizations, such as the Library of Congress, for developing digital library technologies (see, e.g., [ACM95]). Various conferences and workshops devoted entirely to digital libraries have also been established (see, e.g., [DIGI95]).

Various technologies have to be integrated to develop digital libraries. Some of the important ones are data mining, multimedia database management, and heterogeneous database integration. Other important information management technologies include agents, hypermedia, distributed object management, knowledge management, and mass storage. Figure 2.6 illustrates the various digital library technologies.

Integration of these technologies is a major challenge. Appropriate Internet access protocols first have to be developed. In addition, interface definition languages play major roles in the interoperability of different systems. Because of the large amount of data, integration of mass storage with data management is critical. Data mining is needed to extract information from the databases. Multimedia technology combined with hypermedia technology is necessary for browsing multimedia data. Distributed object management plays a major role, especially because the number of data sources to be integrated may be large.

An example of a digital library is illustrated in Figure 2.7. The idea is that a certain number of sites are participating in this library. In theory, the library could also have an unlimited number of users, however, many organizations want to share the data among a certain number of groups.

The information in the form of servers, databases, and tools belongs to the library. The participating sites could place this information or it could be placed by

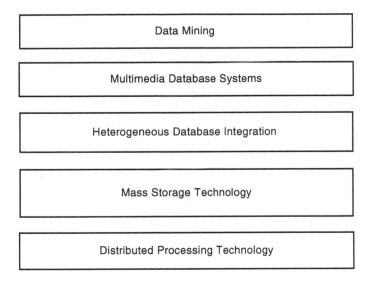

FIGURE 2.6 Some technologies for digital libraries.

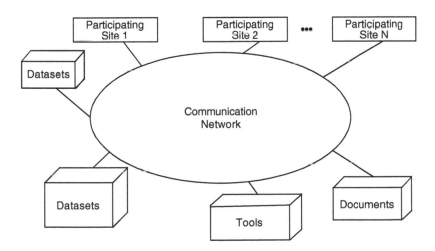

FIGURE 2.7 Digital library example.

someone who is designated to maintain the library. Users then query and access the information in the library.

Figure 2.8 illustrates the use of agents to maintain the library. These agents locate resources for users, maintain the resources, and even filter out information so those users only get the information they want. Agents are essentially intelligent processes. They may communicate with each other in conducting a specific task. The role of agents in query processing for digital libraries is illustrated in Figure 2.9.

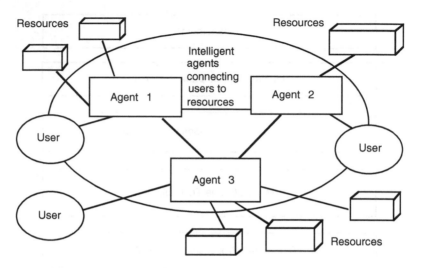

FIGURE 2.8 Agents for locating resources.

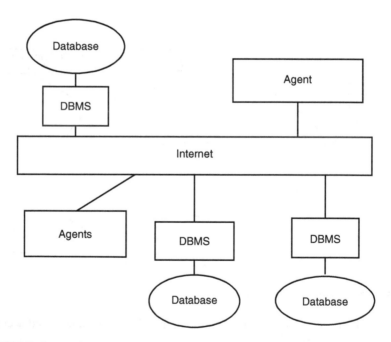

FIGURE 2.9 Agents for query processing.

One can also take advantage of the digital library technology for collaborative work environments. As illustrated in Figure 2.10, suppose an organization wants to develop some technology such as integrating heterogeneous databases. The representatives of the firm access the WWW and find out the names of other organizations

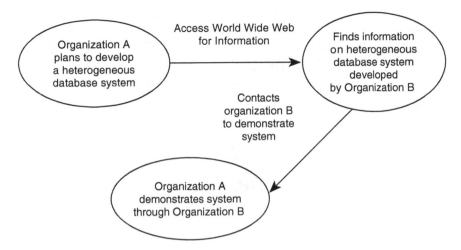

FIGURE 2.10 Collaboration through the Internet.

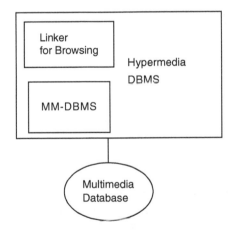

FIGURE 2.11 Hypermedia database management system.

that already have developed such systems. They may like what is said about the system developed by organization B. They contact organization B and get a demonstration of the system through the Internet.

2.4.4 HYPERMEDIA SYSTEMS

For the completion of the general aspects that support Web data management, I discuss hypermedia technologies. As illustrated in Figure 2.11, a hypermedia database management system includes both a multimedia database management system (MM-DBMS) and a linker. The linker is the component of a hypermedia database system that facilitates browsing of various data sources. For example, by following

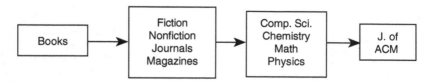

FIGURE 2.12 Linking various topics.

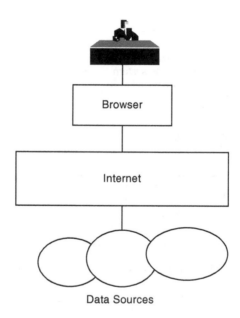

Data Sources

FIGURE 2.13 Browsing on the Internet.

links, it is possible for users to go through large amounts of information in a short space of time. An example of linking various data sources is illustrated in Figure 2.12. With the emergence of the Internet, many are familiar with the various browsers that are now available. The relationships among the user, the browser, and the Internet are illustrated in Figure 2.13.

Although significant developments have been made, it is still very difficult for the users to manage these large quantities of data. With current browsers one can go from one topic to another by following links. One can also get quite lost in what has been called cyberspace. Very quickly, the whole task of browsing can become quite overwhelming. Needed are intelligent browsers that help the users to determine where they are, and how they can backtrack in a meaningful way. Agents can play a major role in intelligent browsing. In addition, appropriate metadata management techniques are also critical. Metadata may include information about the various data sources as well as dynamic information such as the current status of various users browsing the data sources.

2.4.5 REVIEW OF **HTML**

HTML (Hypertext Markup Language) consists of a collection of tags. This language is used to generate Web pages. Tags are enclosed in brackets and are case sensitive. An example of a tag follows:

```
<tag>...</tag>,
```

where <tag> is the beginning and </tag> is the end. An example of an HTML document is as follows:

```
<HTML> ...
<HEAD> ...
<TITLE>Document Title</TITLE> ...
</HEAD> ...
<BODY> ...
</BODY> ...
</HTML> ...
```

The preceding document can generate an empty Web page with no content. The document starts with the statement HTML followed by HEAD, TITLE of document, and BODY, which is the content. In this example we have four sets of tags, HTML, HEAD, TITLE, and BODY. Note that there is a lot of syntax that needs to be studied to understand HTML. For a short introduction to HTML, refer to [HTML]. Numerous books have also been written on this subject. Remember that XML evolved from HTML and SGML. SGML is briefly discussed in Chapter 5. For further details on HTML, refer to [HTML].

2.5 WORLD WIDE WEB CONSORTIUM AND XML

The World Wide Web Consortium (W3C) consists of several members including corporations such as Microsoft and Oracle. W3C was formed in 1996 to establish standards for the Web. It has rapidly evolved into one of the most prominent consortiums. Because of the tremendous interest about the WWW, this consortium is expected to remain for many more years.

W3C consists of many working groups promoting standards for different aspects of information management. The activities of the consortium can be found in www.w3c.org. The standards developed include those for security, data modeling, metadata, query language, and interoperability. This consortium links to other organizations such as the OMG. Figure 2.14 illustrates the various technical activities of W3C.

One of the notable developments of W3C is XML, which is rapidly becoming the standard document exchange language. It is a metalanguage for describing a document, which can then be interchanged on the Web without any ambiguity. It promotes interoperability. Since the inception of XML, various groups are developing XML standards for different applications such as chemical, financial, and medical

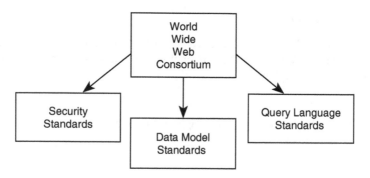

FIGURE 2.14 W3C activities.

as well as for technologies such as multimedia and e-commerce. For example, financial groups are specifying XML domain-type definitions (DTDs) for financial documents, which include information about securities. Those working in the financial fields across states, countries, and continents can then understand such documents. Many are convinced that XML will soon become the global language for the Web. It will be used not only to exchange documents but also to integrate heterogeneous databases and information sources on the Web. (For more details on XML, see Part II).

2.6 SUMMARY

This chapter provides an overview of the WWW. It starts with a discussion of the evolution of the Web and then discusses how corporations are taking advantage of the Web. Then some supporting technologies for the Web including Java, hypermedia, and HTML are mentioned. Finally, the chapter provides an overview of W3C and the origins of XML. That is, the previous sections describe the evolution of the Web and some of the main ideas behind it. The remaining parts of this book describe XML, in particular, the supporting technologies for XML such as data management and information retrieval, details of XML, and applications of XML to various areas including e-business.

The next five chapters in this part discuss various data and information management technologies for the Web and XML. This establishes the foundations for the remaining chapters of the text, which focus on XML, databases, the semantic Web, e-commerce, and their relationships with one another.

3 Web Database Management and XML

3.1 OVERVIEW

As mentioned in Chapter 1, Part I describes various key supporting technologies for XML and the Web. I provided an overview of the Web in Chapter 2. This chapter describes another major supporting technology for XML: Web data management. That is, managing databases on the Web has had a major impact on the development of XML.

As mentioned in Chapter 2, loosely related to Web data management are digital libraries and Internet database management. Digital libraries are essentially digitized information distributed across several sites. The goal is for users to access this information in a transparent manner. The information could contain multimedia data such as voice, text, video, and images. The information could also be stored in structured databases such as relational and object-oriented databases. I also discuss digital libraries in Chapter 2. Sometimes, the terms *digital libraries, Web databases,* and *Internet databases* are used interchangeably.

The explosion of the users on the Internet and the increasing number of World Wide Web (WWW) servers are rapidly advancing Web data management. Users can access the various information sources across the Internet. There is no single technology for Web data management. It is a combination of many technologies including heterogeneous database management, query management, intelligent agents and mediators, and data mining. For example, the heterogeneous information sources have to be integrated so that users access the servers in a transparent and timely manner. Security and privacy are becoming major concerns for Web data management, as are other issues such as copyright protection and ownership of the data. Policies and procedures have to be set up to address these issues.

Figure 3.1 illustrates the developments in data management technology for the Web. Database management system vendors are now building interfaces to the Internet. Query languages like Structured Query Language (SQL) are embedded into Internet access languages. In the example of Figure 3.1, database management system (DBMS) vendors A and B make their data available to applications C and D. DBMS vendors are also developing interfaces to the Java programming environment (see Section 3.3). This all means that heterogeneous databases are integrated through the Internet.

This chapter provides an overview of Web data management functions. In particular, models, functions, and architectural aspects relating to Web data management are discussed. Key aspects of Web data management is the subject of Section 3.2, in particular, database representation, such as data modeling, database system functions for Web data management, and semistructured databases. Note that semistructured databases are discussed in Part II. Data mining on the Web is the subject of

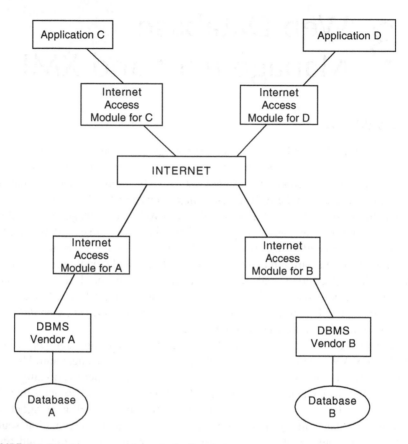

FIGURE 3.1 Database access through the Internet.

Section 3.3. Note that Web data mining is an aspect of Web data management. Much of the remainder of the chapter is devoted to various dimensions of architectures. Section 3.4 focuses on architectures for data management on the Web, particularly, database access and three-tier computing. In addition, Section 3.4 covers interoperability and migration issues and discussions of models of communications on the Web, such as the publish and subscribe models, the impact of client–server computing on the Web, and a note on federated computing. Finally, the relationships to the contents of this chapter and XML are discussed in Section 3.5. (In Part III of this book, I take many of the issues discussed in this chapter and then examine the impact of XML in more detail.) The chapter is summarized in Section 3.6.

3.2 WEB DATABASES

3.2.1 OVERVIEW

This section discusses the core concepts in Web data management. As stated earlier, many of the developments of XML have been influenced by the management of databases on the Web. One of my earlier books was devoted mainly to Web data management and its application to electronic commerce (e-commerce). This section summarizes some of the discussions.

In Section 3.2.2, I discuss data modeling aspects. Database functions are addressed in Section 3.2.3. Finally, special types of databases that integrate text with structured data, called semistructured databases, are discussed in Section 3.2.4. (Note that semistructured databases are covered in Part II. Also, topics such as data mining, security, and interoperability are also addressed in different sections of this chapter.

3.2.2 DATA REPRESENTATION AND DATA MODELING

A major challenge for Web data management researchers and practitioners is coming up with an appropriate data representation scheme. The concern is whether there is a need for a standard data model for digital libraries and Internet database access. Is it at all possible to develop such a standard? If so, what are the relationships between the standard model and the individual models used by the databases on the Web?

Back in 1996, when we gave presentations at various conferences on data representation for Web databases, many felt that it would be impossible to come up with a standard notation. Some even felt that because relational representation was popular, one might need some form of relational notation and SQL-like language to access the various data sources on the Web. There were also discussions on variations of an object model for the Web. Representation schemes such as Uniform Modeling Language (UML) (see, e.g., [FOWL97]) were emerging, and it was thought that perhaps such schemes would be popular for Web data modeling. At that time, various data representation schemes such as Generalized Markup Language (SGML), Hypertext Markup Language (HTML), and Office Document Architecture (ODA) were examined (see, e.g., [ACM96]). The question was whether they are sufficient or another representation scheme is needed.

The significant development for Web data modeling came in the latter part of 1996 when the World Wide Web Consortium (W3C) was formed. This group believed that Web data modeling was an important area and began addressing the data modeling aspects. Then sometime around 1997, interest in XML began through an effort of the W3C. XML is not a data model. It is a metalanguage for representing documents. The idea is that if documents are represented using XML, then these documents can be uniformly represented and therefore exchanged on the Web. Since 1998, one of the significant developments for the Web is XML. Currently, numerous groups are working on XML and proposing extensions to XML for different applications. (I revisit XML in Part II.) Figure 3.2 illustrates the evolution of data model discussion for Web databases.

3.2.3 WEB DATABASE MANAGEMENT FUNCTIONS

Examples of database management functions for the Web include query processing, metadata management, security, and integrity. In [THUR96a], I have examined various database management system functions and discussed the impact of Internet database access on these functions. Some of these issues are discussed in this text.

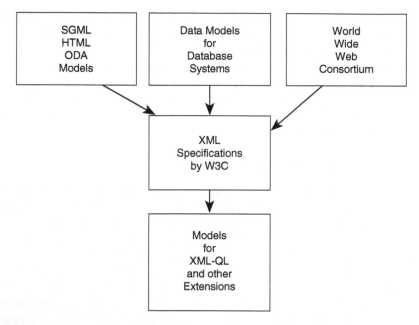

FIGURE 3.2 Data modeling for the Web.

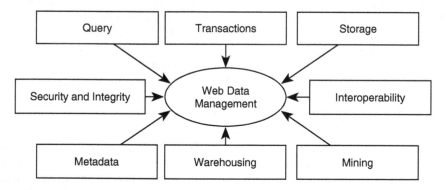

FIGURE 3.3 Web database functions.

Figure 3.3 illustrates the functions. Querying and browsing are two of the key functions. An appropriate query language first is needed. Because SQL is a popular language, appropriate extensions to SQL may be desired. XML Query Language (XMLQL), to be discussed later, is moving in this direction. Query processing involves developing a cost model. Are there special cost models for Internet database management? With respect to browsing operation, the query processing techniques have to be integrated with techniques for following links. Hypermedia technology has to be integrated with database management technology.

Updating digital libraries could mean different things. One could create a new Web site, place servers at that site, and update the data managed by the servers. The concern is whether a user of the library can send information to update the data at a Web site. The issue is security privilege. If users have write privileges, then they could update the databases that they are authorized to modify. Agents and mediators could be used to locate the databases and to process the update.

Transaction management is essential for many applications. There may be new kinds of transactions on the Internet. For example, various items may be sold through the Internet. In this case, the item should not be locked immediately when a potential buyer makes a bid. It has to be left open until several bids are received and the item is sold. That is, special transaction models are needed. Appropriate concurrency control and recovery techniques have to be developed for the transaction models.

Metadata management is a major concern for digital libraries. What are metadata? Metadata describe all the information pertaining to the library. This could include the various Web sites, types of users, access control issues, and policies enforced. Where should the metadata be located? Should each participating site maintain its own metadata? Should the metadata be replicated or should there be a centralized metadata repository? Metadata in such an environment could be very dynamic, especially because the users and the Web sites may be changing continuously.

Storage management for Internet database access is a complex function. Appropriate index strategies and access methods for handling multimedia data are needed. In addition, due to the large volumes of data, techniques for integrating database management technology with mass storage technology are also needed.

Security and privacy are major challenges. Once you put the data at a site, who owns the data? If users copy the data from a site, can they distribute the data? Can they use the information in papers that they are writing? Who owns the copyright to the original data? What role do digital signatures play? Mechanisms for copyright protection and plagiarism detection are needed. In addition, some of the issues discussed in [THUR97] on handling heterogeneous security policies will be of concern.*

Maintaining the integrity of the data is critical. Because the data may originate from multiple sources around the world, it will be difficult to keep tabs on the accuracy of the data. Data quality maintenance techniques need to be developed for digital libraries and Internet database access. For example, special tagging mechanisms may be needed to determine the quality of the data.

Other data management functions include integrating heterogeneous databases, managing multimedia data, and mining. Integrating various data sources is the subject of Section 3.4. when I address interoperability. Managing multimedia data are addressed in Chapter 5, with mining discussed in Section 3.3. Some of the other functions addressed in this chapter, such as data representation and metadata, are revisited in Chapter 7 and in Parts II and III of this book.

---

* Also, there have been many discussions on the notion of a "firewall" to protect the internal information from external users. I do not address firewall issues in this chapter. For more details, I refer the reader to [FIRE] and [CHES94].

3.2.4 Semistructured Databases

Since Codd published his paper on the relational data model [CODD70], a lot of work has been completed to develop various data models. These models mainly represent structured data. Structured data means data that has a well-defined structure such as data represented by tables, with each element belonging to a data type such as integer, string, real, or Boolean.

However, with multimedia data, there is very little structure. Text data could be many characters with no structure. Images could be a collection of pixels. Video and audio data also have no structure, or no organized way to represent such multimedia data. These types of data have come to be known as unstructured data.

It is nearly impossible to represent unstructured data. Therefore, to better represent such data, one introduces some structure. For example, text data could be represented as title, author, affiliation, and paragraphs. Such data are called semistructured data, or data that are not fully structured like relational structures, but they have partial structure.

During the past 5 years or so, researchers have focused on developing models to represent semistructured data. Some of the early models were object based. Object-relational models were also being proposed for semistructured data. With the advent of the Web and W3C, however, there is much interest in developing models for text data. One of the most popular representation schemes is XML. Note that XML is not a data model, but instead is a metamodel to represent various documents. Documents such as memos, letters, books, and journal articles are represented with XML. In other words, XML defines the structure to represent such textual documents. (I revisit XML later in Part II because it is the heart of this book.)

The approach taken to represent text data with XML is adopted to represent various types of data such as video, chemical structures, financial securities information, and medical imagery. XML extensions are also proposed for e-commerce. In a way, all these representations can be regarded to be representations for semistructured data. Semistructured data models can be used as the global data models in the integration of structured data with, for example, text data as shown in Figure 3.4, or they can be used to directly represent semistructured databases as shown in Figure 3.5. Some extensive research on semistructured databases has been conducted at Stanford University in the Lore project [WIDO98]. Various other research efforts on semistructured databases have also been reported [IEEE98]). With the advent of XML, we can expect the research and practice of semistructured databases to grow tremendously.

3.3 DATA MINING AND THE WEB

3.3.1 Overview

With information overload on the Web, it is highly desirable to mine the data and extract patterns and relevant information for the user, making the task of browsing on the Internet so much easier. Therefore, there has been a lot of interest in mining the Web, which is also now called Web mining. This is basically mining the databases

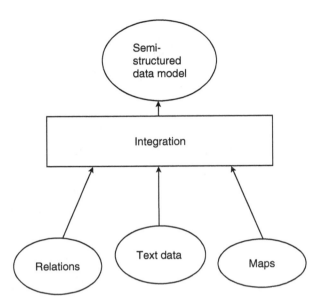

FIGURE 3.4 Integration of structured and semistructured data.

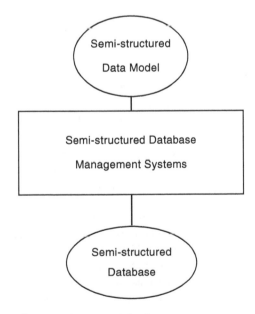

FIGURE 3.5 Representing a semistructured database.

on the Web or mining the usage patterns so that helpful information can be provided to the user.

Data mining and the Web developed as independent technology areas in the mid-1990s. Although it was believed that mining the data on the Web would be useful

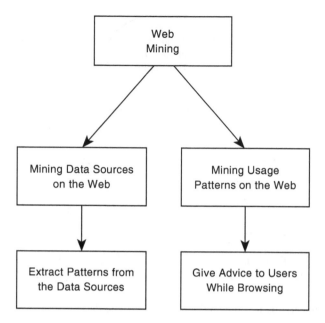

FIGURE 3.6 Taxonomy for Web mining.

to help the information overload problem, the extent to which Web mining would help key areas such as e-commerce was not well understood until recently. It was only about a year or two ago that researchers and practitioners seriously started to think about Web mining. The Web-mining workshop held during the Knowledge Discovery in Databases Conference in 1999 was one of the first [WDM99]. Initial work on Web mining was not implemented until the Web-mining panel at the International Conference on Tools in Artificial Intelligence Conference in November 1997 [ICTA97].

Cooley [COOL98] has specified a taxonomy for Web mining, by dividing it into two categories. One is to mine and get patterns from the Web data. The other is to mine the uniform resources locators (URLs) and other Web links to help the user with various Web activities. Figure 3.6 illustrates this taxonomy. Closely related to Web usage mining is mining to support e-commerce. The two aspects of it are to mine and get information about competitors; and to mine usage patterns, get customer profiles, and conduct targeted marketing. The organization of this chapter is as follows: data mining on the Web is the subject of Section 3.3.2, Web usage mining is described in Section 3.3.3; applications and directions are given in Section 3.3.4; and security and privacy concerns are addressed in Section 3.3.5.

3.3.2 MINING DATA ON THE WEB

Mining the data on the Web is one of the major challenges faced by the data management and mining community as well as those working on Web information management and machine learning. So much data and information on the Web make extracting the useful and relevant information for the user the real challenge. When

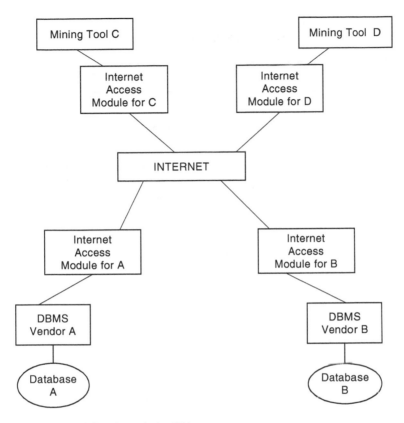

FIGURE 3.7 Data mining through the Web.

users scan through the Web, it becomes quite daunting, and soon they become overloaded with data. The problem is how to convert these data into information and subsequently knowledge so that users only get what they want. Furthermore, what are the ways of extracting information previously unknown from the data on the Web? This section covers various aspects of Web mining.

One simple solution is to integrate the data mining tools with the data on the Web. This is illustrated in Figure 3.7. This approach works well, especially if the data are in relational databases. Therefore, one needs to mine the data in the relational databases with the data mining tools that are available. These data mining tools have to develop interfaces to the Web. For example, if a relational interface is provided as in the Junglee system (see, e.g., [JUNG98]), then SQL-based mining tools can be applied to the virtual relational database as illustrated in Figure 3.8.

Unfortunately, the Web world is not as straightforward. Much of the data are unstructured and semistructured, and a lot of imagery data and video data exist. Providing a relational interface to all such databases may be complicated. The problem is how to mine such data. In Chapter 4, I discuss various aspects to mining multimedia data. In particular, I focus on mining text, images, video, and audio data. One needs to develop tools first to mine multimedia data and then to focus on developing tools to mine such data on the Web. I illustrate a scenario for multimedia mining on

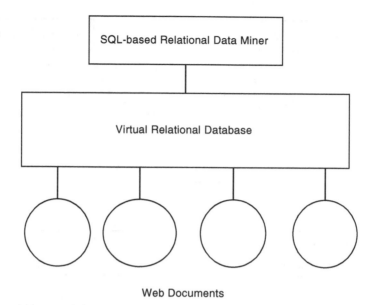

FIGURE 3.8 Web mining on virtual relational databases.

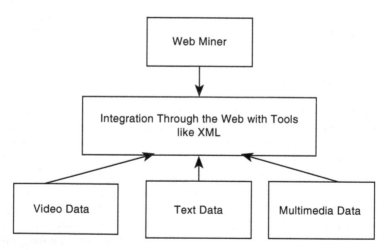

FIGURE 3.9 Multimedia Web mining.

the Web in Figure 3.9 where multimedia databases are first integrated and then mined. Much of the previous discussion has focused on integrating data mining tools with the databases on the Web. In many cases, the data on the Web are not in databases, but on various servers. Therefore, the challenge is to organize the data on these servers. Some form of data warehousing technology may be needed here to organize the data to be mined. A scenario is illustrated in Figure 3.10. Some work is underway on developing some sort of data warehousing technology for the Web to facilitate mining.

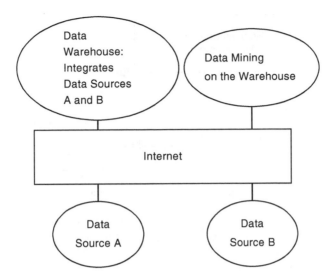

FIGURE 3.10 Data warehousing and mining on the Internet.

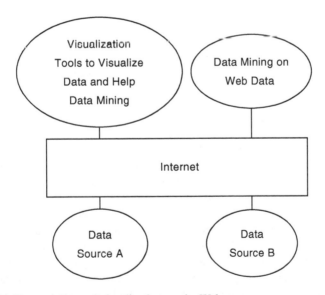

FIGURE 3.11 Data mining and visualization on the Web.

Another area that really needs attention is visualization of the data on the Web [THUR96b]. Much of the data are unorganized and difficult for the user to understand. Furthermore, as discussed in [THUR98], mining is greatly facilitated by visualization. Therefore, developing appropriate visualization tools for the Web greatly facilitates mining the data. These visualization tools could aid in the mining process as illustrated in Figure 3.11.

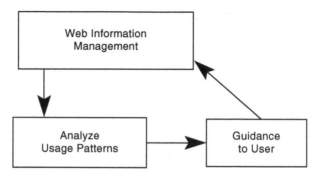

FIGURE 3.12 Analyzing usage patterns and predicting trends.

Various standards have been developed by organizations such as the International Standards Organization (ISO), W3C, and Object Management Group (OMG) for Internet data access and management. These include models, specification languages, and architectures. One of the developments is XML for writing what is called a document-type definition (DTD) that allows the document to be interpreted by the person receiving it (see, e.g., [XML1] and [XML2]). Relationships between data mining and standards such as XML are largely unexplored, however, one could expect data mining languages to be developed for the Web.

In summary, several technologies have to work together to effectively mine the data on the Web. These include data mining on multimedia data, mining tools to predict trends and activities, technologies for data management, data warehousing, and visualization. Active research in Web mining is under way and we can expect to see much progress in this area.

3.3.3 Mining Usage Patterns

Another aspect to mining on the Web is to collect various statistics and determine which Web pages are likely to be accessed based on various usage patterns. Research in this direction is being conducted by various groups including by Morey [MORE98a]. Based on usage patterns of various users, trends and predictions are made as to the likely Web pages a user may want to scan. Therefore, based on this information, users can have guidance as to the Web pages they may want to browse, as illustrated in Figure 3.12. This facilitates the work a user has to do with respect to scanning various Web pages. Note that whereas the previous paragraphs in this section focus on developing data mining tools to mine the data on the Web, this section focuses on using mining to help with the Web browsing process. Many results are expected in this area.

Mining can also be used to give only selective information to the user. For example, many of us are flooded with electronic mail (e-mail) messages daily. Some of these messages are not relevant for our work. One can develop tools to discard the messages that are not relevant. These tools can be simple filtering tools or sophisticated data mining tools. Similarly, these data mining tools can also be used to display only the Web pages of interest to a user.

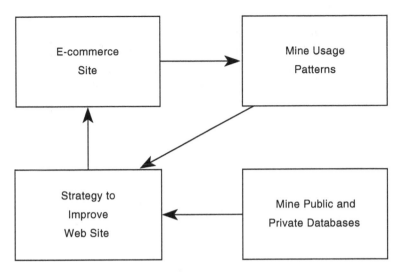

FIGURE 3.13 Web mining for e-commerce.

3.3.4 APPLICATIONS AND DIRECTIONS

One of the major applications of Web mining is e-commerce. Corporations want to have the competitive edge and are exploring numerous ways to market effectively. Major corporations including retail stores have e-commerce sites now. Customers can order products such as books, clothing, and toys through these sites. The goal is to provide customized marketing. For example, user group A may prefer literature novels whereas user group B may prefer mystery novels. Therefore, new literature novels have to be marketed to group A and new mystery novels have to be marketed to group B. How does an e-commerce site know about these preferences? The solution is in data mining. The usage patterns have to be mined. In addition, the company may mine various public and private databases to get additional information about these users. That is, both types of data mining described in the taxonomy have to be performed. Figure 3.13 illustrates the application of Web mining to e-commerce.

Web mining can also be used to provide entertainment on the Web. This is also a variation of e-commerce. Web access and Web data may be mined for user preferences on movies and record albums, with corporations able to carry out targeted marketing.

As more developments are made on data mining and the Web, we can expect better tools to emerge, both to mine the data and to mine the usage patterns. We can expect to hear a lot about Web mining in coming years.

Data mining can help e-commerce sites and also users to find information. For example, one e-commerce site manager mentioned to me that the major problem he has is users finding his e-commerce site. He has advertised in various magazines, but those who do not have access to the magazines find it difficult to access his sites.

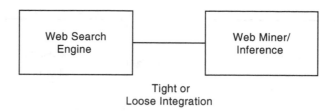

FIGURE 3.14 Web mining for search engines.

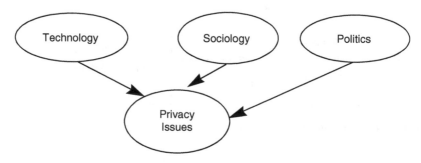

FIGURE 3.15 Privacy issues.

One solution is to have a third-party agent making the connection between the site and the user. Another solution would be to make the search engines more intelligent. Data mining could help in this instance. The data miner could take the requirements of the user, match the requirements to what is offered by the e-commerce sites, and connect the user to the right site. Work has begun in this area, but much remains. This is illustrated in Figure 3.14.

3.3.5 SECURITY AND PRIVACY CONCERNS

At the International Federation for Information Processing (IFIP) working conference on database security in 1997, the group began discussions on privacy issues and the role of Web, data mining, and data warehousing (see, e.g., [IFIP97]). This discussion continued at the IFIP meeting in 1998, and it was thought that the IFIP group should monitor the developments made by the security working group of the W3C. The discussions included those based on technical, social, and political aspects (Figure 3.15). In this section, we examine all these aspects.

First, with the WWW, one can now obtain within seconds an abundance of information about individuals. This information could be obtained through mining or just from information retrieval. Therefore, one needs to enforce controls on databases and data mining tools. This is a very difficult problem, especially with respect to data mining, as seen in the previous section. In summary, one needs to develop techniques to prevent users from mining and extracting information from the data whether they are on the Web or on servers.

These prevention techniques go against all that has been said about mining in the previous chapters. That is, mining has been portrayed as something that is critical for users to have so they can get the right information at the right time. Furthermore, they can also extract patterns previously unknown. This is all true, however, we do not want the information to be used in an incorrect manner. For example, based on information about a person, an insurance company could deny insurance or a loan agency could deny loans. In many cases, these denials may not be legitimate. Therefore, information providers have to be very careful about what they release. Also, data mining researchers have to ensure that security aspects are addressed.

Second, let us examine the social aspects. In most cultures, privacy of the individuals is important, but in certain cultures it is impossible to ensure privacy. These could be related to political or technological issues or the fact that people have been brought up believing that privacy is not critical. Places exist where people divulge their salaries without thinking twice about it; but in many countries, salaries are very private and sensitive. It is not easy to change cultures overnight, and in many cases you do not want to change them, because preserving cultures is very important. What overall effect does this social concern have on data mining and privacy issues? We do not have an answer to this yet because we are only beginning to look into the problem.

Third, let us examine the political and legal aspects. We include policies and procedures under this. What sort of security controls should one enforce for the Web? Should these security policies be mandated or should they be discretionary? What are the consequences of violating the security policies? Who should be administering, managing, and implementing these policies? How is data mining on the Web impacted? Can one control how data are mined on the Web? Once we have made technological advances on security and data mining, can we enforce security controls on data mining tools? How is information transferred between countries? Again, we have no answers to these questions. We have, however, begun discussions. Note that some of the issues discussed in this section are related to privacy and data mining, and others are related to just privacy, in general.

I have raised some interesting questions on privacy issues and data mining as well as privacy in general. Again, data mining is a threat to privacy. The challenge is on protecting the privacy but at the same time not losing all the great benefits of data mining. At the 1998 Knowledge Discovery in Database Conference, an interesting panel met to consider the privacy issues for Web mining. It appears that the data mining as well as the security communities are interested about security and privacy issues. Much of the focus at that panel was on legal issues [KDD98].

So far, I have mainly dealt with privacy issues. Security is also a major consideration for Web. The main concern for e-commerce security is Web security. Web security involves three components in general: secure client, secure server, and secure network.

I discuss network security issues in Part I. Network protocols and basic transmission have to be secured. Encryption provides this type of security. Data are encrypted at the sender's side and decrypted at the receiver's side The main issue

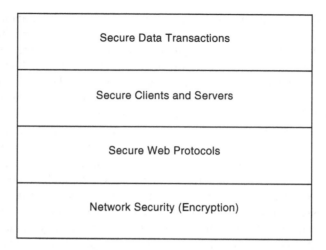

FIGURE 3.16 Secure protocols stack.

is how to maintain the encryption keys. Various techniques such as private key encryption, public key encryption, and certification methods have been used and are discussed in Part III. In addition to network protocol security, the Web protocols such as Hypertext Transfer Protocol (HTTP) have to be secure.

Traditional client–server security methods are used to ensure that clients and servers are secure on the Web. Furthermore, because of the nature of the Web and e-commerce transactions, additional security measures are needed. For example, user A may want to transfer funds from his account to user B's account, but a Trojan horse could lurk in the system transferring the funds to the account of user C instead. If A and B are multinational corporations, millions of dollars could be lost. We hear about such security breaches all the time in the news. Various secure payment protocols and transactions methods have been developed to limit these types of breeches. (These are addressed Part III). Figure 3.16 illustrates the security layers for the Web.

3.4 ARCHITECTURAL ASPECTS

3.4.1 OVERVIEW

Various dimensions to Web data management architectures exist and these dimensions are discussed in the remainder of this chapter. Architectures include those for data access, interoperability, publish and subscribe, client–server, federation, and migration, among others.

Database access architectures are the subject of Section 3.4.2. Three-tier computing is covered in Section 3.4.3. Section 3.4.4 discusses interoperability of heterogeneous data sources on the Web. Migration issues are briefly addressed in Section 3.4.5. Models of communication such as publish and subscribe architectures are the topics of Section 3.4.6. An alternative to client–server computing, which is federated computing, is considered in Section 3.4.7.

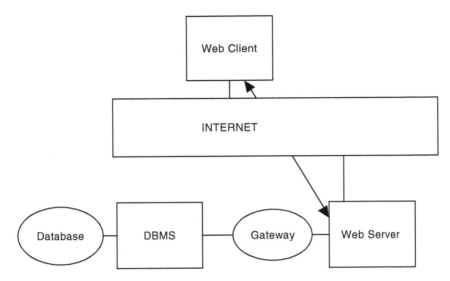

FIGURE 3.17 Database access via gateways.

3.4.2 DATABASE ACCESS

In the earlier sections of this chapter, a high-level illustration of database access is given. One approach is to embed SQL calls into Java programs and access relational databases via Java Database Connectivity (JDBC). The approaches have been extended to include object databases as well as object-relational databases.

Although JDBC-based approaches are the way of the future, unfortunately many Web clients cannot understand the concepts in relational databases. These Web clients only understand the results of Web servers, and database management systems are not Web servers in general. Therefore, as discussed in the various articles in [IEEE98], one of the approaches currently being adopted for Web database access is to use gateways between the database system and the Web servers. These gateways take the output of the database systems and then format it in a way that the Web servers can manage. Then Web clients and Web servers can communicate with each other through the various protocols discussed in Chapter 2. As illustrated in Figure 3.17, when a client issues a request to the server, the data from the databases are retrieved via the gateway. The results are then delivered to the user.

One of the advantages of standards such as XML is to eliminate the need for such gateways. If all the documents are expressed in XML, then the database outputs are represented using XML, these outputs can then be interpreted by Web servers as well as clients. This way the need for gateways can be eliminated, as illustrated in Figure 3.18.

When numerous applications have to access databases on the Web, performance becomes a major consideration. One of the trends is to use various application servers that are based on Enterprise Java Bean (EJB) technology. Application servers can coordinate between the various applications. These application servers either communicate directly with the database systems or go through a data server. A data

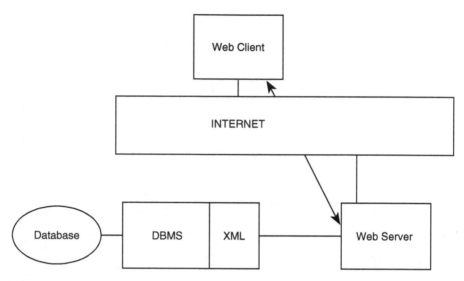

FIGURE 3.18 Database access without gateways.

server has two parts: one is access to the back-end database systems and the other is access to the application servers. The data server can schedule various transactions and access the back-end database system.

Such a system is illustrated in Figure 3.19. This technology is becoming very popular, with various application and data servers now available on the market.

3.4.3 THREE-TIER COMPUTING

Another concept that is extremely popular for the Web is three-tier computing. I discussed some of these aspects in [THUR00]. The front end has the client and the logic for presentation. The middle tier is the Web server. The third tier is the database server.

I have used three-tier computing in a number of applications for data management as well as knowledge management. Figure 3.20 illustrates such an example. The client displays maps to the user. The Web server is based on EJB technology and is a collection of business objects to conduct the functions of the application. One could use a database system to manage the Web server objects. The back end may be a relational database system.* Other aspects of middleware include transaction processing (TP) monitors and message-oriented middleware (MOM). In the future, we can expect object request brokers (ORBs), TPs, and MOM to be integrated.

3.4.4 INTEROPERABILITY

Whereas the previous sections discuss various aspects of Web data management and architectures, the next few sections focus on issues such as interoperability and

---

* I thank Eric Hughes and Tim Frangioso for discussions and information on three-tier computing for the Web.

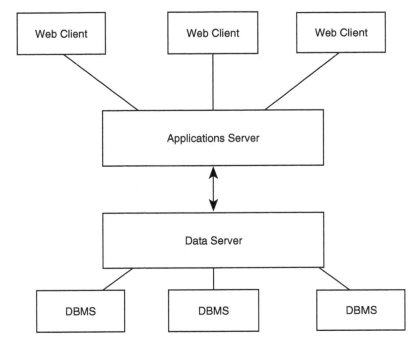

FIGURE 3.19 Application server and data server.

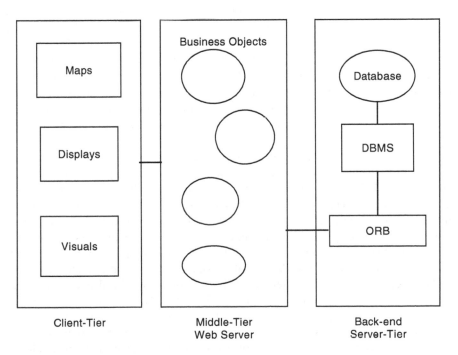

FIGURE 3.20 Three-tier computing.

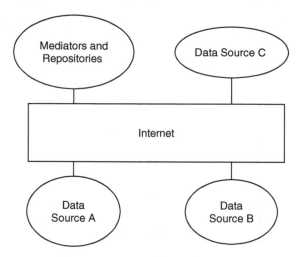

FIGURE 3.21 Integrating data sources on the Internet.

migration on the Web. Again, one of the main goals of this text is to explore the relationship between XML and Web technologies. Therefore, once we understand what the interoperability and migration issues are, we can discuss in more detail the implications of using XML for both interoperability and migration.

Heterogeneous database access, data warehousing, and data mining are important functions of digital libraries. The various heterogeneous data sources have to be integrated to provide transparent access to the user as illustrated in Figure 3.21. In some cases, the data sources have to be integrated into a warehouse. Data mining helps the users to extract meaningful information from the numerous data sources. Because the data in the libraries could have different semantics and syntax, it is difficult to extract useful information. Sophisticated data mining tools are needed for this purpose. A discussion on interactive data mining and its impact on the WWW is given in [THUR96b]. In an earlier section, I illustrate data warehousing and data mining on the Internet.

One way to interoperate heterogeneous databases is to use ORBs (Figure 3.22). A major challenge in ORB-based interoperability is to develop appropriate interfaces between the ORB and the Internet. That is, extensions to Interface Definition Language (IDL) are needed for Internet database access. Another challenge with the Internet is to connect different components of the database management system. Different vendors may provide different components. For example, a query module may be developed by vendor A and a transaction module, possibly with real-time processing capability, may be developed by vendor B. The two modules may need to be accessed through the Internet. ORB technology would also facilitate such integration. This is illustrated in Figure 3.23. The OMG Internet special interest group (SIG) is focusing on ORB interfaces to the Internet. Alternatives to the OMG Common Object Request Broker Architecture (CORBA) technology, such as the OLE/COM distributed by the Microsoft Corporation, are also viable technologies for Internet database access.

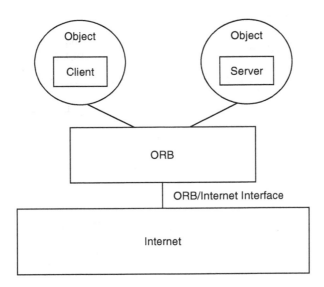

FIGURE 3.22 Internet-ORB-based interoperability.

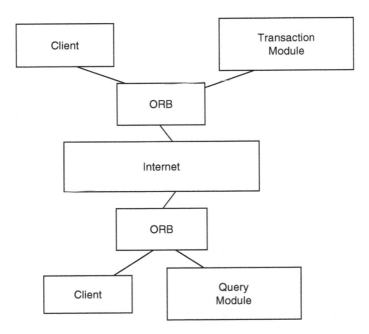

FIGURE 3.23 ORB-based component integration.

3.4.5 NOTE ON MIGRATION

In Part I, I discuss various aspects of migrating legacy databases, both migrating databases as well as applications. For database migration, one needs to develop schemas for the new environment and then migrate the data. This is the easier part of the migration

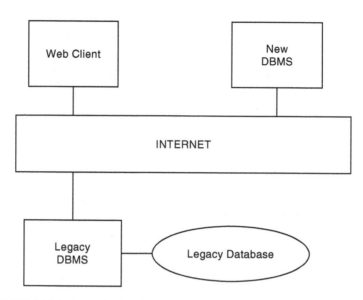

FIGURE 3.24 Initial phase of migration.

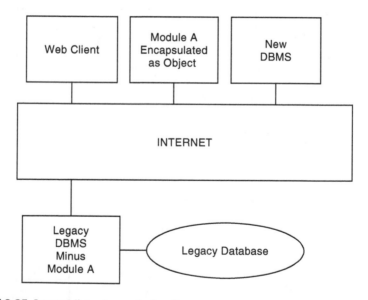

FIGURE 3.25 Intermediate phase of migration.

effort. Migrating applications is more difficult. The applications could be based on complex codes and have many relationships. The challenge is to extract the relationships and then migrate the applications to run on the new environment.

What impact does the Web have on migrating legacy databases and applications? At this point, it does not appear that the Web has any significant impact on the migration process. Figures 3.24 to 3.26 illustrate the steps to migrating a legacy

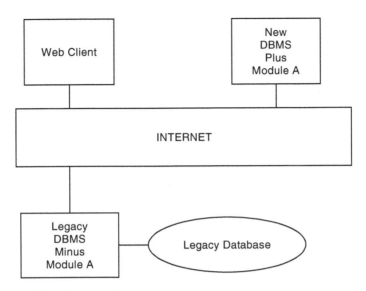

FIGURE 3.26 Final phase of migration.

database accessed on the Web. As in the case of a non-Web environment, the module that is to be migrated may be extracted as objects and then integrated with the new database. Various issues on migrating databases and applications, and the role of object technology for migration are addressed in [THUR97]. The impact of the Web needs to be investigated.

Data modeling will be impacted by the Web. For example, how can XML be used to represent the module A that is extracted for the legacy database? Can XML or similar technology be used to access the legacy databases? That is, does one need a mediator that understands XML at the client side and then access the legacy databases as illustrated in Figure 3.27? We are just at the beginning of the migration revolution on the Web, and we can expect to find answers to some of these questions within the next couple of years. At this time, however, legacy migration on the Web is still premature.

3.4.6 MODELS OF COMMUNICATION

In this section, I examine various models for communication on the Web. By communication I do not mean networking, but instead the paradigms for communicating data between the client and the server. The server is the producer of the data and the client is the consumer. Thus, the communication is between the producer and the consumer via the Web.*

In the first model of communication, the consumer requests data. The Web agents search for the appropriate producers of the data and get the data for the consumer. This model is illustrated in Figure 3.28. In the second model, also sometimes referred to as the push model, the consumer does not request the data. As the producer

---

* I thank Mike Hebert for discussions on push–pull models.

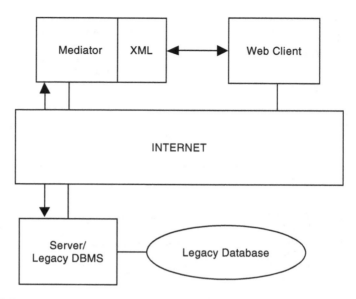

FIGURE 3.27 Mediator approach to migration.

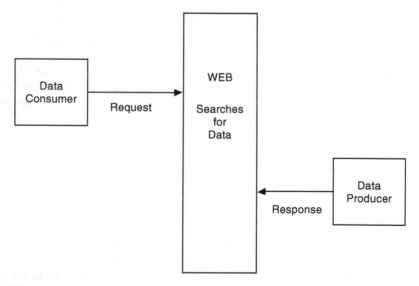

FIGURE 3.28 Request–response between producer and consumer.

generates the data, they are pushed to the consumer. This model is illustrated in Figure 3.29. A variation of this model is when the consumer publishes its need for the data. As the data are produced, the producers push the data to the consumer. Another variation is when the producer pushes the data to the consumer depending on consumer profiles. In this case, the consumer gets personalized services.

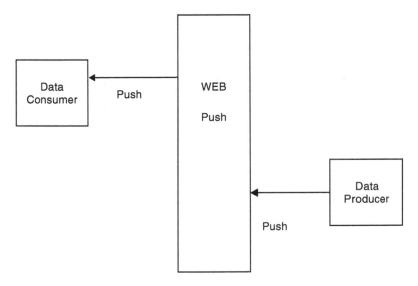

FIGURE 3.29 Push data to consumer.

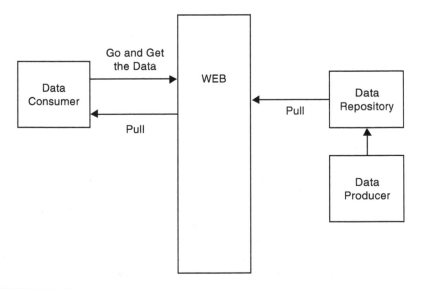

FIGURE 3.30 Consumer pulls data.

A third model is a pull model where the consumer pulls the data from the producers. Producers may place the data at a certain repository and the consumers may only pull the data from the repository. This model is illustrated in Figure 3.30. Several variations of these models have been proposed. Although the different models necessitate different processing routines, some of the essential routines are

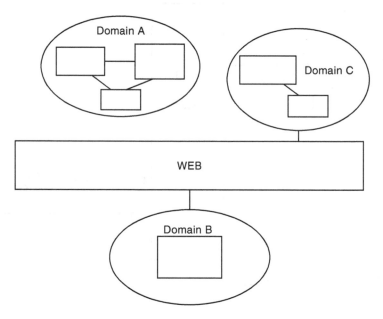

FIGURE 3.31 Federated computing on the Web.

the same. These routines are for processing queries, executing transactions, extracting metadata, and accessing complex storage media. As we get to know more about the Web, the number of models of communication also increases.

3.4.7 NOTE ON FEDERATED COMPUTING

Another computing model that is worth mentioning is the federated computing model. In Part I, I discuss federated databases. This model for computing is becoming popular for the Web. Each group or domain may form its own federation. Various federations have to communicate with each other. With federated computing, one needs to ensure that collaboration and yet autonomy are maintained. Figure 3.31 illustrates federated computing on the Web. Many of the techniques and issues discussed in Appendix B apply in this section.

However, the details of the impact of the Web on federated computing are not well understood at present. This is an area that needs a lot of research. For example, how can users share data and collaborate with one another? What about security concerns? How can data quality be maintained? Some of these issues are discussed in the chapters on knowledge management and collaboration.

3.5 RELATIONSHIP TO XML

I have discussed several aspects of Web database management including discussions on Java, database functions, data mining, security aspects, interoperability, and

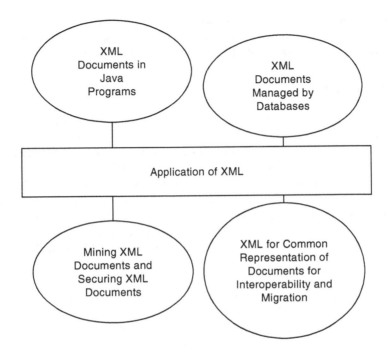

FIGURE 3.32 Applications of XML.

migration, among others. This section briefly explains the relationship to XML, with the relationships explored in more detail in Parts II and III.

With Java and XML closely connected, there is now support for exchanging XML documents in programs written in Java. Many vendors have followed in this direction. Furthermore, standards are evolving such as Java 2 Enterprise Edition (J2EE), Microsoft Simple Object Access Protocol (SOAP), and e-business XML (ebXML) standards, among others. Microsoft Corporation has come up with its family of products called the DOT-NET strategy. All these are discussed in Part III.

With respect to databases, several database vendors are now providing support to store and manage XML documents. That is, they are claiming that their databases are XML databases. This means relations, objects, and other structures are being translated into XML documents.

The data mining and XML connection has not been explored in any detail. Nevertheless, the XML documents have to be mined and therefore one needs to develop appropriate mining techniques. Security for XML is an area that is receiving some attention. Bertino et al. at the University of Milano are conducting extensive research in this area (see [BERT00], [BERT02]).

With respect to interoperability and migration, XML is being touted as the major solution. For example, legacy databases are publishing their schemas and these are represented in XML. This way, XML is being used as the common interchange format. Figure 3.32 illustrates the various relationships that XML has to a number of technologies. (See Parts II and III for more details.)

Another area that is closely related to XML and Web databases is content management. Organizations are interested in ensuring that users access data based on content. XML tagging based on content remains a challenge.

3.6 SUMMARY

This chapter provides a broad overview of the developments and challenges on Web database management and the relationship to XML. I first give an introduction to Java issues and discuss digital libraries. Next, I discuss issues on accessing databases on the Web, in particular, presenting an overview of JDBC and data modeling for the Web. This is followed by a discussion of database functions. Then I focus on Web mining as well as privacy and security aspects. Finally, I describe architectural aspects, including architecture for database access, three-tier computing, interoperability, migration, client–server paradigm, push–pull computing, and the federated model. This chapter ends with a discussion of the relationship of XML to all the technologies considered including Web databases, data mining, security, and interoperability.

This chapter addresses some essential components of Web data management: models, functions, and architectures. One of the key developments on Web database management is the emerging standard XML. XML and other similar technologies can facilitate data management and interoperability on the Web. (See Parts II and III of this book for further elaboration on this topic.)

4 Information Retrieval Systems and XML

4.1 OVERVIEW

Information retrieval systems provide support for managing documents. The functions include document retrieval, document update, and document storage management, among others. These systems are essentially database management systems for managing documents. The various types of information retrieval systems include those for image, video, and audio.

Recall that XML evolved from HTML and SGML. SGML was developed specifically for tagging text. HTML was developed for tagging text on the Web. Therefore, XML was conceived for tagging text data, providing support for exchanging text documents on the Web. Over the years, however, XML has provided support for managing not only text documents but also images, video, and all types of structured and unstructured documents on the Web.

This chapter provides an overview of information retrieval systems and then discusses the relationship to XML. Sections 4.2 to 4.5 discuss various information retrieval systems, particularly text, image, video, and audio retrieval. Multimedia data types are the subject of Section 4.6. Because XML has evolved from SGML, I provide an overview of SGML in Section 4.7. Finally, the relationship of XML to information retrieval systems is covered in Section 4.8, with the chapter summarized in Section 4.9.

4.2 TEXT RETRIEVAL

A text retrieval system is a database management system for handling text data. Text data could be documents such as books, journals, and magazines. In this section, I discuss some of the various issues that need to be considered.

One first needs a good data model for document representation. A considerable amount of work has gone into developing semantic data models and object models for document management. For example, a document could have paragraphs and a paragraph could have sections (and subsections), as shown in Figure 4.1. Then you need an architecture for the system. A functional architecture would have the following modules: query manager, browser, editor, update manager (which may overlap with the editor), storage manager, and metadata manager. In addition, you need an integrity and security manager to maintain integrity and security. An architecture for a text processing system is illustrated in Figure 4.2.

Querying documents could be based on many factors. One could specify keywords and request the documents with the keywords to be retrieved. One could also

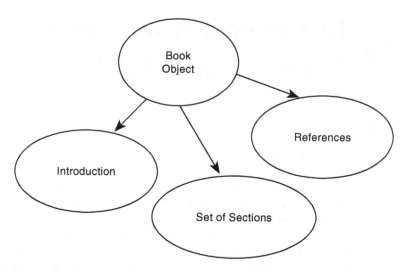

FIGURE 4.1 Data model for text.

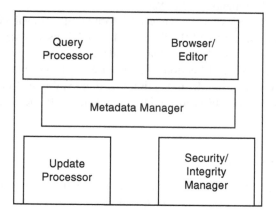

FIGURE 4.2 Functional architecture for text-processing system.

retrieve documents that have some relationship with one another. Is a system that supports relationships a text-processing system or a text-mining system? The answer is very subjective. In this discussion on taxonomy, I examine different levels of complexity for document management. In the next section, I cover text mining.

Much of the information is now in textual form, such as data on the Web, library data, or electronic books. One of the problems with text data is that they are not structured as relational data. In many cases, they are unstructured, but in other cases they are semistructured. Semistructured data, for example, may include an article that has a title, author, abstract, and paragraphs. The paragraphs are not structured, whereas the format is structured (see [CLIF97]).

Information retrieval systems and text processing systems have been developed for more than a few decades. Some of these systems are quite sophisticated and can

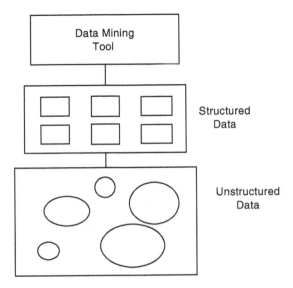

FIGURE 4.3 Converting unstructured data to structured data for mining.

retrieve documents by specifying attributes or keywords. Text-processing systems can also retrieve associations between documents. What is the difference between information retrieval systems and text mining systems?

I define text mining to be data mining on text data. Text mining is all about extracting patterns and associations previously unknown from large text databases. The difference between text mining and information retrieval is analogous to the difference between data mining and database management, really no clear difference. Some information retrieval and text processing systems discover associations between words and paragraphs, and therefore can be regarded as text mining systems.

Next, let us examine the approaches to text mining. Many of the current tools and techniques for data mining work for relational databases. Even for data in object-oriented databases, rarely do we hear about data mining tools for such data. Therefore, current data mining tools cannot be directly applied to text data. Some of the current directions in mining unstructured data include the following:

- Data and metadata are extracted from the unstructured databases possibly by using tagging techniques, storing the extracted data in structured databases, and applying data mining tools on the structured databases. This is illustrated in Figure 4.3.
- Data mining techniques are integrated with information retrieval tools so that appropriate data mining tools can be developed for unstructured databases. This is illustrated in Figure 4.4.
- Data mining tools are developed to operate directly on unstructured databases. This is illustrated in Figure 4.5.

While converting text data into relational databases, one has to be careful so that no loss of key information occurs. Unless you have good data, you cannot mine

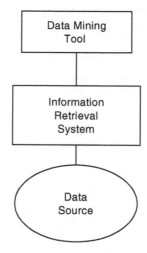

FIGURE 4.4 Augmenting an information retrieval system.

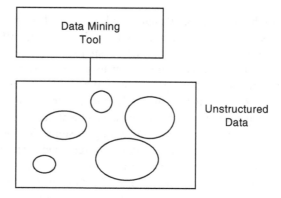

FIGURE 4.5 Mining directly on unstructured data.

the data effectively and expect to get useful results. One needs to create a sort of a warehouse first before mining the converted database. This warehouse is a relational database that has the essential data from the text data. In other words, one needs a transformer that takes a text corpus as input and outputs tables that have, for example, the keywords from the text.

As an example, in a text database that has several journal articles, one could create a warehouse with tables containing the following attributes: author, date, publisher, title, and keywords. From the keywords, one can form associations. The keywords in one article could be "Belgium, nuclear weapons" and the keywords in another article could be "Spain, nuclear weapons." The data miner could make the association that authors from Belgium and Spain write articles on nuclear weapons.

This example illustrates only the beginning of text mining. In the longer-term approach, we would want to develop tools directly to mine text data. These tools

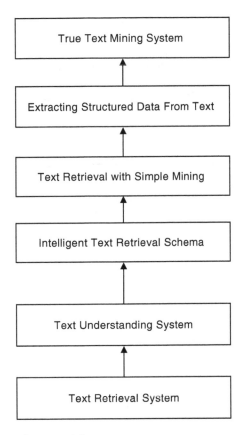

FIGURE 4.6 Taxonomy for text mining.

have to read the text, understand the text, put out pertinent information about the text, and then make associations between different documents. The discipline is far from developing such sophisticated text mining tools, although the work reported by Tsur et al. (see, e.g., [TSUR98]) is the first step in the right direction toward text mining. Some interesting early work on text mining was reported in [FELD95].

Taxonomy for text retrieval and text mining is illustrated in Figure 4.6. At the bottom is text retrieval and at the top is a true text mining system. In between may be multiple levels. At one level, an intelligent text mining system may exist that may make deductions and inferences. Another layer may have a text understanding system. A third layer may include a semitext mining system that may make partial correlations. A fourth layer may have a system that extracts structured data from text and mines the structured data. As the taxonomy goes higher and higher, a true text mining system is reached where text is mined directly.

Note that this text mining taxonomy is somewhat subjective and depends on whose viewpoint it is. Nevertheless, somewhat of a distinction between text mining and text retrieval can be made. At the one end is a simple query system for retrieving documents. At the other end is a true text mining system. In between, many layers of increasing levels of sophistication exist.

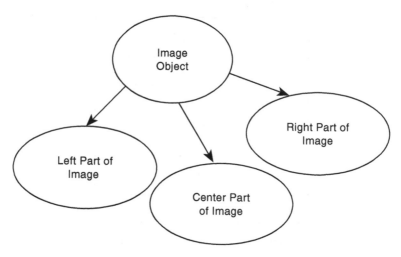

FIGURE 4.7 Data model for image.

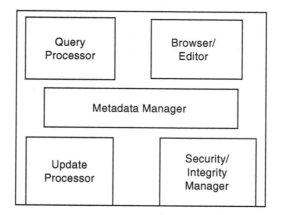

FIGURE 4.8 Functional architecture for image processing system.

4.3 IMAGE RETRIEVAL

An image retrieval system is a database management system for handling image data. Image data could be X-rays, pictures, satellite images, and photographs. Various issues need to be considered, some of which are explored in this section.

One first needs a good data model for image representation. Some work has gone into developing semantic data models and object models for image management (see, e.g., [THUR93]). For example, image could consist of a right and left image as shown in Figure 4.7 (an example is an X-ray of the lungs). An architecture for an image processing system, as illustrated in Figure 4.8, is the same as that described for Figure 4.2.

Querying images could be based on many factors. One could extract text from images and then query the text. One could tag images and then query the tags. One could also retrieve images from patterns. For example, an image could contain several squares. With a picture of a square, one could query the image and retrieve all the squares in the image. Is a system that finds associations or relationships an image processing system or an image mining system? The answer is very subjective. In the discussion on taxonomy, I examine different levels of complexity for image management, followed by a discussion of image mining in the next section.

If text mining is still in the early research stages, image mining is an even more immature technology. Image processing has been around for quite a while. Image processing applications exist in various domains including medical imaging for cancer detection, satellite image processing for space and intelligence applications, and also hyperspectral image handling. Images include maps, geological structures, biological structures, and many other entities. Image processing has dealt with areas such as detecting abnormal patterns that deviate from the norm, retrieving images by content, and matching patterns.

The main question is what is image mining? How does it differ from image processing? Again, no clear-cut answers have been found. Although image processing focuses on detecting abnormal patterns and retrieving images, image mining is all about finding unusual patterns. Therefore, image mining deals with making associations between different images from large image databases.

Clifton [CLIF98] and associates have begun work in image mining. Initially, their plan was to extract metadata from images and then conduct mining on the metadata. This would essentially be mining the metadata in relational databases, however, after some consideration they believed that images could be mined directly. The challenge is to determine what type of mining outcome is most suitable. One could mine for associations from images, cluster images, and classify images, as well as detect unusual patterns. One area of research being pursued by Clifton and associates is to mine images and find out whether there is anything unusual. Thus, the approach is to develop templates that generate several rules about the images, and to apply these data mining tools to see whether unusual patterns can be obtained; however, the mining tools cannot tell us why these patterns are unusual. Figure 4.9 shows an image with some unusual patterns.

Detecting unusual patterns is not the only outcome of image mining, but this is just the beginning. More research is needed on image mining to determine whether data mining techniques can be used to classify, cluster, and associate images. Image mining is an area with applications in numerous domains including space, medical, and geologic images.

Taxonomy for image retrieval and image mining, as illustrated in Figure 4.10, is similar to the description of that for Figure 4.6.

4.4 VIDEO RETRIEVAL

A video retrieval system is a database management system for handling video data. Video data could be documents such as books, journals, and magazines. Various issues need to be considered and some are discussed in this section.

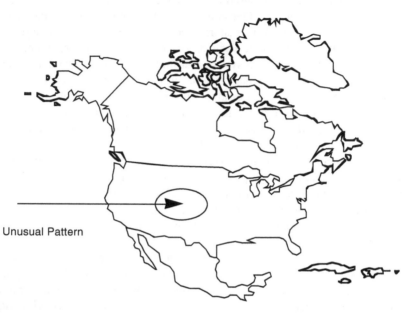

FIGURE 4.9 Image mining.

One needs a good data model for video representation. For work on developing semantic data models and objects models for video data management, see [WOEL86]. For example, a video object could have advertisements, main film, and coming attractions as shown in Figure 4.11. The architecture for the video processing system, as illustrated in Figure 4.12, is similar to that described for Figure 4.2.

Querying documents could be based on many factors. One could extract text from the video and query the text. One could also extract images from the video and query the images. One could store short video scripts and conduct pattern matching. That is, "find the video that contains the following script." One could also video documents that have some relationship to one another. Is a system that finds relationships a video processing system or a video mining system? The answer is very subjective. In the discussion on taxonomy, many different levels of complexity are shown for video data management. In the next section, I discuss video mining.

Mining video data is even more complicated than mining image data (Figure 4.13). One can regard a video to be a collection of moving images, much like animation. Video data management has been the subject of much research. The important areas include developing query and retrieval techniques for video databases, including video indexing, query languages, and optimization strategies. What is the difference between video information retrieval and video mining? Unlike image and text mining, we do not have any clear idea of what is meant by video mining. For example, one could examine video clips and find associations between different clips. Another example would be to find unusual patterns in video clips. How is this different from finding unusual patterns in images? Thus, the first step to successful video mining is to have a good handle on image mining.

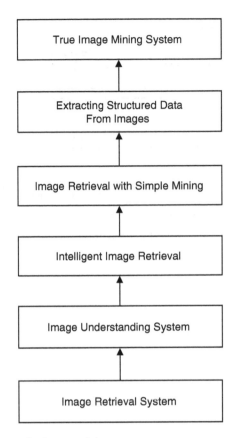

FIGURE 4.10 Taxonomy for image mining.

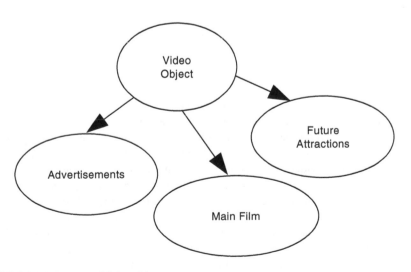

FIGURE 4.11 Data model for video.

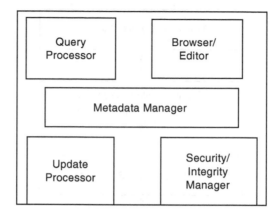

FIGURE 4.12 Functional architecture for video processing system.

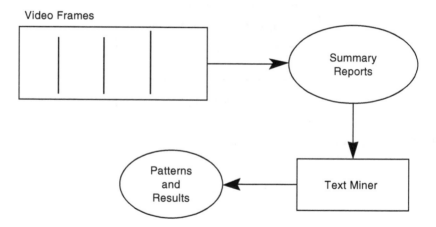

FIGURE 4.13 Mining text extracted from video.

Let us examine pattern matching in video databases. Should one have predefined images and then match these images with the video data? Is there any way one can execute pattern recognition in video data by specifying what one is looking for and then to extract the feature for the video data? If this is video information retrieval, what then is mining video data? To be consistent with our terminology, we can say that finding correlations and patterns previously unknown from large video databases is video mining. By analyzing a video clip or multiple video clips, one comes to conclusions about some unusual behavior. People in the video who are unlikely to be there, yet have occurred two or three times, could mean something significant. Another way to look at the problem is to capture the text in video format and make the associations one would conduct with text, but this time use the video data instead.

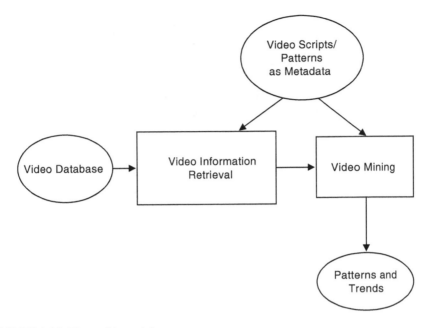

FIGURE 4.14 Direct video mining.

Unlike text and image mining where the ideas have been less vague, the discussion on video mining is quite preliminary. This is mainly because there is so little known about video mining. Even the term video mining is something very new. To date, no concrete results have been reported on this, but a lot of information is available on analyzing video data and producing summaries. One could mine these summaries, which would amount to mining text, as shown in Figure 4.13. One good example of this effort is the work on summarizing video news by Merlino [MERL97]. Converting the video mining problem to a text mining problem is reasonably well understood, but the challenge is mining video data directly, and more important, knowing what we want to mine. With the emergence of the Web, video mining becomes even more important. An example of direct video mining is illustrated in Figure 4.14.

Another point is that one can use techniques for image mining for video mining. That is, one can detect abnormal patterns in void data. One may use neural networks to train normal video such as who usually appears with whom. Then if something abnormal occurs, such as "John appearing with Mary" for the first time, the system flags this as something abnormal. Anomaly detection for video mining needs further investigation.

A taxonomy for video retrieval and video mining can be described by using a flow chart similar to Figure 4.6, and is illustrated in Figure 4.15.

Similar to those of text and image mining, video mining taxonomy is somewhat subjective, depending on the viewpoint. The distinction between video mining and video retrieval progresses from a simple query system for retrieving documents to a true video mining system, with many in-between layers of increasing sophistication.

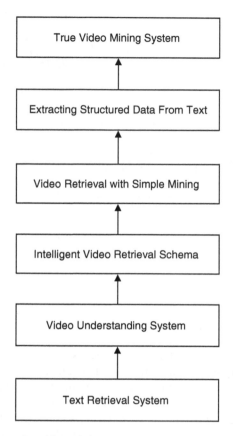

FIGURE 4.15 Taxonomy for video mining.

4.5 AUDIO RETRIEVAL

An audio retrieval system is a database management system for handling audio data. Audio data could be documents such as books, journals, and magazines. Some of the various issues that need to be considered are discussed in this section.

Start with a good data model for audio representation. Some work has gone into developing semantic data models and object models for audio data management (see [WOEL86]). For example, a audio object could have advertisements, main film, and coming attractions, as shown in Figure 4.16. The functional architecture needed for such a system, with modules similar to those shown in Figures 4.2, 4.8, and 4.12, is illustrated in Figure 4.17.

The many factors affecting querying documents follow. One could extract text from the audio and query the text. One could also store short audio scripts and conduct pattern matching, that is, "find the audio that contains the following script." One could also audio documents that have some relationship to one another. Is a system that finds relationships an audio processing system or an audio mining system? The answer is very subjective. In the discussion on taxonomy, different

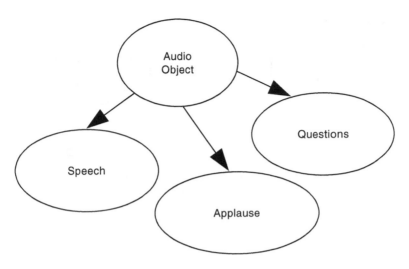

FIGURE 4.16 Data model for audio.

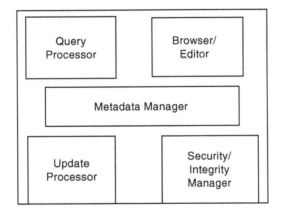

FIGURE 4.17 Functional architecture for audio processing system.

levels of complexity for audio data management are considered. In the next section, audio mining is the focus.

Because audio is a continuous media type like video, the techniques for audio information processing and mining are similar to video information retrieval and mining. Audio data could be in the form of radio, speech, or spoken language. Even television news has audio data, and in this case audio may have to be integrated with video and possibly text to capture the annotations and captions.

To mine audio data, one could convert it into text using speech transcription techniques and other techniques such as keyword extraction and then mine the text data as illustrated in Figure 4.18. On the other hand, audio data could also be mined directly by using audio information processing techniques and then mining selected audio data. This is illustrated in Figure 4.19.

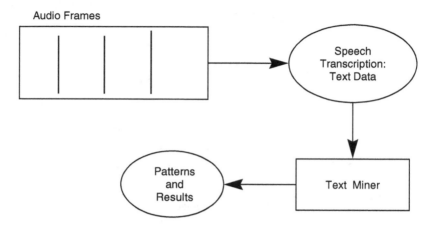

FIGURE 4.18 Mining text extracted from audio.

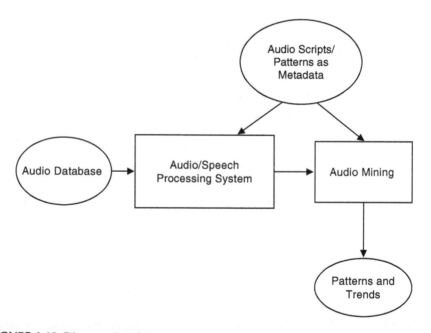

FIGURE 4.19 Direct audio mining.

In general, audio mining is even more primitive than video mining. Although a few articles have appeared on text mining and even fewer on image and video mining, work on audio mining is just beginning.

Another point worthy of note is that one could also use image mining techniques for audio mining. One could detect abnormal patterns in audio data. In this situation, one may use neural networks to train normal audio data such as who speaks what, and when something abnormal occurs, for the first time. Then the system flags this

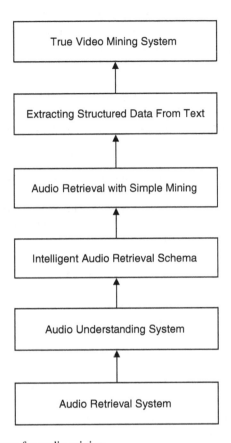

FIGURE 4.20 Taxonomy for audio mining.

as something abnormal. Anomaly detection for audio mining needs further investigation.

A taxonomy for audio retrieval and mining is illustrated in Figure 4.20, which is similar to the preceding figures for text, image, and video retrieval and mining (see Figures 4.6, 4.10, and 4.15).

The taxonomy for audio mining is also somewhat subjective, depending on the viewpoint. Nevertheless, the distinction between audio mining and retrieval varies from a simple query system for retrieving documents to a true sophisticated audio mining system.

4.6 MULTIMEDIA DATA TYPES

The previous sections discuss retrieval and mining for individual data types such as text, images, video, and audio, otherwise known as information retrieval and mining systems; however, we need to manage combinations of data types and the systems that manage them are multimedia database systems.

A multimedia database system includes a multimedia database management system and a multimedia database. A multimedia database management system (MM-DBMS) manages the multimedia database, which contains multimedia data. Multimedia data may include structured data as well as semistructured and unstructured data such as audio, video, text, and images. An MM-DBMS provides support for storing, manipulating, and retrieving multimedia data from a multimedia database. In a sense, a multimedia database system is a type of heterogeneous database system, because it manages heterogeneous data types. Heterogeneity is due to the media of the data such as text, video, and audio.

An MM-DBMS must provide support for typical database management system functions. These include query processing, update processing, transaction management, storage management, metadata management, security, and integrity. In many cases, the various types of data such as voice and video have to be synchronized for display; therefore, real-time processing is also a major issue in an MM-DBMS.

If we are to mine multimedia data, we need to mine combinations of two or more data types such as text and images, text and video, or text, audio, and video. In this section, I briefly discuss some of the issues on multimedia data mining.

Handling combinations of data types is very much like dealing with heterogeneous databases. For example, each database in the heterogeneous environment could contain data belonging to multiple data types. These heterogeneous databases could be first integrated and then mined, or one could apply mining tools on the individual databases and then combine the results of the various data miners. These two scenarios are illustrated in Figures 4.21 and 4.22. In both cases, the Distributed Multimedia Processor (DMP) plays a role. If the data are to be integrated before mining, then this integration is conducted via the DMPs. If the data are to be mined first, the data miner augments the corresponding MM-DBMS and the results of the data miners are integrated via the DMPs.

Because there is much to be done on mining individual data types such as text, images, video, and audio, mining combinations of data types are still challenging. Once we have a better handle on mining individual data types, we can then focus on mining combinations of data types.

4.7 MARKUP LANGUAGES AND SGML

Markup languages provide the support to tag any entity of interest. These entities could be person, place, or some object. Markup languages can provide structure to unstructured data such as text. Details on one of the earliest markup languages Standard Generalized Markup Languages (SGML), can be found in numerous texts including [SGML]. I briefly discuss some of the essential points in this section.

SGML is a descriptive language as opposed to a procedural language. It uses markup codes to markup the document. Procedural languages specify the processing to be executed. In SGML, instructions to process the document are separated from the descriptive markup, which is the set of markup codes. With descriptive markup, the document can be independent of the system that processes it. One can markup

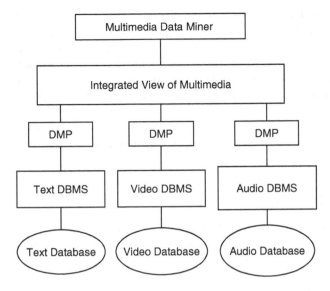

FIGURE 4.21 Integration and then mining.

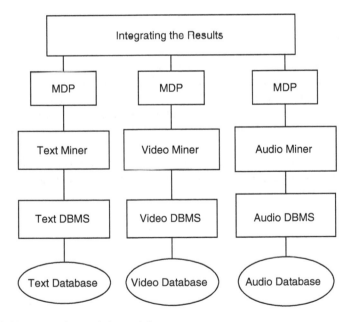

FIGURE 4.22 Integration and then mining.

the names, the places, or entities, with the processing program able to handle various parts of the document.

Document type and document-type definitions (DTDs) are introduced in SGML and also are now used in XML. Documents have types. The type is defined by the structure of the document. For example, a book document type may contain title, front matter, introduction, set of chapters, references, appendices, and index. A document parser can check to see whether the document conforms to its specified type.

The design goal of SGML was to ensure that a document written in one system can be transported to another without any loss of information. This means that there has to be a way of independently and consistently representing strings, letters, numbers, characters, etc. in a machine. SGML provokes support for such representations.

It is impossible to give an overview of SGML in a few paragraphs. Nevertheless, I have discussed some of the key points, noting that XML has been influenced greatly by the developments with SGML.

4.8 RELATIONSHIP TO XML

XML, having evolved from HTML and SGML, was primarily developed to tag text. However, XML is now used to tag all kinds of documents including images, video, audio, and multimedia. XML is also used for music, math, and e-business documents. XML has become key to the exchange of not only text documents but also any type of document, included relations and tables on the Web.

This chapter has only briefly explored the relationship of XML to information retrieval systems. (See Part III for more details.)

4.9 SUMMARY

In this chapter, I mainly address information retrieval systems and mining individual data types. I introduce mining to show the importance of extracting entities, for example, from text through tagging. This requires the use of markup languages such as SGML. Then I discuss SGML and finally end the chapter with a discussion of the relationship of XML to information retrieval systems. (See Part III for more discussion of the application of XML.)

Based on this overview of information retrieval and XML as well as databases and XML, we can now explore information management technologies and XML. These are the subjects of Chapter 5.

5 Information Management Technologies and XML

5.1 OVERVIEW

Chapter 3 describes Web databases and XML whereas Chapter 4 describes information retrieval and XML. This chapter focuses on information management technologies such as collaboration, knowledge management, and multimedia systems and agents; and then on the relationship to XML. (XML applications in information management will be elaborated on further in Part III).

I have tried to separate data management and information management. That is, data management focuses on database systems technologies such as query, transaction, and storage management. Information management is much broader than data management and I have included many topics in this category. Information retrieval is also a particular aspect of information management. I have devoted a separate chapter to information retrieval systems such as text, image, and video because they have a special relationship to XML. That is, XML was conceived for document representation.

The organization of this chapter is as follows. Collaboration and data management are the subject of Section 5.2, with multimedia information management discussed in Section 5.3. Knowledge management is covered in Section 5.4. Decision support is the topic in Section 5.5 and agents are described in Section 5.6. Many of the other information management technologies are explored in Section 5.7 and relationship to XML is the subject of Section 5.8, followed by a summary in Section 5.9.

5.2 COLLABORATION AND DATA MANAGEMENT

Although the notion of computer supported cooperative work (CSCW) was first proposed in the early 1980s, only recently has much interest been shown in this topic. Several research articles have now been published in collaborative computing and prototypes and products have been developed. Collaborative computing enables people, groups of individuals, and organizations to work together with one another to accomplish a task or a collection of tasks. These tasks could vary from participating in conferences, solving a specific problem, or working on the design of a system. Specific contributions to collaborative computing include the development of team workstations (where groupware creates a shared workspace supporting dynamic collaboration in a work group), multimedia communication systems supporting distributed work groups, and collaborative computing systems supporting

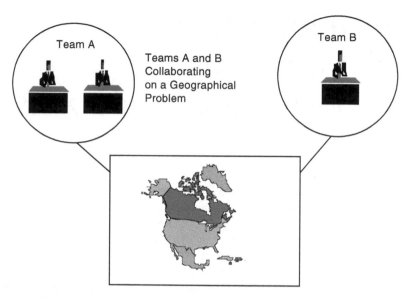

FIGURE 5.1 Collaboration example.

cooperation in the design of an entity (such as an electrical or a mechanical system; see [ACM91]). Several technologies including multimedia, artificial intelligence, networking and distributed processing, and database systems as well as disciplines such as organizational behavior and human computer interaction have contributed significantly toward the growth of collaborative computing.

One aspect of collaborative computing of particular interest to the database community is work flow computing. Work flow is defined as the automation of a series of functions that comprise a business process such as data entry, data review, and monitoring performed by one or more people. An example of a process that is well suited for work flow automation is the purchasing process. Applications can range from simple user-defined processes such as document review to complex applications such as manufacturing processes. Original custom-made work flow systems developed over the past 20 years for applications such as factory automation were built using a centralized database. Many commercial work flow system products targeted for office environments are based on a messaging architecture. This architecture supports the distributed nature of current work teams, however, the messaging architecture is usually file based and lacks many of the features supported by database management systems such as data representation, consistency management, tracking, and monitoring. Although the emerging products show some promise, they do not provide the functionality of database management systems.

Figure 5.1 illustrates an example where teams A and B are working on a geographic problem such as analyzing and predicting the weather in North America. The two teams must have a global picture of the map as well as any notes that go with it. Any changes made by one team should be instantly visible to the other team and both teams communicate as if they are in the same room.

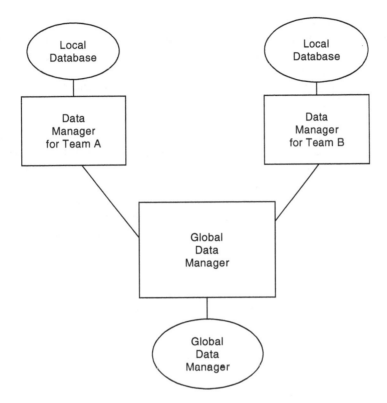

FIGURE 5.2 Database support.

To enable such transparent communication, data management support is needed. One could utilize a database management system to manage the data or some type of data manager that provides some of the essential features such as data integrity, concurrent access, and retrieval capabilities. In the preceding example, the database may consist of information describing the problem the teams are working on, data that is involved, history data, and metadata information. The data manager must provide appropriate concurrency control features so that when both teams simultaneously access the common picture and make changes, these changes are coordinated.

One possible scenario for the data manager is illustrated in Figure 5.2 where each team has its own local data manager and a global data manager maintains any global information, including the data and the metadata. The local data managers communicate with the global data manager. The global data manager illustrated in Figure 5.2 is at the logical level. At the physical level the global data manager may also be distributed. The data managers coordinate their activities to provide features such as concurrency control, integrity, and retrieval.

The Web has increased the need for collaboration even further. Users now share documents and work on papers and designs on the Web. Corporate information infrastructures promote collaboration and sharing of information and documents.

Therefore, the collaborative tools have to work effectively on the Web. Although the Web promotes collaboration, collaboration also benefits the Web. That is, collaboration is a key information technology to enhance the Web. Therefore, the two technologies can benefit from each other.

The challenge is to use these tools to work effectively on the Web. In the simple case you build Web interfaces, although many of the tools were not developed with the Web in mind, for example, database systems. Building Web access is the easy part. There are many challenges such as data formats, transactions, and metadata management on the Web. Such challenges are also present for collaboration. Some of the collaborative tools work with the understanding that the people are located in the same building. Although for corporate intranets this may not be a problem, with the Internet this could pose some major problems. Scalability of the tools is also an important issue. Typically, the tools have been developed for tens of users. With the Web, these tools have to work for tens of thousands of users. These requirements have to be taken into consideration.

Collaboration and the Web will go hand in hand. In the future, collaboration tools will have to work with multimedia data. Therefore, I address multimedia data in the next section. For some interesting articles published on collaboration and the impact of the Web on the collaboration tools, see [IEEE99].

5.3 MULTIMEDIA DATA MANAGEMENT

A multimedia database management system (MM-DBMS) provides support for storing, manipulating, and retrieving multimedia data from a multimedia database. In a sense, a multimedia database system is a type of heterogeneous database system, because it manages heterogeneous data types. Heterogeneity is due to the media of the data such as text, video, and audio.

An MM-DBMS must provide support for typical database management system functions. These include query processing, update processing, transaction management, storage management, metadata management, security, and integrity. In many cases, the various types of data such as voice and video have to be synchronized for display; therefore, real-time processing is also a major issue in an MM-DBMS.

Various architectures are under examination to design and develop an MM-DBMS. In one approach, the DBMS is used just to manage the metadata, and a multimedia file manager is used to manage the multimedia data. Then there is a module for integrating the DBMS and the multimedia file manager. In this case, the MM-DBMS consists of the three modules: the DBMS managing the metadata, the multimedia file manager, and the module for integrating the two.

The second architecture is the tight coupling approach. In this architecture, the DBMS manages both the multimedia database and the metadata. That is, the DBMS is an MM-DBMS. The tight coupling architecture has an advantage because all the DBMS functions could be applied on the multimedia database. This includes management of query processing, transactions, metadata, storage, security, and integrity. Note that with the loose coupling approach, unless the file manager performs the DBMS functions, the DBMS only manages the metadata for the multimedia data.

Other aspects pertaining to architectures also exist, as discussed in [THUR97]. For example, a multimedia database system could use a commercial database system such as an object-oriented database system to manage multimedia objects; however, relationships between objects and the representation of temporal relationships may involve extensions to the database management system. A DBMS together with an extension layer provides complete support to manage multimedia data. In the alternative case, both the extensions and the database management functions are integrated so that there is one database management system to manage multimedia objects as well as the relationships between the objects. Multimedia databases could also be distributed. In this case, we assume that each MM-DBMS is augmented with a multimedia distributed processor (MDP).

The British Broadcasting Corporation, American Broadcasting Corporation, *Financial Times of London, Wall Street Journal,* and Cable News Network disseminate news from all over the world. Many of the organizations that are producers of such multimedia information now want to put their information on the Web. Because of the quantity of data, it is almost impossible to get quality presentations of multimedia data on the Web. This is especially true with continuous media such as video and audio.

Network communication problems have to be overcome. Although there is progress and hardware is becoming less expensive, developing good software to ensure quality of service and timely access and presentation of these data remains the challenge. We have come a long way over the past few years in implementing delayed broadcast services. For example, important speeches by heads of countries are posted on the Internet within minutes. We are still a long way from live video broadcast as well as live movies on the Web. This does not mean live entertainment is not yet possible. The service we get today is not of good quality.

The biggest consumer of multimedia data on the Web is the entertainment, broadcasting, and journalism industries. A huge market exists for these industries and these organizations have tapped into only a small portion of it. As technology becomes more mature we can expect major players in the entertainment industry to be very active. In a way this is all part of electronic commerce (e-commerce). Although this does not deal with buying and selling music and video on the Internet, it deals with playing video and music on the Internet. Some of the technical challenges for data management include synchronizing presentation with storage and security, and ensuring that quality of service is maintained. Figure 5.3 illustrates multimedia on the Web with a three-tier approach where the middle tier does all the Web-based multimedia data processing. Another application area for multimedia on the Web is for training and distance learning. I discuss this application in the next section.

5.4 KNOWLEDGE MANAGEMENT

Knowledge management is the process of using knowledge as a resource to manage an organization. It could mean sharing expertise, developing a learning organization, teaching the staff, and learning from experiences, as well as collaboration. Basically,

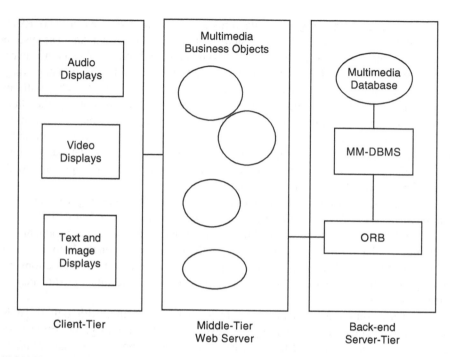

FIGURE 5.3 Three-tier multimedia computing on the Web.

knowledge management includes data management and information management, but this is not a view shared by everyone. Various definitions of knowledge management have been proposed. A good text on knowledge management is that by Davenport [DAVE97]. Knowledge management is a discipline invented mainly by business schools. The concepts have been around for a long time, but the term *knowledge management* was coined as a result of information technology and the Web.

In the collection of articles on knowledge management by Morey et al. [MORE01], knowledge management is divided into three areas as shown in Figure 5.4. These are strategies such as building a knowledge company and making the staff knowledge workers; process such as techniques for knowledge management including developing a method to share documents and tools; and metrics that measure the effectiveness of knowledge management. In the *Harvard Business Review* on knowledge management there is an excellent collection of articles describing a knowledge creating company, building a learning organization, and teaching people how to learn [HARV96]. Organizational behavior and team dynamics play major roles in knowledge management.

Knowledge management essentially changes the way an organization functions. Instead of competition it promotes collaboration. This means managers have to motivate the employee to share ideas and to collaborate by giving awards and other incentives. Team spirit is essential for knowledge management. People often get threatened with imparting knowledge because their jobs may be on the line. They are reluctant to share expertise. This type of behavior could vary from culture to

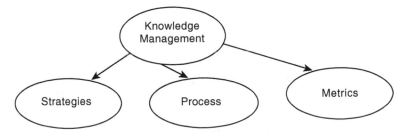

FIGURE 5.4 Knowledge management components.

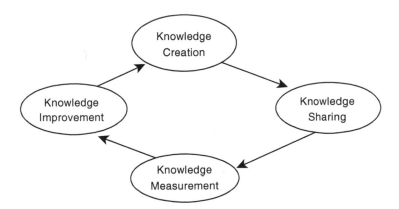

FIGURE 5.5 Knowledge management cycle.

culture. It is critical that managers eliminate this kind of behavior not by forcing the issue but by motivating the staff and educating them about all the benefits available to everyone with good knowledge management practices.

Teaching and learning are two important aspects of knowledge management. Both the teacher and the student have to be given incentives. Teachers can benefit by getting thank-you notes and write-ups in the company newsletter. Students may be rewarded by certificates, monetary awards, and other similar gestures. Knowledge management also includes areas such as protecting company intellectual properties, job sharing, changing jobs within the company, and encouraging change in an organization. Effective knowledge management eliminates dictatorial style and promotes more collaborative style. Knowledge management follows a cycle of creating, sharing, and integrating the knowledge; evaluating the performance with metrics; and then giving feedback to create more knowledge. This is illustrated in Figure 5.5. Variations of this cycle have been proposed in the literature [MORE98b].

The major question is what are knowledge management technologies? This is where information technology comes in. Artificial intelligence researchers have conducted a considerable amount of research on knowledge acquisition. They have also developed expert systems. These are also knowledge management technologies. Other knowledge management technologies include tools for collaboration, for organizing information on the Web, and for measuring the effectiveness of the knowledge

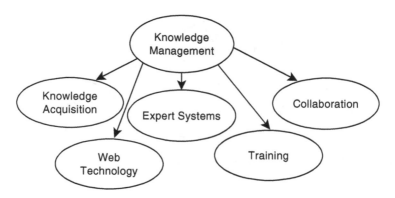

FIGURE 5.6 Knowledge management technologies.

gained such as collecting various metrics. Knowledge management technologies include data and information management. Figure 5.6 illustrates some of the knowledge management technologies. As can be seen, Web technologies play a major role in knowledge management. The impact of the Web is the subject of the next subsection.

Knowledge management and the Web are closely related. Although knowledge management practices have existed for many years, the Web has promoted these practices. Remember, knowledge management is building a knowledge organization. No technology is better than the Web for sharing information. You can travel around the world in seconds, with much knowledge to be gained by browsing the Web.

Many corporations now have intranets, the single most powerful knowledge management tool. Thousands of employees are connected through the Web in an organization. Large corporations have sites all over the world and the employees are becoming well connected with one another. Electronic mail (e-mail) can be regarded to be one of the early knowledge management tools. Now many tools are available such as search engines and e-commerce tools.

With the proliferation of Web data management and e-commerce tools knowledge management can become an essential part of the Web and e-commerce. Figure 5.7 illustrates the knowledge management activities on the Web such as creating Web pages, building e-commerce sites, sending e-mail, and collecting metrics on Web usage.

5.5 DECISION SUPPORT

Whereas data mining deals with discovering patterns from the data, machine learning deals with learning from experiences to make predictions and analyses; knowledge management deals with developing a learning organization; and decision support systems deal with tools that managers use to make effective decisions. Well-defined theory and principles, otherwise known as decision theories, are developed for decision support systems. In practice, however, the decision support techniques encompass various types of data, information, and knowledge management systems. For example, one can consider data mining tools to be special kinds of decision

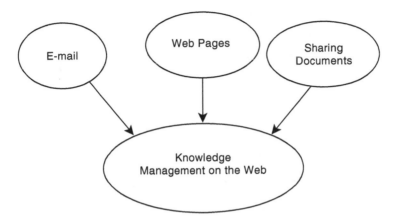

FIGURE 5.7 Knowledge management on the Web.

support tools. Are the tools based on machine learning, as well as tools for extracting data, from data warehouses? In fact, data warehouses are often referred to as systems used by managers to make effective decisions. In summary, decision support tools belong to a broad category (see, e.g., [DECI00]).

Decision support tools could include those that remove unnecessary and irrelevant results obtained from data mining. They could also be tools such as spreadsheets, expert systems, hypertext and Web information management systems, and any other system that helps analysts and managers to effectively manage the large quantities of data and information. One can also regard knowledge management to be a kind of decision support system [MORE98b]. This includes storing and managing the information, as well as developing tools to extract useful information. Some of the knowledge management tools also help in decision support. Collaboration tools are also special kinds of decision support tools. Various user modeling tools and human computer interaction tools also help analysts make decisions. An excellent introduction to decision support is given [TURB97]. In this text, a decision support system is viewed as any tool that can be used to get any data, information, or knowledge.

In summary, decision support is a technology that overlaps with data mining, data warehousing, knowledge management, machine learning, statistics, and others that help to manage knowledge and data of an organization. This is illustrated in Figure 5.8.

Now that I have discussed some of the essential points in decision support, I consider how the Web is significantly impacting it. Although the principles of decision support have not changed, the way decisions are made has. Managers and analysts no longer have to go through the laborious process of getting the data ready so that the decision support tools can be applied. Lots of data are now available, with more and more tools available to organize the data. Therefore, within a short space of time the decision support tools can be applied to the data and we can get answers. That is, effective data, information, and knowledge management on the Web are key to effective decision support.

With the Web, the distinction among data management, information management, and knowledge management is becoming vague. The problems include the

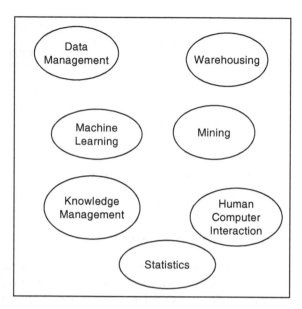

FIGURE 5.8 Decision support technologies.

great quantities of data and the challenges of extracting useful information to make decisions. Therefore, the various decision support tools have to be interfaced to the Web. We are seeing progress in this area. Web data management, warehousing, mining, and many other technologies such as knowledge management and collaboration play a role in making decisions by utilizing the Web. Because the infrastructure already exists for the Web, one can then keep on adding the various tools. The challenges include the scalability of the tools and making sense out of the available data.

At present, decision support on the Web is still premature. With the emphasis on e-commerce and various knowledge management and collaboration technologies, we can expect significant developments in this area.

5.6 AGENTS FOR THE WEB

Ever since the development of the Web in the early 1990s, we have heard the term *agents*. The problem is that it has been very difficult for people to agree with what agents mean. Various views of agents have been proposed. Some say agents are simply processes and some others say agents are Java applets. Yet a third group says that agents are processes that can jump from machine to machine and can execute everywhere. A fourth group says that agents are processes that have to communicate according some well-defined protocol. In fact, all these definitions are correct. Agents are processes that function on behalf of other processes and users, but they have to satisfy some agreed on method of communication.

Agents conduct many functions. These include locating resources on the Web or otherwise retrieving and filtering data for security purposes, and executing code.

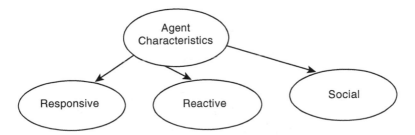

FIGURE 5.9 Agent characteristics.

Agents also may be self-describing, decentralized and autonomous, or distributed and heterogeneous. Various agent architectures have been proposed. These architectures describe frameworks for agent communication. Commutation also occurs based on well-defined protocols and languages. Although agents conduct security features like performing access controls and filtering, the agents themselves have to be secure. Furthermore, recent research investigates real-time and fault-tolerant aspects of agents. Agents have to react in a timely manner and recover from failures gracefully.

After examining the various definitions of agents given earlier, DiPippo et al. cite the following definition in [DIPI99]:

> [An agent is] a computer system, situated in some environment, that is capable of flexible autonomous action in order to meet its design objectives.

DiPippo also defines agents as having three major characteristics, as illustrated in Figure 5.9. They are:

- Responsive — reacting to environment
- Proactive — taking opportunistic, goal-directed initiatives
- Social — interacting with other agents (and users)

For example, agents have to take certain actions when certain situations occur such as getting data to the right users when the data become available, as described in the push model in Chapter 3.

Various types of agents have been proposed. These include the following:

- Data retrieval agent: retrieves data, knows when a user (or another agent) requires certain data, autonomously retrieves the data on behalf of the user (or agent)
- Data filtering agent: sorts incoming data — e-mail, news, etc. — and determines relevance place in appropriate location
- Resource locating agent: locates various resources such as database and files
- Situation monitoring agent: monitors a situation; when an event occurs, executes triggers

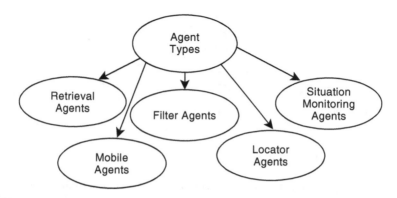

FIGURE 5.10 Agent types.

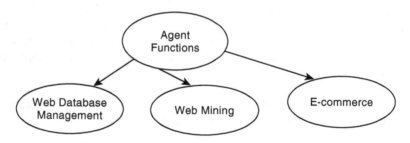

FIGURE 5.11 Agent functions.

- Mobile agent: migrates from machine to machine and executes code in different environments
- Data management agent: executes various functions such as query and transactions, mining, and e-commerce

Note that although the first five types can be regarded to be basic agents, they may also conduct activities for database management, data mining, and e-commerce. Thus, I have separated the agent types and functions in Figures 5.10 and 5-11. Note that agents do not necessarily have to function on the Web, however, the Web has really expanded agent technology. Agents now perform Web mining and database management, and e-commerce. The relationship between agents and the Web is illustrated in Figure 5.12.

Although they are agents, mobile agents are essentially those on the Web that execute at different locations and sites. These are processes that migrate from one environment to another and execute in a new environment. An example of a simple mobile agent is a Java applet. As stated in Chapter 2, an applet is a piece of code that resides in the server. The applet is brought into the browser environment when requested by a Web page and executes in the browser environment. Another alternative is a servlet, which executes in the server environment and the results are brought to the client.

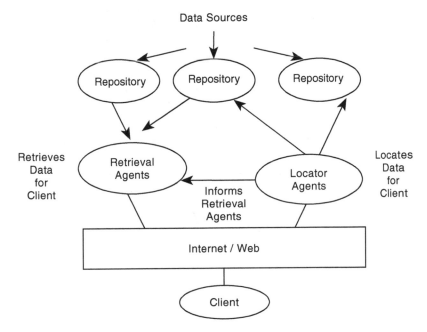

FIGURE 5.12 Agents and the Web.

An applet is a mobile agent because it migrates from a server to the client environment where it executes. Security is a major consideration for applet execution. An applet may be untrusted and therefore could corrupt the client resources. This is why in general applets execute in what is called a sandbox and cannot corrupt the client's resources.

Mobile code is not just restricted to an applet. This code is any process that exists on any of the machines, either client or server, and executes in any environment. The advantages with this approach are that you need to execute processes in the server environment and bring the results to the client. This could have a performance impact. By bringing the process into the client environment, speed may be enhanced, especially if the server environment is slow. Also, a server may execute many requests and priority may not be given to a client's request. By bringing the process into the client, this problem is avoided. Mobile code can execute between servers. For example, a mobile agent can move from one server to another.

Various aspects of mobile code are under examination. I believe security is most important for the reasons mentioned earlier. In addition to trusting mobile code, other security issues include access control and execute permissions. Appropriate access control and execution rules have to be enforced. The challenge is who is to enforce these rules in a Web environment. When a code migrates from system to system, what privileges does it have? Does it use the privileges originally granted to it or does it modify the privileges depending on the execution environment? A good discussion of secure mobile agents is given in [CORR99], where the focus is not only on securing the agents, but also ensuring that untrusted hosts do not corrupt the agents or spy on the agents. Protecting the agents is also an issue. Other research

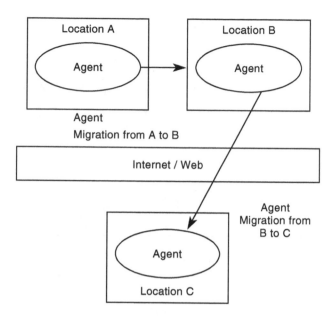

FIGURE 5.13 Mobile agents.

issues for mobile agents include real-time computing where these agents have to migrate, execute, and give results within a certain time. Fault tolerance is also a major consideration, because mobile agents have to recover from faults.

Ultimately, whether an agent is a mobile agent or another type such as a retrieval agent, there is little difference. For example, a mobile agent can perform retrieval facilities. A retrieval agent can migrate to different environments. Research and practice on mobile agents and code can be expected to explode. Java and similar developments are just the beginning. Figure 5.13 illustrates an example of mobile agents.

The ideal goal is to get the right information at the right time to the users. This could be achieved through the push model where information is pushed to the user, a pull model where the user goes out to get the data, or a combination of both models. In Chapter 3, I discuss various models for communications including the push and pull models. The main concern is information dissemination. Producers generate all kinds of information. This information has to be disseminated to the users in an appropriate manner. Following examination of various aspects of agents, I discuss the role of agents in information dissemination.

As stated earlier, agents could be the locator, retrieval, situation monitoring, or filtering types that retrieve data either by monitoring or when requested, monitor situations for events, and filter unwanted information, respectively. All these types of agents play a role in information dissemination. Figure 5.14 illustrates an instance where situation agents monitor for information production, and this information is then retrieved, filtered, and given to the consumer. Figure 5.15 illustrates the case where the consumer requests information, the locator agent locates the producers, and then the retrieval agents retrieve the information.

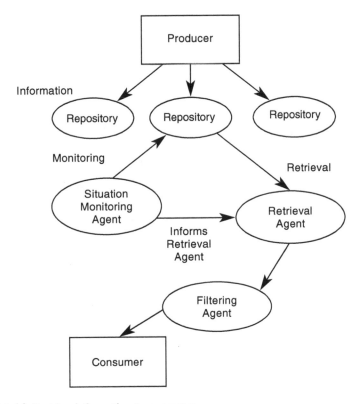

FIGURE 5.14 Pushing information to consumer.

Information dissemination technologies have expanded due to the Web. The challenge is to get the information to the user without overloading the user. Because this is such a big challenge, we cannot expect this problem to be solved completely. However, technologies under development show much promise so that information dissemination will be enhanced.

5.7 SOME OTHER INFORMATION TECHNOLOGIES

5.7.1 OVERVIEW

This section describes a collection of other important technologies for Web information management. These include training and distance learning; real-time processing and high-performance computing; visualization; quality of service; and some other technologies such as knowledge management, decision support, and agents. Some of these are discussed in this section.

The organization of this section is as follows: training and distance learning, which are becoming important technologies for the Web, are the subject of Section 5.7.2. Visualization is examined Section 5.7.3. The data on the Web have to be visualized for better understanding. Quality of service, which makes trade-offs between features such as security and real-time processing, is the subject of

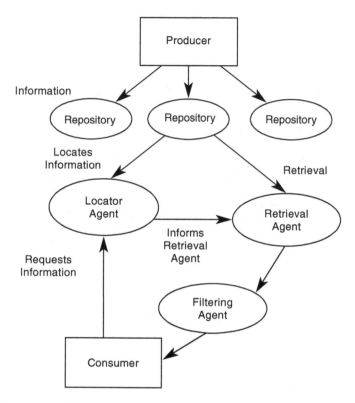

FIGURE 5.15 Pulling information from producer.

Section 5.7.4. Wireless information management covered in Section 5.7.5. Some other technologies are described in Section 5.7.6.

5.7.2 TRAINING AND DISTANCE LEARNING

Computer-based training (CBT), a hot topic these days, is all about preparing course materials and placing them electronically so that trainees can learn at their own paces. Because the instructor often is not present, several user interface issues and human computer interaction aspects come into play. The challenge is how to provide a personalized service to the trainees. For example, in a course on data management, financial workers may want additions on e-commerce, whereas defense workers may want information on data management for government applications. Instructors have to interview users, gather requirements, and prepare the material according to the requirements.

Closely related to CBT is CBT on the Web. This is also a form of distance learning. Various universities are now offering degrees on the Web, based on distance learning. The challenge is not only preparing the material to satisfy the users but also delivering the material in a timely manger. Multimedia on the Web is an import technology for this application, because live teaching may be desired at times. Although CBT is extremely useful, from time to time, students may want contact

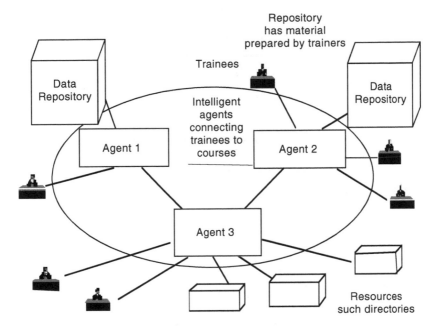

Repository
has material
prepared by trainers

Trainees

Data
Repository

Intelligent
agents
connecting
trainees to
courses

Data
Repository

Agent 1

Agent 2

Agent 3

Resources
such directories

FIGURE 5.16 Computer-based training on the Web.

with the instructor who may be thousands of miles away. Distance learning is not restricted to the boundaries of a country. It is now being implemented across continents. Figure 5.16 illustrates CBT on the Web. Several technologies have to work together, not just CBT but also multimedia, real-time processing, and all the technologies for Web data management. We can expect to hear a lot of about CBT on the Web and distance learning over the next several years.

5.7.3 VISUALIZATION

Visualization technologies graphically display the data in the databases. Much research has been conducted on visualization and the field has advanced a great deal, especially with the advent of multimedia computing. For example, the data in the databases could be rows and rows of numerical values. Visualization tools take the data and plot them in some form of a graph. The visualization models could be two-dimensional, three-dimensional, or even higher. Several visualization tools have been developed to integrate with databases, and workshops are devoted to this topic [VIS95]. An example illustration of integration of a visualization package with a database system is shown in Figure 5.17.

Subsequently, there has been much discussion on using visualization for data mining and also on using data mining to help the visualization process. When considering visualization as a supporting technology, however, it is the former approach that is getting considerable attention (see, e.g., [GRIN95]). As data mining techniques mature, it will be important to integrate them with visualization techniques. Figure 5.18 illustrates interactive data mining. The database management

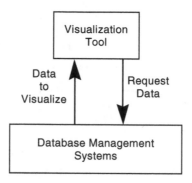

FIGURE 5.17 Database and visualization.

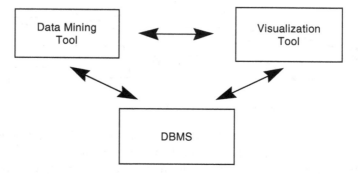

FIGURE 5.18 Interactive data mining.

system, visualization tool, and machine learning tool all interact with each other for data mining.

Let us reexamine some of the issues on integrating data mining with visualization. Of the four possible approaches, one is to use visualization techniques to present the results that are obtained from mining the data in the databases. These results may be in the form of clusters or they could specify correlations between the data in the databases. The second approach applies data mining techniques to visualization. The assumption in this instance is that it is easier to apply data mining tools to data in the visual form. Therefore, instead of applying the data mining tools to large and complex databases, one captures some of the essential semantics visually, and then applies the data mining tools. The third approach is to use visualization techniques to complement the data mining techniques. For example, one may use data mining techniques to obtain correlations among data or to detect patterns, but visualization techniques may still be needed to obtain a better understanding of the data in the database. The fourth approach uses visualization techniques to steer the mining process. The various data visualization tools now have to work on the Web. For example, these tools need to access the various data sources on the Web and visualize them to understand the data.

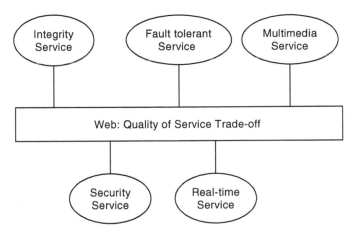

FIGURE 5.19 Qualify of service trade-offs.

5.7.4 QUALITY-OF-SERVICE ASPECTS

Because of the many Web data management technologies such as database management, security, multimedia, and integrity, it will be a challenge to make all work
together effectively. For example, how can we guarantee that the stock information
meets the timing constraints for delivery to the trader and yet maintain 100%
security? This will be very difficult. If we add the task of ensuring integrity of the
data and techniques for recovering from faults, and presenting multimedia data in
a timely manner, the problem becomes nearly impossible to solve. What do we do?
This is when quality of service (QoS) becomes involved. It is almost impossible to
satisfy all the requirements all the time. Thus, QoS specifies policies for trade-offs.
For example, if security and real time are both constraints that have to be met, then
perhaps at some instances it is not absolutely necessary to meet all the timing
constraints and we need to focus on security. In other instances, meeting timing
constraints may be crucial. As another example, consider multimedia presentation.
In some instances, we can live with low resolution, whereas in others we may need
perfect pictures.

Although much work has been implemented on QoS, a model has yet to be found
that takes into consideration all factors of QoS. This is a difficult problem and with so
many research efforts under way, we can expect to see progress. Users specify what
they want and these requirements get mapped down to the database system, operating
system, and networking requirements. Figure 5.19 illustrates an approach to QoS on
the Web. The ideas are rather preliminary and much work is needed.

5.7.5 WIRELESS INFORMATION MANAGEMENT

During the past decade, we have heard a lot about mobile information management
or wireless information management. Although mobile agents are an important
aspect of wireless information management, many other issues have to be taken into
consideration.

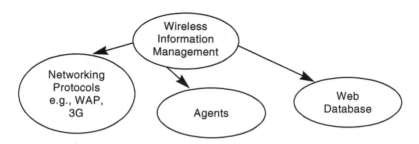

FIGURE 5.20 Wireless information technologies.

In today's world, we are becoming increasingly wireless with handheld digital and personal digital assistants. Managing the information and representing the information displayed on wireless devices are becoming critical. Various standards are proposed for wireless technology. These include networking standards as well as information management standards. For example, Wireless Access Protocol (WAP) enables information in disks to be displayed on wireless devices such a mobile phones. Third generation (3G) wireless protocols also are available. Finally, XML extensions have also been proposed for wireless technologies.

The database community has been examining data management issues for mobile computing for the past decade [IMIE92]. Wireless technologies have advanced rapidly, but information management technologies have not kept up with them. A research and development program is needed to ensure that appropriate data and information management technologies are developed. These include query processing techniques and indexing strategies. In addition, data modeling and display technologies are also important. Figure 5.20 illustrates wireless information management technologies.

5.7.6 SOME DIRECTIONS

This chapter discusses various technologies and services for the Web. Much of the discussion focuses on collaboration and multimedia technologies and services. I also briefly address knowledge management, decision support, training and distance learning, and visualization aspects.

Many of the technologies such as data, information, and knowledge management are used ultimately for managers, policymakers, and other people in authority to make effective decisions. Therefore, decision support is an important technology area for the Web because, in the future, we can expect these managers and policymakers to access the Web and make effective decisions based on the information they obtain.

Finally, technologies for accessing the resources on the Web as well as processing these resources are critical for effective data management. The technology that is vital for these services is agent technology. Different types of agents are used. Some agents locate resources, some conduct mediation, and some are mobile and execute in different environments. A Java applet can be regarded to be a simple agent.

Therefore, in addition to data, information, and knowledge management technologies, other technologies for Web data management and e-commerce include

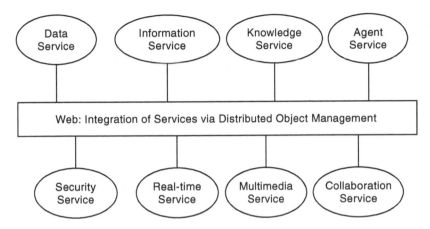

FIGURE 5.21 Integration of services on the Web.

security, collaboration, visualization, real-time processing, training, and multimedia. Several other technologies that I have not mentioned include data quality, fault tolerance, mass storage, fuzzy systems and soft computing, and data administration. All these technologies and services have to work together to make Web information management a success. Figure 5.21 illustrates how a distributed object management system can integrate the various technologies and services to provide effective Web data and information management.

5.8 RELATIONSHIP TO XML

This chapter has described a number of information management technologies for the Web. What the relationship is between these technologies and XML is the main goal of this publication, which explains the concepts of XML and shows how they can be applied to information management.

XML is extended for many of the information management technologies. For example, collaboration tools are using XML to specify the metadata as well as to exchange information. XML is extended to markup multimedia data such as images and video. XML is used for training application for data interchange. There is an interest in exploring QoS aspects for XML [ALLE01]. XML is also explored for wireless information management including Wireless Markup Language (WML). Agent markup languages are under development and are discussed further in Part II. In other words, XML is examined extensively for many of the information and data management technologies. Figure 5.22 illustrates XML for different information management technologies.

5.9 SUMMARY

This chapter provides an overview of a number of information management technologies. These include collaboration, multimedia, knowledge management, training, and

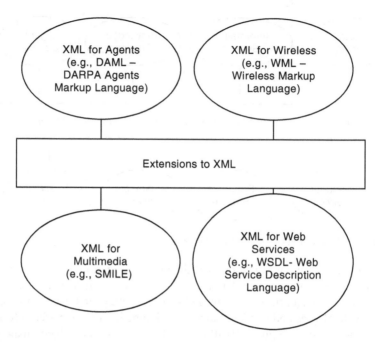

FIGURE 5.22 Extensions to XML.

agents as well as technologies such as visualization and decision support. I then briefly examine the relationship of these technologies to XML.

The chapter further provides the background for a more in-depth exploration of XML in Part III of this book. In particular, I review the XML extensions examined for a number of information management technologies in Part III.

6 E-Commerce and XML

6.1 OVERVIEW

I am now ready to embark on what is currently referred to as the killer application for the Web — electronic commerce (e-commerce). What is e-commerce? Simply stated, e-commerce is all about conducting commerce on the Web. It is about conducting transactions on the Web that involve buying and selling products. Earlier in this book, I mentioned that e-commerce on the Web could be as simple as putting up a Web page or as complicated as merging two corporations. We also have heard the term e-business, which is much broader than e-commerce and means conducting any business on the Web. Therefore, e-commerce has come to be known as conducting transactions on the Web, and tasks such as putting up Web pages and other activities are known as e-business. Figure 6.1 illustrates how one does a normal transaction (that is, a non-Web transaction), and Figure 6.2 illustrates how one carries out a business transaction on the Web.

This chapter provides a broad overview of e-commerce. More specialized topics are addressed in the next three chapters. I first discuss e-business and its relationship to e-commerce. This gives the reader some idea about the latest buzzwords in e-commerce. Then I describe some models for e-commerce, particularly business-to-business (B-to-B) e-commerce and business-to-consumer (B-to-C) e-commerce models. Models for e-commerce are immature; as we know more about e-commerce, various models will emerge. Then I discuss architectures for e-commerce. These include centralized as well as distributed and interoperable architectures. E-commerce functions are covered next, followed by how information technologies may be applied to e-commerce. Many other considerations such as the use of Java, applications of telecommunications, and legal and social issues are not discussed here. For more details, refer to [THUR00].

The organization of this chapter is as follows. Section 6.2 discusses e-business and its relationship to e-commerce with models of e-commerce the subject of Section 6.3. Architectures are described in Section 6.4; e-commerce functions, in Section 6.5; and information technologies for e-commerce, in Section 6.6. The relationship to XML is given in Section 6.7, with the conclusion presented in Section 6.8.

6.2 E-BUSINESS AND E-COMMERCE

We often hear the term e-business these days. Many companies prefer to be doing e-business instead of e-commerce because they believe e-commerce may be too narrow and e-business encompasses e-commerce. As far as I am concerned,

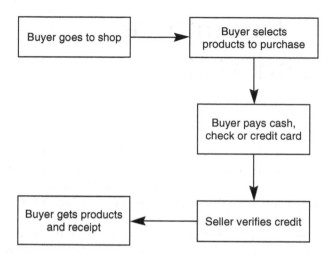

FIGURE 6.1 Non-Web process of commerce.

e-commerce on the Web can be considered to be as broad as putting up a Web page, listening to music, or conducting transactions. However, to be consistent with the terminology that is emerging, let me explain the differences between e-business and e-commerce, even though these two terms are often used interchangeably.

Those who differentiate between e-business and e-commerce state that e-commerce is all about conducting transactions on the Web, although e-business on the Web is much broader and includes learning and training, entertainment, putting up Web pages, hosting Web sites, conducting procurement, conducting supply chain management, handling help for telephone repairs or other services, and conducting almost anything else. E-business and some of its various components are illustrated in Figure 6.3.

Various types of corporation are now in e-business. One group consists of corporations that simply have Web pages. A second group consists of corporations that conduct e-commerce. A third group consists of corporations that help other corporations formulate e-business strategies. A fourth group consists of corporations that provide solutions and products for e-business. Other groups include those that conduct e-learning, e-training, and e-procurement, or provide e-helpdesks. With e-helpdesks, the time it takes to handle customer problems is greatly reduced and the need for too many human operators is also eliminated.

Corporations that provide consulting as well as solutions and products include Fortune 100 corporations such as International Business Machines (IBM) or smaller corporations such as the dot-com companies. For example, some of these small corporations can connect consumers with health care providers, lawyers, real estate agents, and others who furnish services. Consulting companies come in, assess the state of a corporation and its business practices, and advise the corporation on how to develop e-business solutions. One of the latest trends is to provide fully integrated enterprise resource management and business process reengineering on the Web. Corporations such as SAP AG are active in this area.

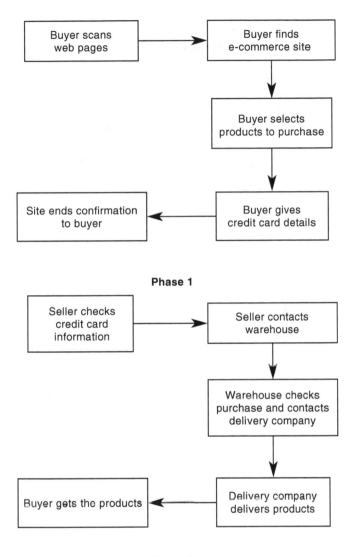

FIGURE 6.2 Web process of e-commerce.

Figure 6.4 illustrates the building blocks of e-business. For example, in Figure 6.4(a), the building blocks are the Web, information management technologies, and business processes (such as the business processes supported by the SAP product). These building blocks support e-commerce. Figure 6.4(b) illustrates the building blocks for e-music (i.e., entertainment on the Web). These include the Web, information management technologies, and the music business.

Figure 6.4(c) illustrates building blocks for universities and schools. These include Web, information management, and school or university business activities.

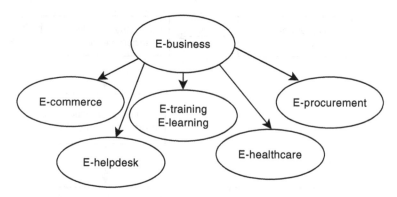

FIGURE 6.3 E-business and its components.

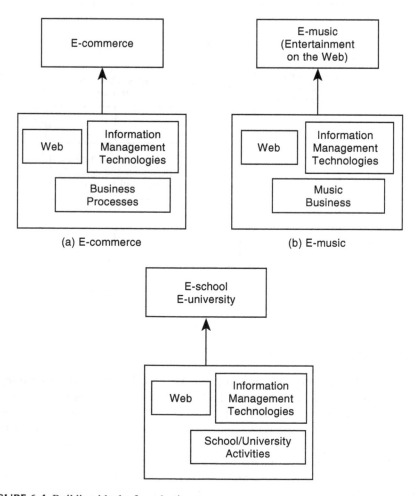

FIGURE 6.4 Building blocks for e-business.

As stressed in this book, to conduct good e-commerce, we need technologies and also good business practices. I have approached the subject from a technological point of view because we are technologists, not business specialists. Nevertheless, we need business specialists to build an e-commerce organization.

In summary, we will hear quite a lot about e-business in the future. Often, the terms e-business and e-commerce are used interchangeably. Some debate exists as to whether e-business is mainly about business or about information technology. After reading more about this subject and thinking about it, I believe a strong business component is essential for e-business. Technology will provide only the tools to make e-business more efficient. One can draw an analogy to health care. Good medical practices and policies are essential for good health care. Technology only makes the management of health care more efficient.

6.3 MODELS FOR E-COMMERCE

Again, no well-defined models exist for e-commerce. Two paradigms, however, which we can consider to be models, are emerging. They are B-to-B e-commerce and B-to-C e-commerce. Discussions on both these models, with examples, follow.

As its name implies, B-to-B e-commerce is all about two businesses conducting transactions on the Web. As an example, suppose corporation A is an automobile manufacturer and needs microprocessors to be installed in its automobiles. It then purchases the microprocessors from corporation B who manufactures the microprocessors. Another example is when an individual purchases some goods such as toys from a toy manufacturer. This manufacturer then contacts a packaging company via the Web to deliver the toys to the individual. The transaction between the manufacturer and the packaging company is a B-to-B transaction. B-to-B e-commerce also involves one business purchasing a unit of another business or two businesses merging. The main point is that such transactions have to be conducted on the Web.

B-to-C e-commerce is when a consumer such as a member of the mass population makes purchases on the Web. In the toy manufacturer example, the purchase between the individual and the toy manufacturer is a B-to-C transaction. Although B-to-C e-commerce showed much promise in the late 1990s, it has not lived up to its expectations. Many believe that the real future will be in B-to-B e-commerce, because this will involve millions of dollars.

The major difference between the two models is the way business is conducted. This is similar to the real world. In a B-to-C transaction, people can give credit cards, cash, or checks to make a purchase. In the Web world, credit cards are used most often, although the use of e-cash and checks is also being investigated. In B-to-B transactions, corporations have company accounts that are maintained and the corporations are billed at certain times. This is the approach used in the e-commerce world also. That is, corporations have accounts with one another, and these accounts are billed when purchases are made. Figures 6.5 and 6.6 illustrate examples of B-to-B and B-to-C transactions, respectively.

Regardless of the type of model, one of the major goals of e-commerce is to complete the transaction on time. For example, in the case of B-to-C e-commerce,

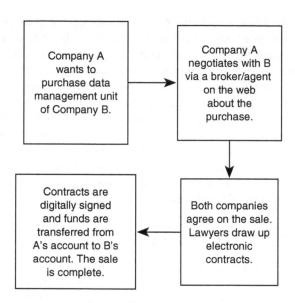

FIGURE 6.5 Business-to-business e-commerce.

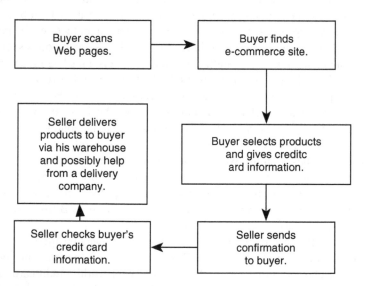

FIGURE 6.6 Business-to-consumer e-commerce.

the seller has to minimize the time between the time of purchase and the time the buyers receive their goods. The seller may have to depend on third parties such as packaging and tracking companies to achieve this goal. It should also be noted that with e-commerce the consumer has numerous choices for products. In a typical shop, consumers do not have access to all the products that are available. They cannot see the products displayed at the shop. In an e-commerce world, however, the consumer has access to all the products that are available to the seller.

Another key point to note is the issue of trust. How can the consumer trust the seller and how can the seller trust the consumer? For example, consumers may give the credit card number of a seller who is a fraud. The consumer may be a fraud and not send a check on receipt of the goods. The best model is known as the B-to-C relationship, but this is not always the case in the e-commerce world. Some of the challenges of trust are not very different from the mail order and the catalog world. If the goods do not arrive, consumers can write to their credit card companies, which is possibly a lengthy and a legal process. Another solution is for the seller to establish an account with a credit card company, thereby establishing some credibility. That is, a vendor from some unknown company called XXX may not be able to establish a relationship with a credit card company and therefore the buyer may not be in danger. In the e-commerce world, several additional security measures exist such as secure wallets and cards. These aspects are discussed in the chapter on security for e-commerce and also in the section on Java for e-commerce later in this chapter.

6.4 ARCHITECTURES FOR E-COMMERCE

In the previous sections, I discuss the process and models for e-commerce. In particular, Section 6.1 illustrates a process for e-commerce and Section 6.3 covers two models for e-commerce. Section 6.2 describes the relationship between e-commerce and e-business, in addition to architectures for e-commerce. Architectures can be viewed in two ways. One is centralized vs. distributed architecture and the other is client–server vs. federated architecture. I also discuss my views of the architectures suitable for the models described earlier. Then I provide an overview of interoperability issues and the role of object request brokers (ORBs) for e-commerce as well as a discussion of three-tier computing for e-commerce.

In the centralized architecture, illustrated in Figure 6.7, assume that all information at the e-commerce site is centralized. Many of the issues discussed for centralized data management would apply here. The challenges include maintaining all the data, which could be in databases, on Web pages, and in files. The data mining component may also be part of the central e-commerce server. The functions of a central e-commerce manager are illustrated in Figure 6.8. Assume that the e-commerce business functions as well as data management functions are conducted by the e-commerce server. An alternative in the three-tier computing architecture is illustrated later.

In a distributed architecture, the information managed by the e-commerce server is distributed. This could be because the corporation assets may be distributed across multiple sites. For example, major corporations have sites all over the world and each site may host components of the e-commerce server. The servers may be connected by a distributed processor, called e-distributed processor (EDP). Figure 6.9 illustrates a distributed architecture.

Currently, e-commerce is conducted in a client–server environment. Typically, browsers run in the client environment. We use browsers to access the commerce sites and specify the items we want to purchase. This is typically a client–server environment and is illustrated in Figure 6.10. Note that this is a two-tier, client–server system where the server is responsible for data as well as Web page management.

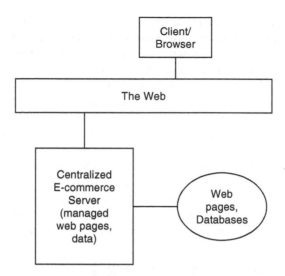

FIGURE 6.7 Centralized architecture for e-commerce.

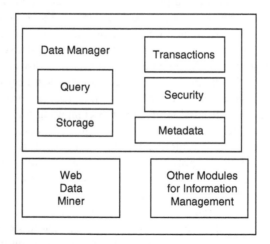

FIGURE 6.8 Modules of an e-commerce server.

A current trend is to move toward a three-tier environment. In this case, the client is responsible for presentation, the database server is responsible for managing databases, and the middle tier (the e-commerce server) is responsible for managing business objects that will implement the business functions of e-commerce such as brokering and mediation. Three-tier computing is illustrated in Figure 6.11.

Although client–server is the current trend, in a B-to-B e-commerce environment many corporations may have to collaborate with one other. That is, a federated environment may be needed. This is illustrated in Figure 6.12 where the e-commerce sites are connected through e-federated distributed processors (EFDPs). The various e-commerce servers form a federation and have to cooperate with one another. They

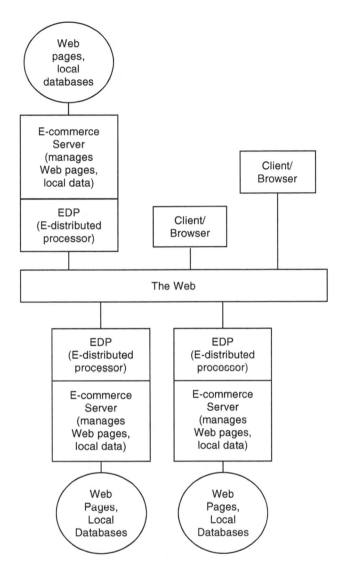

FIGURE 6.9 Distributed architecture for e-commerce.

also have to maintain some kind of autonomy. The issues, problems, and solutions for federated architectures are still unknown. As we conduct more research on e-commerce and get practical experience, some of the architectural issues will become clearer.

Next, let us look at interoperability aspects for e-commerce. The Object Management Group (OMG) has a special interest group (SIG) that focuses on services for e-commerce. The idea is for any e-commerce client to talk to any e-commerce server. That is, heterogeneous applications and systems have to interoperate on the Web in order to conduct e-commerce. Figure 6.13 illustrates an example where ORB services such as mediation and brokering help clients to communicate with servers.

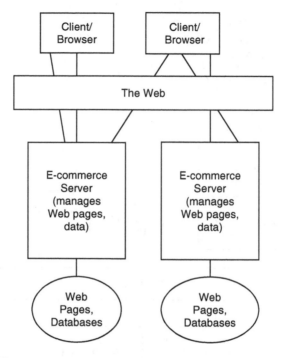

FIGURE 6.10 Client–server architecture for e-commerce.

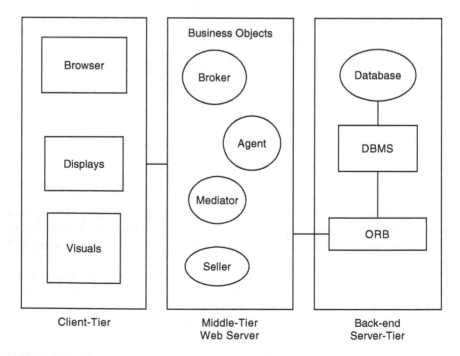

FIGURE 6.11 Three-tier computing for e-commerce.

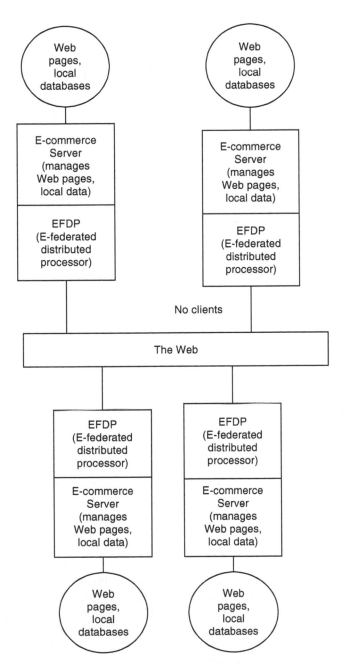

FIGURE 6.12 Client–server architecture for e-commerce.

6.5 E-COMMERCE FUNCTIONS

Three aspects to discussing e-commerce functions exist and are illustrated in Figure 6.14. The first aspect involves e-commerce client–server functions, which are

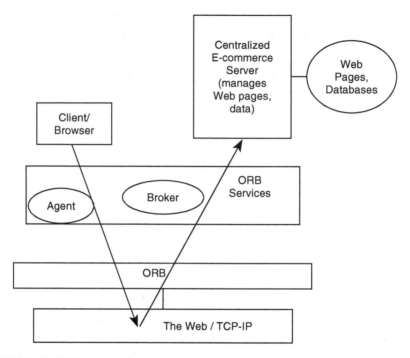

FIGURE 6.13 ORB services for e-commerce.

the information management functions; the second, the business functions for commerce; and the third, the distribution functions. Let us look at all aspects.

E-commerce server functions are illustrated in Figure 6.14. The modules of the e-commerce server may include modules for managing the data and Web pages, mining customer information, security enforcement, and transaction management. E-commerce client functions may include presentation management, user interface, caching data, and hosting browsers. A middle tier can also exist, which may implement the business objects for conducting the business functions of e-commerce. These business functions may include brokering, mediation, negotiations, purchasing, sales, marketing, and other e-commerce functions.

The business functions are those that are conducted in business transactions. Additional issues for e-commerce include the legal, ethical, and political considerations to be discussed later in this chapter. The e-commerce server functions are impacted by the information management technologies for the Web. These technologies are discussed in detail in the next chapter. In addition to the data management and business functions, the e-commerce functions also include those for managing distribution, federations, and heterogeneity.

6.6 INFORMATION TECHNOLOGIES FOR E-COMMERCE

In the previous section, I focus on various e-commerce functions. Data and information management plays a critical role for e-commerce. In one of my previous

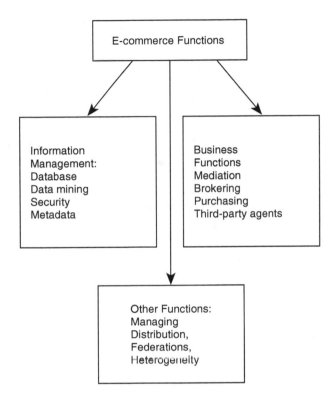

FIGURE 6.14 E-commerce functions.

books, I elaborated on information technologies for e-commerce. I summarize that information in this section. With the various data and information management technologies, e-commerce cannot be a reality. E-commerce also includes nontechnological aspects such as policies, laws, and social and psychological impacts. We are now doing business in an entirely different way and therefore we need a paradigm shift. We cannot do successful e-commerce if we still want the traditional way of buying and selling products. We have to be more efficient and rely on the technologies much more to gain a competitive edge.

A number of information management technologies are essential for e-commerce. These include data management, data mining, security management, transaction management, multimedia, collaboration, and knowledge management. Figure 6.15 illustrates the overall picture of the technologies that may be applied to e-commerce. In addition to these technologies, other areas such as Java and telecommunications also play major roles for e-commerce. Some of the details are given in [THUR00].

6.7 RELATIONSHIP TO XML

Metadata technology is another critical component for e-commerce. Metadata include information about the e-commerce site, with internal information such as

FIGURE 6.15 Information technologies for e-commerce.

how the site is structured as part of the metadata. Metadata also include information about the users of the site. Various ontologies are under development for e-commerce. These ontologies are common definitions for various e-commerce terms. Finally, XML is under examination for e-commerce. XML specification for e-commerce would include information about specifying e-commerce site-specific data; information about the process for e-commerce; and domain-specific data such as securities information for financial transactions. With XML, both the clients and servers specify documents with common notations and domain-type definitions. Figure 6.16 illustrates an example of XML for conducting Web transactions.

I have briefly discussed how XML may be applied for e-commerce. In Part III, I elaborate on this and discuss the applications of XML to data and information management in more detail.

6.8 SUMMARY

This chapter gives a broad overview of e-commerce. I start with a discussion of the e-commerce process, which is followed by a discussion of the differences between e-business and e-commerce. Then I describe models, architectures, and functions for e-commerce. I also discuss the application of Java and the communications for e-commerce. Finally, I provide an overview of information technologies for e-commerce, ending with a discussion of the relevant relationship to XML.

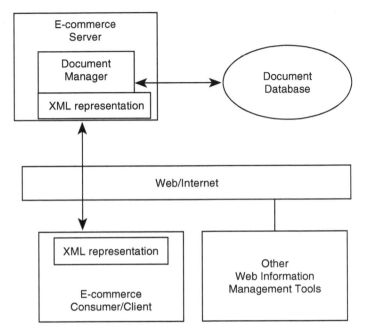

FIGURE 6.16 XML and e-commerce.

7 Metadata, Ontologies, and XML

7.1 OVERVIEW

The previous chapters in Part I discuss various supporting technologies for XML This chapter focuses on metadata and ontologies and provides a brief overview of XML, as the bridge between Part I and the rest of the book.

Metadata is a term that has been defined rather loosely. It originates from data management. Initially it was called the data dictionary or the catalog that described the data in the databases [DATE90]. As discussed in Appendix B, in a relational database the data dictionary has information about the relations and their attributes. Subsequently, data dictionaries included other information such as access control rules, integrity constraints, and information about data distribution. As a result, this information came to be known as metadata. With data warehousing, multimedia, and Web information management, the definition of metadata started expanding. Finally, with integration of heterogeneous databases, applications, and systems, the term metadata is now used synonymously with repository technology.

Although I could have included metadata as part of the discussion on technologies addressed in Part I of this book, I chose not to do so because metadata is still a new topic for Web data management and mining; and because the technologies are emerging, the definition of metadata is also expanding. Therefore, I have devoted a chapter on metadata under emerging Web data management technologies. This is an area that will change with technological developments.

The role of metadata in mining is now a subject of much research (see, e.g., [META96]). Two aspects are considered: one is mining the metadata to extract patterns, and the other is to use the metadata to guide the mining process. This chapter also provides a preliminary discussion of metadata mining. Section 7.2 provides some background information on what metadata is all about for various types of systems. Metadata technology for the Web is introduced in Section 7.3. In Section 7.4, metadata mining is discussed with the Web as a key part of this. A note on ontologies is given in Section 7.5, with the subject revisited in the discussion of the semantic Web. XML, an emerging standard for Web documents, is the subject of Section 7.6. That is, after discussing XML briefly in previous chapters, it is seriously introduced in Section 7.6. The chapter is summarized in Section 7.7. The conclusion to Part I is given in Section 7.8.

7.2 BACKGROUND ON METADATA

Let us revisit the discussion of metadata in Appendix B. In the example we give, the database consists of two relations EMP and DEPT. The metadata include information

Data

FIGURE 7.1 Metadata for image data.

about these relations, the number of attributes of each relation, the number of tuples in each relation, and other information such as the creator of the relation. Metadata also include information on the three-schema architecture discussed in Appendix B. That is, the external, conceptual, and internal views, as well as the mapping between the three layers, are part of the metadata. In addition, metadata include information such as "John has read access to EMP and write access to DEPT." Metadata also have information on access methods and index strategies.

Next, let us take it one step further and consider the distributed and heterogeneous databases discussed in Appendix B. Metadata have information on how the data are distributed. For example, EMP relation may have multiple fragments distributed across multiple sites. Metadata also include information to handle heterogeneity. For example, the fact that at site 1 an object is interpreted as a ship and at site 2 it is interpreted as a submarine is part of the metadata. The three-schema architecture discussed in Appendix B has been extended to multiple layers to handle heterogeneous schema (see the discussion in [THUR97]). Metadata guide the schema transformation and integration process in handling heterogeneity. Metadata are also needed to migrate legacy databases. Information about the legacy databases is stored as part of the metadata. These metadata are used to transform the legacy database systems to new systems.

Multimedia on the Web is becoming an important technology area and was addressed in [THUR01]. Metadata that describe multimedia data could be in different formats. As illustrated in Figure 7.1, in the case of image databases, metadata that describe images could be in text format. Metadata about video and audio data could be in relations or in text. Metadata could be multimedia data such as video and audio. Metadata for the Web include information about the various data sources, the locations, the resources on the Web, the usage patterns, and the policies and procedures.

Metadata for data warehousing include data for integrating the heterogeneous data sources as well as metadata to maintain the warehouse. Metadata can also be generated in the mining process. As data mining is performed, metadata could be gathered about the steps involved in mining. Metadata are also collected for visualization, decision support, machine learning, and statistical reasoning.

In summary, whether it be data mining, data management, Web information management, data warehousing, visualization, or decision support, metadata are the central components common to all technologies. These are illustrated in Figure 7.2.

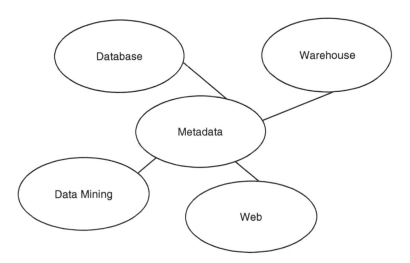

FIGURE 7.2 Metadata as a central component.

7.3 METADATA FOR THE WEB

Some of the metadata management issues for Internet database management have been discussed. Maintaining appropriate metadata is critical for intelligent browsing. As one goes through the cyberspace, the metadata, which describe the navigation patterns, should be updated. These metadata are consulted periodically so that users can have some idea as to where they are. Metadata become like a map. Furthermore, the Internet metadata manager should continually give advice to the users.

Appropriate techniques are needed to manage the metadata. These include querying and updating the metadata. The Internet environment is very dynamic. This means that the metadata must be updated continually as users browse through the Internet and as data sources get updated. Furthermore, as new data sources get added, the changes have to be reflected in the metadata. Metadata may also include various security policies. The metadata must also be available to the users in a timely manner. Finally, appropriate models for the metadata are also needed. These models may be based on the various data models or may utilize the models for text and multimedia data.

Metadata repositories may be included with the various data servers or may be provided as separate repositories for the metadata. A scenario having multiple data servers and metadata repositories is illustrated in Figure 7.3.

Much research is being conducted on metadata management for the Internet (see, e.g., [AIPA95], [AIPA96], and [META96]), however, much remains to be done before efficient techniques are developed for metadata representation and management. Defining the metadata is also a major issue.

7.4 MINING AND METADATA

Metadata technology is becoming key for various tasks such as data management, data warehousing, Web searching, multimedia information processing, and data

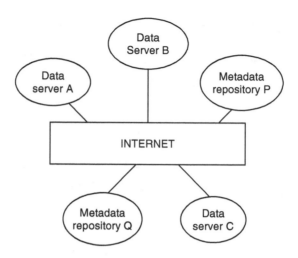

FIGURE 7.3 Metadata repositories on the Internet.

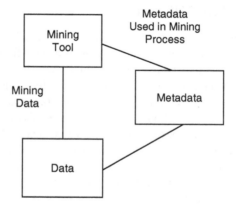

FIGURE 7.4 Metadata used in data mining.

mining. Because metadata have been so closely aligned with databases in the past, a discussion is included in this book about the impact of metadata technology on data mining.

Metadata technology plays an important role in data mining. Metadata could guide the data mining process. That is, the data mining tool could consult the metadatabase and determine the types of queries to pose to the DBMS. Metadata may be updated during the mining process. For example, historical information as well as statistics may be collected during the mining process, and the metadata have to reflect the changes in the environment. The role of metadata in guiding the data mining process is illustrated in Figure 7.4. Extracting metadata from the data and then mining the metadata are illustrated in Figure 7.5.

With the many discussions on the role of metadata for data mining [META96], many challenges have emerged. For example, when is it better to mine the metadata?

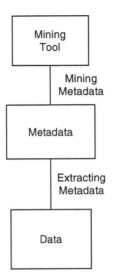

FIGURE 7.5 Metadata mining.

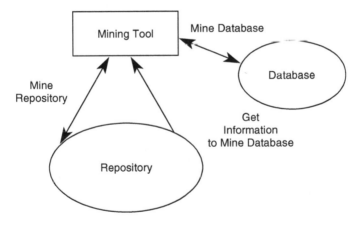

FIGURE 7.6 Repository and mining.

What are the techniques for metadata mining? How does one structure the metadata to facilitate data mining? Researchers are working on addressing these questions.

Closely associated with the metadata notion is that of a repository. A repository is a database that stores possibly all the metadata, the mappings between various data sources when integrating heterogeneous data sources, information needed to handle semantic heterogeneity such as "ShipX and SubmarineY are the same entity," policies and procedures enforced, and information on data quality. Thus, the data mining tool may consult the repository to conduct the mining. On the other hand, the repository itself may be mined. Both these scenarios are illustrated in Figure 7.6.

Metadata technology plays an important role in various types of mining. For example, in the case of mining multimedia data, metadata may be extracted from

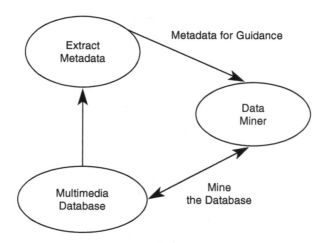

FIGURE 7.7 Metadata for multimedia mining.

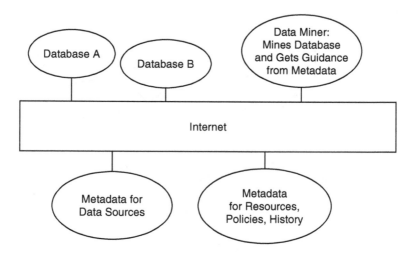

FIGURE 7.8 Metadata for Web mining.

the multimedia databases and then used to mine the data. For example, as illustrated in Figure 7.7, the metadata may help in extracting the key entities from the text. These entities may be mined using commercial data mining tools. In the case of textual data, metadata may include information such as the type of document, the number of paragraphs, and other information describing the document but not its contents.

Metadata are also critical in the case of Web mining discussed in Chapter 3. Because so much information and data are available on the Web, mining these data directly could become quite challenging. Therefore, we may need to extract metadata from the data, and then either mine the metadata or use them to guide in the mining process. This is illustrated in Figure 7.8. Languages such as XML, to be briefly discussed in the next section, play a role in describing metadata for Web documents.

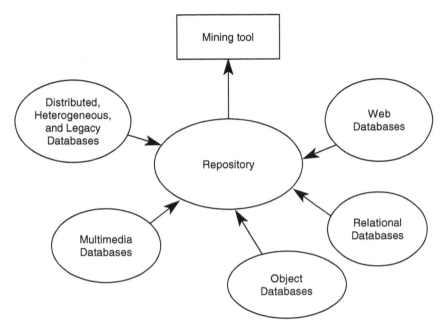

FIGURE 7.9 Metadata as the central repository for mining.

Chapter 3 addresses security and privacy issues for data mining, with policies and procedures key issues for determining the extent of protecting the privacy of individuals. These policies and procedures can be regarded as part of the metadata. Therefore, such metadata have to guide the process of data mining so that privacy issues are not compromised through mining.

In almost every aspect of mining, metadata play crucial roles. Even in the case of data warehousing, regarded to be a preliminary step to mining, it is important to collect metadata at various stages. For example, in the case of a data warehouse, data from multiple sources have to be integrated. Metadata guide the transformation process from layer to layer in building the warehouse (see the discussion in [THUR97]). Metadata also help in administering the data warehouse, in addition to extracting answers to the various queries posed.

Because metadata are key to all kinds of databases including relational; object, multimedia; distributed, heterogeneous, and legacy; and Web databases, one could envisage building a metadata repository that contains metadata from the different kinds of databases and then mining the metadata to extract patterns. This approach is illustrated in Figure 7.9 and could be an alternative if the data in the databases are difficult to mine directly.

7.5 NOTE ON ONTOLOGIES

In recent years, we have been hearing a lot about ontologies. That is, the terms have evolved from data dictionary to metadata and now to ontology. What then is an ontology? Fikes [FIKE96] has defined an ontology to be a specification of concepts to be used for expressing knowledge. This would include entities, attributes, reationships, and constraints (see the discussion in [ONTO] about this work).

One may argue that we have been talking about entities and relationships for over two decades. So what additional benefits do ontologies give us? Ontologies are essentially an agreed on way to specify knowledge. Fikes [FIKE96] states that ontologies are distinguished not by their form but by the role they play in representing knowledge. One can have ontologies to represent persons, vehicles, animals, and other general entities such as tables, chairs, and chemistry. For example, a group of people could define an ontology for a person and this ontology could be reused by someone else. Another group may want to modify the ontology for a person and have its own ontology for a person. That is, different groups could have different ontologies for the same entity. Once these ontologies are used repeatedly, a standard set of ontologies may evolve. Efforts are being made to standardize ontologies by different programs. In addition, standards organizations are also attempting to specify ontologies.

Why are ontologies useful? They are needed whenever two or more people have to work together. For example, ontologies are very important for collaboration, agent-to-agent communication, or knowledge management; and for different database systems to interoperate with each other. Ontologies are also useful for education and training, genetics, and modeling and simulation. In summary, many fields require ontologies. A good example is different groups collaborating on a design project. They could define ontologies so that they all speak the same language. If ontologies are previously defined by other design groups, they could reuse these ontologies to save time.

We often hear about domain-specific ontologies. What are they? One can arbitrarily come up with ontologies for aircraft, but groups working in various Air Force organizations may have their own specialization for aircraft. These are domain-specific ontologies. One challenge when interoperating heterogeneous databases is whether you can find a common set of ontologies for semantic integration of the databases or you need to take each pair of databases and treat them separately. To determine a common set of ontologies, it is sometimes necessary to examine various pairs, to develop ontologies for these pairs, and then to extract a common set of ontologies. The goal for integrating heterogeneous databases is to find a common set of ontologies from the domain-specific ontologies. This is illustrated in Figure 7.10.

Electronic commerce (e-commerce) applications and Web data management define a new set of ontologies. For e-commerce applications, ontologies include specifications for Web pages to set up e-commerce sites and ontologies for specifying various goods. Web sites are emerging that specify ontologies. These ontologies can be used for various activities such as collaboration and integration.

Computer scientists and also logicians and philosophers are engaged in extensive research on ontologies. Uncertain reasoning, probabilities, and other heuristics are incorporated into ontology research. This is a very dynamic area, and I urge the reader to visit various Web sites specifying ontologies and keep up with the developments.

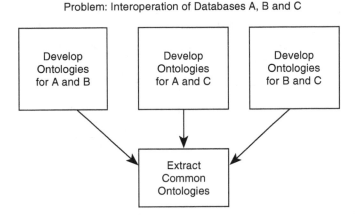

FIGURE 7.10 Common ontologies from domain-specific ontologies.

7.6 RELATIONSHIP TO XML

XML is discussed throughout this book because it is one of the significant developments in information technology from the 1990s. This section introduces XML and discusses the relationship to ontologies and metadata.

Is XML a data model, a metadata model, or something else? Although different views have been given about XML, it can be viewed as all these. Essentially, it specifies a format you can use to represent documents that can be universally understood. These could be documents of text, multimedia, relational data, and financial data. Finally, XML gives us some way to specify features in a common way; and because the Web has millions of users, we need this for document representations.

XML is a specification by the World Wide Web Consortium (W3C) for document representations. It was initially developed to represent text documents. Text documents could be memos, letters, and papers. As stated in [ROSE99], XML is a semistructured format for data with interesting tags. Tags are defined by tagsets called domain-type definitions (DTDs). DTDs can be used to specify memos, letters, and other documents. XML is used only for specification. Its counterpart, Extensible Style Language (XSL), is used for presenting a document. Various application programming interfaces (APIs) are used for accessing XML content. Links between documents are provided by XML Link Lanaguage (Xlink), a form of hyperlinking. XML Pointer Language (Xpointer) is used to point within an XML document.

XML evolved from Hypertext Markup Language (HTML) and Standard Generalized Markup Language (SGML). SGML was developed before the Web and had too many unnecessary details. HTML was developed for the Web and had limitations. For example, HTML has a fixed set of markup tags that do not help in understanding the content. These tags are designed to help a browser know how to display the document. Consequently, the best search engines can index HTML documents based on such items as frequency of words. HTML cannot implement one-to-many linking,

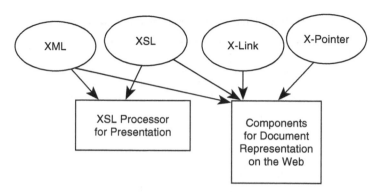

FIGURE 7.11 XML for the Web.

extract pieces of text out of a document, and link to arbitrary portions of Web pages. These are just some of the deficiencies of HTML. XML attempts to overcome these deficiencies (see [ROSE99]).

XML provides the facility for creating one's own set of markup tags. That is, a document can be defined the way you want it. As long the receiver's machine can understand XML tags, then the receiver can look at the document the way it was intended. One can think of XML as a metalanguage, or a language describing how to create one's markup language. By changing the tags, an XML document can take a completely different shape. XSL is used for creating one's own set of presentation rules; Xlink enables one-to-many linking and also enables bidirectional linking; and Xpointer enables one to point into a document without putting any anchor tags into the document. Thus, XML, XSL, Xlink, and Xpointer are the essential components for document representation on the Web. This is illustrated in Figure 7.11.

Various groups are proposing XML for representing documents such as financial securities, chemical structures, e-commerce product information, and multimedia data. One specific area of interest to the data management community is a query language for XML (XMLQL). As stated by Duetch et al. [DEUT99], XMLQL is a declarative and relationally complete query language. Various proposals have been submitted to W3C for XMLQL. A simple XMLQL query extracts data from an XML document. For example, a query could be to extract the author and title from an XML document. A more complex query can perform joins on contents in XML documents as well as other complex operations. Queries can also be nested. An XMLQL has associated with it a data model, which is usually a graphical model. A thorough discussion of one such XMLQL is given in [DEUT99]. Based on proposals such as XMLQL, W3C is standardizing query languages for XML and the result is the effort on XML Query Language (Xquery) (see ACM01]).

One of the current limitations of XML is its inability to specify semantics. Some argue that it is not up to XML to specify semantics. Others argue that ontology work has to be integrated into XML. We can expect some resolution in the next few years. Ontology, which is an important aspect of metadata, is the subject of the next section. XML specifications are continually evolving like many standards. Therefore, I urge the reader to keep track of the developments in www.w3c.org. XML implementations may not conform entirely to the standards. Thus, users need to be aware of such issues before using an XML product.

One of the questions I am often asked is what the difference is between ontologies and XML. Whereas XML specifies the structure of a document, ontologies specify semantics of various applications. The challenge is to integrate the structure with the semantics to provide a complete set of interoperable mechanisms.

7.7 SUMMARY

This chapter is devoted to a discussion of Web metadata management and mining. I first provide an overview of the various types of metadata, and then describe metadata management on the Web. Metadata mining is discussed because it is critical for Web data management and one can extract, for example, usage patterns by mining metadata. Metadata technology is the central component to many kinds of information systems such as decision support, database, and machine learning. I end this chapter with a discussion of ontologies and the relationship to XML.

The notion of metadata is continually changing. Initially, metadata technology was considered to be just the data dictionary. Then it included policies, access control rules, and information about data distribution. Now metadata include information about the various resources on the Web, usage patterns, and repositories. Metadata management and mining on the Web will become an essential part of all aspects of data management and mining. Finally, we can expect developments in both XML and ontologies to explode to benefit effective data management on the Web.

Conclusion to Part I

Part I described various supporting technologies for XML. These involve the Web; Web database systems including architectures, models, and functions; information retrieval systems; information management such as collaboration, multimedia, knowledge management, and training; e-business and e-commerce; and finally meta-data and ontologies. For each of these supporting technologies I discussed the relationship to XML. XML evolved as a result of the developments of the various data and information management technologies as well as the Web.

Part III shows how these technologies relate in more detail to XML. Databases have to be accessed through the Web and XML supports data exchange for this purpose. Furthermore, heterogeneous databases have to be integrated on the Web; even here, schemas can be represented in XML. XML also has applications in e-business and e-commerce. The various documents on the Web have to interoperate with each other. I elaborate on the details in Part III.

Now that the readers have some idea of what motivates XML, they are in the position to examine the concepts of XML, which are the subjects of Part II.

Part II

XML and the Semantic Web

Part II, consisting of four chapters, describes XML, the semantic Web, and semistructured databases, which are some of the essential concepts in XML. Chapter 8 discusses basic Extensible Markup Language (XML), particularly, XML attributes and elements, namespaces, data types, and other aspects. The information in this chapter can give the reader a preliminary understanding of XML, but it is not intended to prepare the reader to be proficient in writing XML documents. Many "how to" books on writing XML documents exist. As I have stressed, my books are written mainly for technical managers who can get an understanding of what the technologies are to manage projects and programs.

Chapter 9 provides an overview of some the advanced concepts in XML including a discussion of semantic issues, domain definition types, Xlink and other concepts, internationalization, XML schemas, and data integration issues. Chapter 10 describes the resource description framework (RDF) and the semantic Web. Many claim that RDF will soon replace XML because it not only uses XML syntax but also describes semantics; as a result, it is a lot more powerful. RDF is the main foundation of the semantic Web. Finally, Chapter 11 provides an overview of semistructured databases. When XML was originally formulated, it was thought to be the model for semistructured databases. It was soon found that XML could be the model for any type of database. Because semistructured databases influenced the development of XML, an overview of this technology is given in Part II. In Part III, however, more details on XML and databases in general are examined.

8 Basic Concepts in XML

8.1 OVERVIEW

Part I covers various supporting technologies for XML. Because of these supporting technologies, XML has gained much popularity. These supporting technologies include the Web, Web databases, information retrieval, metadata, information management, and electronic commerce (e-commerce). In each of the chapters in Part I, the relationship of the technology to XML is mentioned briefly. This gives the reader some idea about XML. This part of the text explores what XML is all about.

As mentioned in [LAUR00], XML documents are containers for information. A container could have information as well as more containers; that is, one could have containers of containers. The containers have labeled information as described in Section 8.2. XML documents conform to certain rules. Well-formed documents are those that satisfy the rules. For a document to be an XML document, it has to be well formed. One could go a step farther and have valid XML documents. These documents are based on what is called document-type definitions (DTDs). These various aspects as well as a sample of a simple XML document are given in Section 8.2. Many other XML concepts such as namespaces, data types, schemas, and XML Link Language (Xlinks) are discussed in this chapter and the next. To make it more understandable, the simple concepts are introduced in this chapter and the more advanced concepts, in the next.

The organization of this chapter is as follows: basic XML concepts are given in Section 8.2; elements and attributes, in Section 8.3; namespaces, in Section 8.4; data types, in Section 8.5; and other aspects, in Section 8.6. Finally, the chapter is summarized in Section 8.7. Figure 8.1 illustrates the various aspects addressed in the chapter. Numerous texts describe the syntax of XML, although much of the information may be outdated, because newer specifications are emerging. That is one of the main reasons I have not given the details of XML syntax. The reader is referred to many excellent texts, but to get up-to-date information on XML syntax and rules, the reader should read World Wide Web Consortium (W3C) Web pages on XML and related standards.

8.2 COMPONENTS OF AN XML DOCUMENT

An XML document has three components: an optional prolog; a root element that is required; and material following the root, which is optional. The prolog has information about XML declarations, white spaces, comments, and other instructions. The root

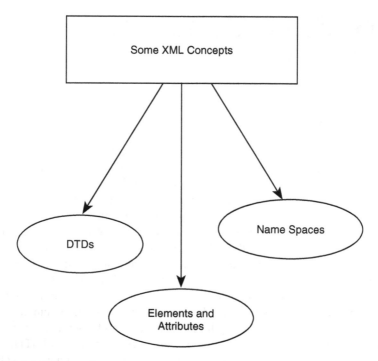

FIGURE 8.1 XML overview.

element is the body of the XML document and has elements and attributes. The optional end material may give information about how to process the document.

The prolog has XML declaration of the form, for example, <"XML version 1.0">, which states that we are using version 1.0 of XML in the document. This may be followed by a series of DTDs of the form:

```
<!DOCTYPE document (title, author) [
<!ELEMENT title (---)>
<!ELEMENT author (---)>
]
{which ends the DTD}
```

The preceding display is a simple DTD that specifies the document with elements title and author. The root has information about the title and the author as shown next. The end material could have some comments. Figure 8.2 illustrates the components of an XML document.

```
<document>
<title> XXX </title>
<author> John </author>
</document>
{the above is the root element}
```

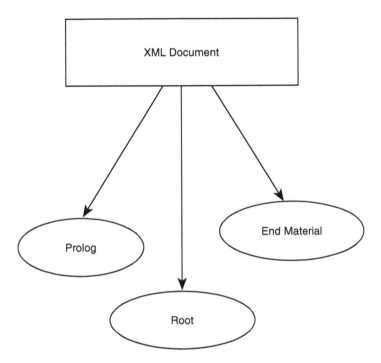

FIGURE 8.2 Components of an XML document.

8.3 CONTAINERS, ELEMENTS, AND ATTRIBUTES

In an XML document, which holds containers and information, the information
specifies the attributes and elements. An element is of the following form:

```
<element> information </element>
```

Consider an example, where Jane Smith's address is specified. This information can
be represented as follows:

```
<label>
<name> Jane Smith </name>
<address>
<street> 270 Burlington Road </street>
  <city> Bedford </city>
  <state> MA 01730 </state>
</address>
</label>
```

Therefore, to specify the name and address of a person in a label, the name is
an element, and the address is a container within the container label. The address
has three elements including the street, city, and state. The street number is included
as part of the city, and the zip code is included as part of the state. In the above

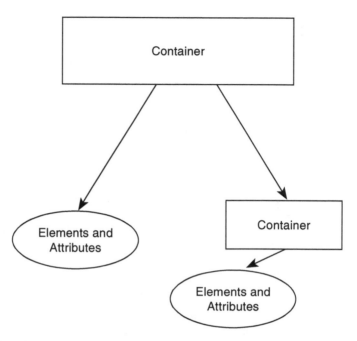

FIGURE 8.3 Containers, elements, and attributes.

example we have used the elements to represent the information. Alternatively, attributes could have been used to represent the information instead of elements. By using attributes, the following results:

```
<address
street = "270 Burlington Road"
city = "Bedford"
state = "MA 01730"
/>
```

Thus, in the first representation we have information presented as elements, whereas in the second representation we have them as attributes. Elements can contain other elements whereas attributes can contain just text. Various rules are available to name the elements and attributes. More details can be found in any of the documents on XML (see, e.g., [LAUR00]). For completely up-to-date information, however, the best reference is the XML specification listed on the W3C Web pages. Figure 8.3 illustrates the components of a root element consisting of elements and attributes.

8.4 NAMESPACES

One of the major issues with XML is that different groups are defining same objects differently. This heterogeneity problem has been extensive in integrating heterogeneous databases, but never before has the problem been so exacerbated. This is because all kinds of groups are using XML to define documents. These include

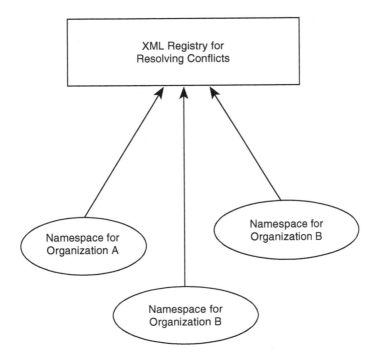

FIGURE 8.4 Namespaces and conflict resolution.

defense, chemical, biological, and many more types of groups. A solution to this heterogeneity problem is namespaces. Although this is not really a desirable solution, there is really no way around it at the present time. Thus, as stated in [LAUR00], namespaces allow developers to uniquely identify their XML vocabularies by using a uniform resource identifier (URI). URIs include uniform resources locators (URLs) as well as uniform resource numbers (URNs). By having a URI with a namespace, the developers can work with their namespaces but we need managers to resolve conflicts. That is, namespaces may conflict with one another. One namespace may specify a definition for an aircraft whereas another name space may have a different definition. The namespace managers have to resolve these conflicts. They may maintain XML registries. That is, when a namespace is developed, it has to be registered in the directory. The URI is registered in the registry. It is a fairly laborious task to go through the registry and identify the conflicting names.

Over the past 2 years, tremendous progress has been made on resolving conflicts with namespaces. The different groups often meet and discuss the potential conflicts. We can expect a lot of progress in this area. Figure 8.4 illustrates namespaces and conflict resolution.

8.5 DATA TYPES

One of the criticisms of XML 1.0 is that it does not support types. That is, XML is not a strongly typed language. As a result, it makes it difficult to write XML

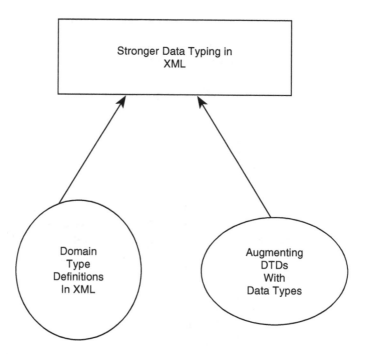

FIGURE 8.5 Data typing in XML.

documents when there is a need for strong typing. XML schemas overcome this problem. Furthermore, DTDs have been extended to include types as well. For example, the types may be simple types such as integer and Boolean or compound types such as address and date. A date type must have day, month, and year. In the same way, an address type may have the street number and name, city, state, and zip code. Then these types can be used in the DTDs.

The solution to include types in DTDs is cumbersome because it was not originally intended, which makes it rather artificial. Advantages of XML include its flexibility and universality — everyone can use it and they are able to interchange documents. By bringing strong typing into the language, however, some of its flexibility is lost. A trade-off always exists as to how much typing should be included. Figure 8.5 illustrates the idea of extending DTDs with data typing. This enables stronger typing in XML.

8.6 OTHER ASPECTS

Several aspects of XML are not included in this chapter, but are emphasized in the next. This is for the purpose of keeping this chapter as simple as possible. It is just a brief introduction to XML without discussing any of the complex ideas. A manager who wants to speak intelligently about XML must at least know what is in this chapter.

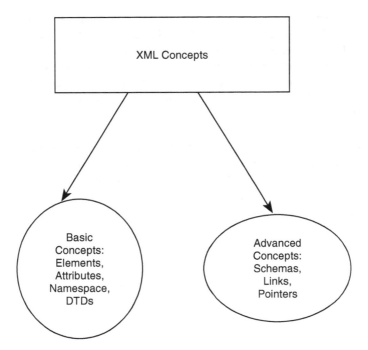

FIGURE 8.6 Basic and advanced concepts.

In the next chapter, I introduce some of the advanced concepts such as schemas, data integration, semantic issues, and some further aspects. Figure 8.6 illustrates the basic and advanced concepts identified in this book.

8.7 SUMMARY

This chapter introduces some of the basic concepts of XML, starting with a definition of a sample XML document with components such as prolog, root, and other information. The prolog has the declaration part of the document and the root has the key elements and attributes of the document. The optional end part has comments and other information. Then containers, elements, and attributes are discussed. These are the key components of an XML document. Namespaces for resolving conflicts are discussed next. That is, different groups have different notations and some way is needed to resolve conflicts. Finally, an overview of data typing in XML is given. For example, the XML DTDs can be extended with data types so that there is more structure to XML documents.

The information provided in this chapter is just the first step toward understanding XML, with a lot more to do. The next chapter discusses some of the advanced concepts. These concepts include semantics, XML schemas, and some other aspects. Numerous books have been produced on XML, describing details and syntax. The reader is encouraged to take advantage of the related developments by checking the

Web pages developed by W3C. As stressed, the goal is not to make the reader proficient in XML and able to write XML documents. Instead the goal is to put XML in a larger context and to discuss how it relates to Web data management, e-commerce, and other information management technologies. Part I provides an overview of the technologies that have impacted XML developments. These are also the technologies that have been impacted by XML. A two-way relationship exists between XML and various information management technologies. Part II describes XML and the semantic Web. It also discusses semistructured databases, which initially influenced the development of XML. Part III discusses the impact of XML on various information management technologies. For example, some of the related standards and protocols, such as Simple Object Access Protocol (SOAP), Universal Description Discovery Integration (UDDI), and Web Services Description Language (WSDL) are examined in Part III.

9 Advanced Concepts in XML

9.1 OVERVIEW

Chapter 8 discusses the basics of XML. In particular, a simple XML document is described; and then concepts such as containers, elements, attributes, and namespaces are explained. Then, the ways in which data types could be incorporated into domain-type definitions (DTDs) are shown. Whereas the concepts in Chapter 8 explained the basics of XML, this chapter discusses some of the more advanced concepts. Similar to Chapter 8, the goal is not to make the reader proficient in XML. The aim is to give the big picture and to discuss the relationship of XML to data management and the semantic Web. Should the reader be interested in writing XML documents, numerous books are available on the syntax, with some of the references given in this book. The topics often become outdated, however, because the field is continually evolving. We hear of numerous commercial XML products as well as XML standards groups in addition to the groups by World Wide Web Consortium (W3C). Therefore, for up-to-date information on XML, the reader is encouraged to keep track of the various W3C Web pages.

The topics covered in this chapter include handling semantic issues, schemas for XML, query languages for XML, and many other concepts such as enhanced DTDs and internationalization. Application of XML to areas such as data management, information management, and e-commerce are the subjects of Part III.

The organization of this chapter is as follows: semantic issues are the topic of Section 9.2; DTDs are revisited in Section 9.3; XML Link Language (Xlink) and some other aspects are covered in Section 9.4; XML schemas are discussed in Section 9.5; query languages for XML are examined in Section 9.6; data integration aspects are discussed in Section 9.7; and internationalization is explored in Section 9.8. Some other aspects are briefly addressed in Section 9.9, with the chapter summarized in Section 9.10. Figure 9.1 illustrates the various topics addressed in this chapter.

9.2 SEMANTIC ISSUES

One of the major criticisms of XML is that it only represents the structure of a document. For example, one could take unstructured text, tag it, and represent the tagged document in XML. It does not, however, attach any meanings to the document. XML was not intended to represent semantics. It was invented entirely to represent structure. As stressed in Part I, XML evolved both from Hypertext Markup Language (HTML) and Standard Generalized Markup Language (SGML).

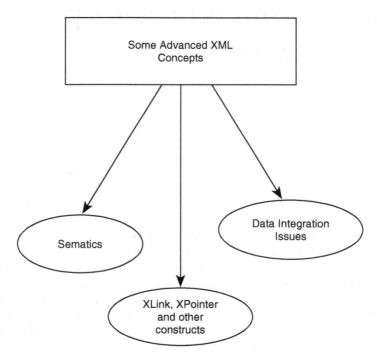

FIGURE 9.1 Some advanced XML concepts.

Extending XML to represent semantics is not an ill-formed notion; however, to take something that was intended for one purpose and make it into another would make the representation cumbersome. Efforts are underway to integrate ontologies, knowledge representation, and XML. For example, each XML document would also have, for example, annotations, which represent the semantics or intended interpretations. Semantics result in a whole new set of problems, one of which is semantic heterogeneity. It is hard enough to deal with namespaces and syntactic differences. It becomes very complicated to deal with semantic differences. Note the big difference between "I doubt X is a good player" and "I believe that X is a good player."

Although it takes considerable effort to incorporate semantics into XML, the semantic Web and resource description framework (RDF) were developed mainly to overcome the semantic problems with XML. Now RDF uses XML syntax, and integrates ontologies and knowledge representation. That is, RDF was conceived right from the beginning to handle semantics. In a sense, RDF can be considered the "semantic XML." The semantic Web and RDF are covered in more detail in Chapter 10. Figure 9.2 illustrates XML and RDF and the differences. Although XML continues to evolve and support numerous communities, RDF can be expected to overtake XML once everyone agrees on RDF. Due to the semantic difficulties and agreement on common terms and interpretations, however, RDF may be more difficult to standardize and to be accepted universally than XML is.

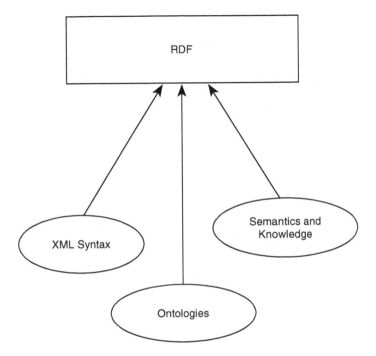

FIGURE 9.2 XML and RDF.

9.3 REVISITING DTDs

In Chapter 8, domain-type definitions (DTDs) are briefly introduced and XML is noted to be built on various components including DTDs. How DTDs could be extended to include data types so that XML can be strongly typed is also discussed. In this section, I examine more extensions to DTDs.

Laurent describes how DTDs can get very complex [LAUR00]. If we are describing a simple document containing names and addresses, then the DTDs are quite simple. If we are describing a document with complex objects and containers within containers, then the DTDs can be quite complex. Processing the DTDs could become a nightmare. Therefore, one needs the DTDs to be modular and even reusable. If we have known DTDs for a document, then we might as well use them because others will also have access to the same DTDs. An XML document is decoded at the receiving end according to the DTDs specified and the DTD processor decodes the document. This way, the document is presented the same way at all sites. Building modular, reusable, and simple DTDs is quite a challenge. To master any language, one needs practice to develop good DTDs. That is, there is nothing magical about DTDs. To master any programming language or language such as Structured Query Language (SQL), one needs experience.

One also needs to develop DTDs that are extensible. It is wasteful and very inefficient to throw away all the DTDs and build ones for each new application, so

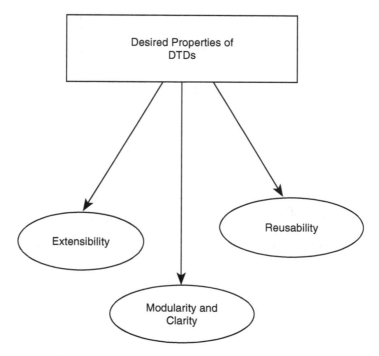

FIGURE 9.3 Desired properties of DTDs.

we want to make the DTDs as extensible as possible. XML provides the hooks for developing extensible DTDs. Figure 9.3 illustrates the desired properties of DTDs.

9.4 XLINK AND OTHER CONSTRUCTS

Up to now, self-contained XML documents have been discussed, but XML documents need to point to each other in a manner similar to HTML documents. The construct that enables XML documents to be linked is XML Link Language (Xlink). Xlink together with two other constructs, XML Pointer Language (Xpointer) and XML Path Language (Xpath), provides very rich capabilities for document linking.

Xlink supports simple links, such as those found in HTML, or more complex links such as those found in cases where developers link their vocabularies to a namespace-based approach. Both simple links and extended links provide support for hypertext-like capability where one can traverse from one document to several other documents; however, one needs to keep track of the type of links in use because it could become unmanageable with so many links to traverse.

Simple links connect two resources, with one connection between the two resources [LAUR00]. The different versions of simple links are explained in the book by Laurent. The extended links implement what is called a set of resources model. One can connect many resources with extended links. The various types of extended links are discussed in [LAUR00].

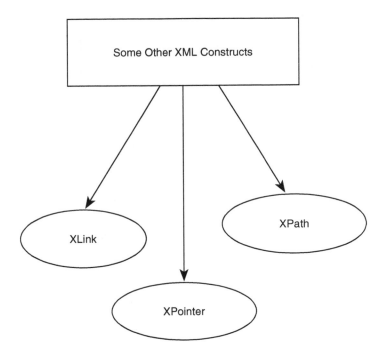

FIGURE 9.4 Other XML constructs.

It is also useful to take note of Xpointer and Xpath. Although Xlink has powerful linking capabilities, it is not sufficient for describing fragments scattered throughout a document. For example, you may want to link one fragment of a document to a fragment of another. Xpointer and Xpath standards provide support for such linking, and are continually evolving.

Another point to note is the Extensible Style Language (XSL). As mentioned in Part I, whereas XML is a specification of the structure of a document, XSL enables the presentation of a document. The XML document is processed by XSL and is presented to the user. Figure 9.4 illustrates the different notions discussed in this section.

9.5 XML SCHEMAS

Schemas are well known in the database world. They mainly describe what is in the database, and whether it is centralized, relational, object-oriented, or distributed. DTDs for XML are schemas for databases. DTDs describe the structure of an XML document, but DTDs have limitations. One is that they are difficult to write, especially for complex documents, and have to be designed modularly. More important, types are not natural to DTDs. One needs to extend DTDs to support types. These limitations have resulted in what is now called XML schemas. Can simple or complex XML documents be described in a clean and consistent way? W3C requested proposals for an approach and received submissions such as SOX and

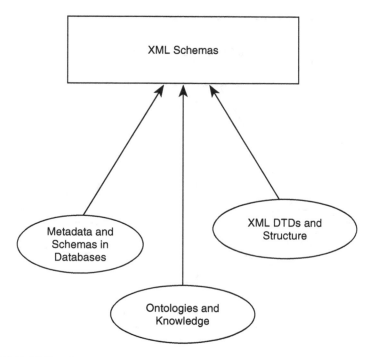

FIGURE 9.5 XML schemas.

DDML. These submissions were then examined and modified as appropriate by the standards groups, with the end result what is now called "XML schemas."

XML schemas have been around for over a year now and are continually evolving as new issues arise. An XML schema is essentially a way to describe an XML document. It has constructs to specify the element and attributes of an XML document. XML schemas have been studied extensively in the past by database researchers and therefore are a more natural way to represent XML databases. This aspect is revisited in Part III. Also, with the use of schemas it is easier to expand to include ontologies and knowledge representation schemes. For example, in the case of databases, the simple schemas have been extended now to include ontologies. Therefore, XML schemas in a way blur somewhat the differences between RDF and XML. This topic is examined again in Chapter 10. Figure 9.5 illustrates the XML schema concept.

9.6 XMLQL

The database community is extremely active in using XML for data management. Although XML has become the standard document representation model for databases, the development in data management can also contribute extensively to the development of XML. XML schemas are certainly one contribution. Other areas include XML techniques such as query languages (QL), query processing, and storage.

Let us examine query languages. Many research efforts on query languages for XML were reported around 1999. A W3C working group began soliciting proposals

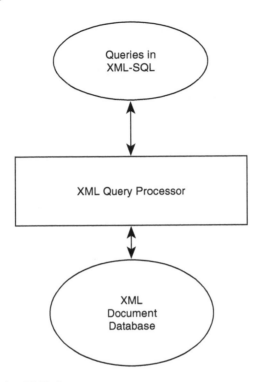

FIGURE 9.6 Querying XML documents.

for XML query languages, with XML Query Language (XMLQL) as one of the initial proposals. W3C then began a standardization effort for query languages for XML, resulting in Xquery (see [ACM01]). The SQL standard is examining XMLSQL, which can query XML documents to retrieve values of elements depending on some condition. XMLSQL, which can also request the retrieval of values of attributes, looks very similar to Xquery. XMLSQL is very new and can be expected to evolve. For example, I expect the support for specifying constraints, rules, and other features. Further details on XML and query languages are given in Part III when XML and data management are discussed.

The database community is also helping to develop techniques for processing XML queries, including query optimization techniques, updating XML documents, executing transactions, and maintaining security and integrity. Some of these issues are examined in Part III. Figure 9.6 illustrates querying XML documents.

9.7 DATA INTEGRATION ISSUES

XML has become a popular tool for integrating data. Many middleware solutions such as transaction monitors, Web servers, and object request brokers connect data sources that have made their schema explicit with XML. Figure 9.7 illustrates this aspect. Different heterogeneous applications and databases interoperate with each other using XML. The challenge is to extract structure for the legacy applications and data and to specify the structures in XML documents.

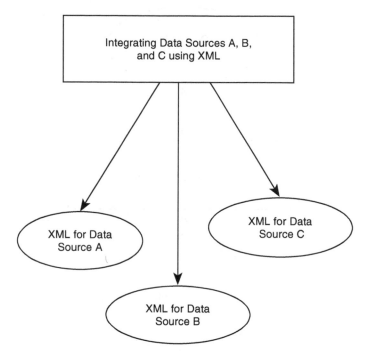

FIGURE 9.7 Data integration with XML.

The issue of semantics remains, and much research is needed in this area. For example, how do you handle the different semantics for the different applications? RDF will eventually be useful in solving this issue. Data integration is reexamined in Part III.

9.8 INTERNATIONALIZATION

Although XML was developed initially for English documents, it is now becoming a common data interchange format for those in a number of other languages. This aspect of XML is called internationalization.

Numerous international organizations, such as the International Standards Organization (ISO), are now working on internationalization. Almost every language is under examination. These include French, German, Italian, Spanish, Japanese, and Chinese as well as the numerous languages spoken in India. XML internationalization is illustrated in Figure 9.7.

9.9 OTHER ASPECTS

Several other points about XML have not been included in this chapter. These include processing XML documents, giving more detailed examples of XML documents, showing how simple links and complex links differ, and exploring many more topics such as detailed discussions of XML schemas and query languages. As stressed

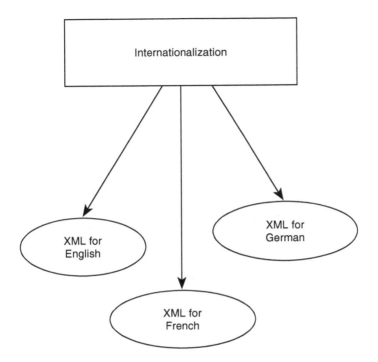

FIGURE 9.7 Internationalization of XML.

throughout, the purpose of this book is to give technical managers enough understanding of XML so that they can comprehend the various developments on XML,
the semantic Web, and RDF.

The next step to be studied is RDF. Some say that RDF will soon replace XML
as it overcomes all the limitations of XML including semantics and other features.
Some argue that with XML schemas, however, RDF may not be needed. Whether
RDF or XML schemas, we need a way to specify semantics in addition to the syntax.
We have come a long way with XML. For once the international community is
agreeing on standards. Furthermore, different user groups are active specifying their
own standards with XML. Although XML may not be the silver bullet, it is here to
stay in some form or another. Figure 9.8 illustrates the directions of XML.

9.10 SUMMARY

This chapter introduces some of the advanced concepts in XML. It begins with a
discussion of semantic issues and then revisits DTDs. Next, Xlinks and related
technologies such as Xpointers and Xpath are exammined. These technologies enable
documents to be linked. A discussion of XML schemas and their use is followed by
a discussion of querying XML documents. Finally, issues such as data integration
aspects and internationalization are addressed.

The information provided in this chapter is just the first step toward understanding some of the more advanced concepts of XML. The reader should not expect to

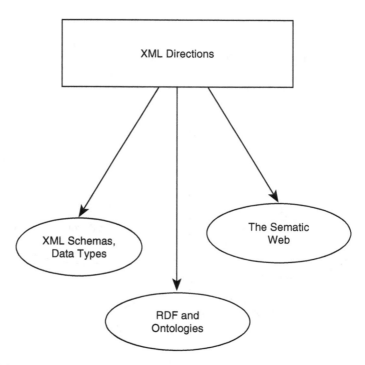

FIGURE 9.8 XML directions.

write XML documents soon after reading this and the preceding chapter, but instead he or she will obtain enough understanding of what XML is all about. Although numerous books have been published on XML syntax, the reader is encouraged to take advantage of the latest developments by checking the Web pages developed by W3C.

Because the next steps beyond XML are the semantic Web and RDF, the next chapter is devoted to these topics. As the Web becomes increasingly sophisticated, RDF and the semantic Web will become integral parts of Web information management.

10 The Semantic Web

10.1 OVERVIEW

A closely related topic to XML is the semantic Web. What is the difference between the Web and the semantic Web? Languages like XML enable one to focus on the syntax of the documents. The Web has objects with complicated relationships. We need a way to specify all these relationships. Furthermore, the Web pages currently are for human consumption and manipulation. We need the Web pages to be understood by machines. This is the idea behind the semantic Web. A semantic Web is not a single entity. Instead it is a collection of XML documents, semistructured databases, and millions of objects on the Web with rich semantics needing to be described. Furthermore, based on information on the Web, the machines and agents need to conduct actions and make decisions. Work on the semantic Web is just beginning, but we need to master this technology to effectively conduct e-business on the Web.

The idea of the semantic Web was conceived by Tim Berners Lee. In his book on weaving the Web, he explains his ideas on going from the Web to the semantic Web [LEE99]. Perhaps one of the best articles on the semantic Web was published by Lee et al. [LEE01]. The authors explain clearly how with the semantic Web, agents are able to effectively conduct all operations from coordinating the activities to keeping appointments and schedules.

The idea behind the semantic Web is to make the Web as intelligent as possible. Therefore, in addition to storing and managing data and information, the Web should enable people to conduct their daily activities. Individuals could have their own personal space on the Web and conduct various activities such as learning, teaching, providing services, and obtaining services. The ultimate goal is for users to get the desired and correct information at the right time displayed on their personal digital assistants (PDAs). Although wireless technology and Web technology have come a long way, we still have a lot of work to do before this goal can be realized.

This chapter explores the various aspects of the semantic Web. Section 10.2 gives a brief overview of the semantic Web concepts, with the remaining sections elaborating on the concepts. The technologies for the semantic Web include resource description framework (RDF) and ontologies. Also discussed are the DARPA Agents Markup Language (DAML) program at the Defense Advanced Research Projects Agency (DARPA) and how the Web can be viewed as a huge database. RDF is described in Section 10.3; ontologies, in Section 10.4; the DAML program, in Section 10.5; database aspects, in Section 10.6; XML, RDF, and interoperability issues, in Section 10.7; and some thoughts on Web vs. the semantic Web, in Section 10.8. The chapter is summarized in Section 10.9.

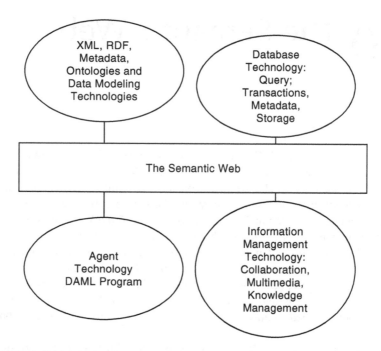

FIGURE 10.1 Technologies for the semantic Web.

The notion of semantic Web is reexamined later in Chapter 16 of Part III, after the discussion of various technologies and applications of XML. In particular, Chapter 16 is devoted to some issues on building the semantic Web. Because the semantic Web is regarded as an application of XML, this discussion is not entirely out of the scope of Part III.

10.2 SEMANTIC WEB CONCEPTS

Although the semantic Web as a concept is still evolving, many developments have been made in this area. These include RDF, ontologies, agents, and databases. Figure 10.1 illustrates the technologies for the semantic Web. Figure 10.2 illustrates a model for the semantic Web. One could envisage a model for the Web where producers publish the services while consumers subscribe for the services.

Figure 10.3 illustrates a sample concept of operation for the semantic Web. As shown, agents of various types, such as brokers, act on behalf of users. These brokers negotiate the best deals for their customers. These services could include managing schedules and appointments, giving advice, and handling all the activities for a customer.

Consider a hypothetical example of John who is a physician. The Web wakes him up depending on the day of the week. Then he is informed of his entire schedule and appointments. He could get information about the optimal routes to get to his destinations. He could also be informed about the location of his personal accessories.

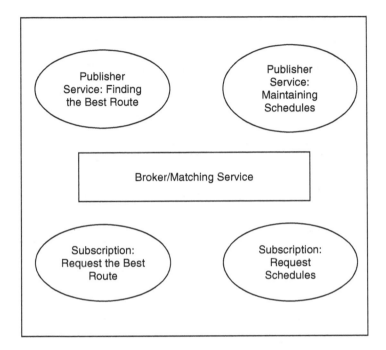

FIGURE 10.2 Model for the semantic Web.

As the day progresses, the Web manages the dynamic situations such as accidents, unexpected traffic, and other unanticipated events. Then the Web also gives him information about his patients such as their histories. When his work is over, the Web makes arrangements for John to meet his wife Mary for dinner and go to the theater.

One could say that the Web has completely taken over John's life, which is the ultimate goal. It would certainly make life a lot easier for John, but in the end it is up to John to follow the advice and directions. John ultimately decides how he should proceed for the day.

After this brief overview of what the semantic Web is, we are now able to explore some of the technologies. In the next four sections, RDF, ontologies, agents, and databases, all relating to the semantic Web, are discussed.

10.3 RDF

RDF (resource description framework) is the foundation of the semantic Web and for processing metadata. An excellent tutorial on RDF can be found in [RDF]. Whereas XML is limited in providing machine understandable documents, RDF handles this limitation. As a result, RDF provides better support for interoperability, searching, and cataloging. RDF also describes contents of documents as well as relationships between various entities within the document. As stated in the tutorial in RDF, RDF complements XML. Whereas XML provides syntax and notations,

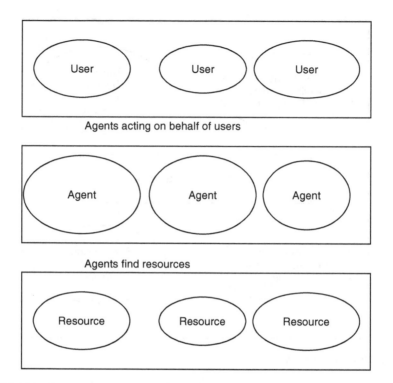

FIGURE 10.3 Concept of operation for the semantic Web.

RDF supplements this by providing semantic information in a standardized way. RDF is the work of many communities collaborating together to represent metadata in a standardized way. These communities include the Web Standardization Community as well as those working on XML, Hypertext Markup Language (HTML), Standard Genaralized Markup Language (SGML), and other related standards.

Let us now examine the basic RDF model as well as some advanced concepts. The basic RDF model has three types: resources, properties, and statements. A resource is any entity described by RDF expressions. It could be a Web page or a collection of pages. Property is a specific attribute used to describe a resource. RDF statements are resources together with a named property plus the value of the property. Statement components are subject, predicate, and object. For example, if we have a sentence of the form "John is the creator of xxx," then xxx is the subject or resource. The property or predicate is "creator," and the object (or literal) is "John." RDF diagrams often exist as, for example, entity-relationship (ER) diagrams or object diagrams to represent statements. RDF descriptions are of the form:

```
<rdf:RDF>

(describes what it is intended to describe such as
John is the creator of xxx)

</rdf:RDF>
```

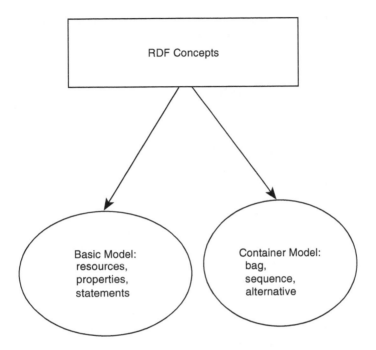

FIGURE 10.4 RDF concepts.

For more details on the various aspects specific to RDF syntax, refer to the documents on RDF published by the World Wide Web Consortium (W3C). Also, it is very important that the intended interpretation be used for RDF sentences. This is accomplished by RDF schemas. A schema is sort of a dictionary and has interpretations of various terms used in sentences. RDF and XML namespaces resolve conflicts in semantics.

More advanced concepts in RDF include the container model and description of statements. The container model has three types of container objects: bag, sequence, and alternative. A bag is an unordered list of resources or literals. It is used to mean that a property has multiple values but the order is not important. A sequence is a list of ordered resources. In this instance, the order is important. An alternative is a list of resources that represent alternatives for the value of a property. Various tutorials in RDF describe the syntax of containers in more detail.

RDF also provides support for making comments about other statements. For example, with this facility one can make comments of the form, "The statement A is false" where A is the statement "John is the creator of xxx." Again, one can use object-like diagrams to represent containers and comments about statements. Figure 10.4 illustrates the various aspects of RDF.

RDF also has a formula model associated with it. This formal model has a formal grammar and is the result of logicians and theoreticians working on RDF. RDF mainly is the work of theoreticians and practitioners. For further information on RDF, refer to the work of W3C, particularly, the work of the RDF model and syntax working group. As in the case of any language or model, RDF continues to evolve.

Therefore, the reader is encouraged to keep up with the latest developments with RDF and to check the W3C Web page from time to time for new developments and pointers.

10.4   REVISITING ONTOLOGIES

Following the discussions of semantic Web concepts and RDF, as well as concepts in XML in the previous two chapters, let us now examine the role of ontologoies. Ontologies describe entities and relationships among entities. The concept of metadata has evolved over the years starting from data dictionaries to database schemas and now to ontologies, XML, XML schemas, RDF, and RDF schemas. XML and RDF are a special way of representing the various ontologies. Ontologies could describe vehicles, people, animals, as well as relationships among people, events, and many other things. Whereas XML has limitations and less semantic power to represent onotlogies, RDF attempts to overcome these limitations. XML and RDF are not the only way to represent ontologies. One can use semantic networks, frames, object models, hypersemantic data models, and many other presentation schemes for ontologies.

Figure 10.5 shows how ontologies can be represented using XML and RDF schemas. As illustrated, ontologies resulted from various metadata concepts. Ontologies can also be represented by semantic nets and other models such as frames. That is, ontologies are essentially semantics about various entities, events, and relationships shared by the entities. Several representational schemes for ontologies exist and RDF is one of them.

In summary, ontologies are vital for developing the semantic Web, which consists of agents that can manage the numerous resources, including Web pages, and can handle activities for people. Therefore, representing semantics and managing the semantics of applications are essential for the semantic Web. Ontologies are a means of describing semantics. The specific syntax chosen could be one of many. Nevertheless, ontologies are at the heart of the semantic Web. Many efforts and discussions have gone into integrating and transforming ontologies. They also are discussed in Chapter 16 along with some directions for building the semantic Web.

10.5   AGENTS AND THE DAML PROGRAM

The DAML (Defense Advanced Projects Research Agency Agents Markup Language) program was initiated by Dr. James Hendler, when he was the program manager at DARPA. The program officially began in 2000 and is ongoing. The goal of this program is to develop a markup language for agents so that they can understand and process the Web information. Although DAML and the semantic Web initially developed independently, the goals are the same. Therefore, one can say that DAML is currently developing technologies for the semantic Web.

DAML researchers are investigating various aspects including RDF, data models, ontologies, logics for RDF, and metadata processing. RDF was under independent development by W3C working groups, however, the DAML research output is now

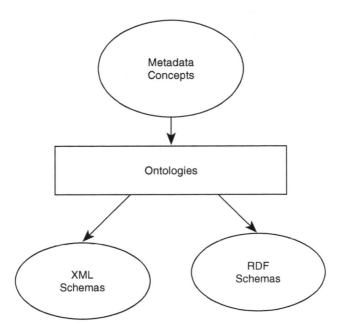

FIGURE 10.5 Ontologies.

under examination by the W3C, with the result that DAML is influencing the development of RDF a great deal. The relationship between DAML and W3C is illustrated in Figure 10.6.

Whereas W3C is involved with developing specifications, DAML complements the work by investigating in depth many of the research issues including ontologies and logics. We need more programs like DAML to develop the semantic Web because the work of W3C alone is not sufficient. The National Science Foundation (NSF) also is working collaboratively with research agencies in Europe to further identify research topics for the semantic Web.

In summary, the semantic Web technologies are in their infancy. Various data and information management technologies have to be investigated to develop the semantic Web. The DAML program is moving in the right direction. The relationship between DAML and W3C is also moving in the right direction, but much work remains.

10.6 SEMANTIC WEB AS A DATABASE

No standard definition of a semantic Web exists. I have adopted the view presented by Lee et al. [LEE01]. Some say that the Web is where agents process the information. Others say it is based on the publish and subscribe model. Another group says that it is an intelligent database and, therefore, all the techniques developed for managing intelligent databases apply here also. This section examines the latter view.

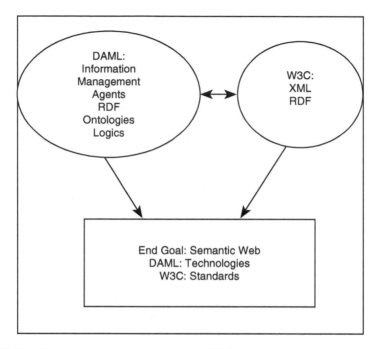

FIGURE 10.6 Relationship between DAML and W3C.

One could consider the semantic Web to be a collection information sources that are interconnected and have to be managed by a database management system. The challenges include modeling the database, integrating the heterogeneous information sources, querying the information and sources, and accessing information; this means developing appropriate indexing techniques. One needs to understand the schemas of the information sources and the integrate of the schemas. One could think of using XML or RDF to represent the schemas. Schema integration issues include handling semantic heterogeneity. We need to examine the developments on integrating heterogeneous data and information sources (see [ACM90]) and then apply them for the semantic Web. Figure 10.7 illustrates the semantic Web as a database.

10.7 XML, RDF, AND INTEROPERABILITY

There have been discussions as to how XML supports interoperability. XML supports common representation of documents. As a result, it is possible for different systems to interpret the document the same say. Common representation is key to interoperability, however, XML does not support semantics. Therefore, various aspects such as semantic heterogeneity cannot be handled by XML. One proposal is to use RDF (resource description framework) to facilitate semantic heterogeneity, as illustrated in Figure 10.8. RDF, with the use of ontologies, supports semantics. This way, one can handle syntactic as well as semantic heterogeneity.

In the case of database interoperability, with both XML and RDF one can represent the schemas of various databases including legacy databases. This in turn

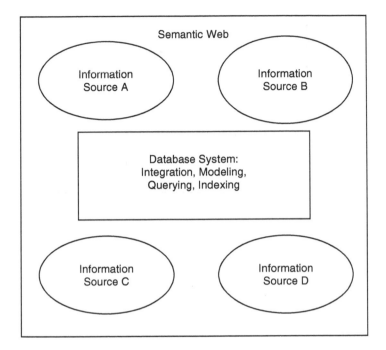

FIGURE 10.7 Semantic Web as a database.

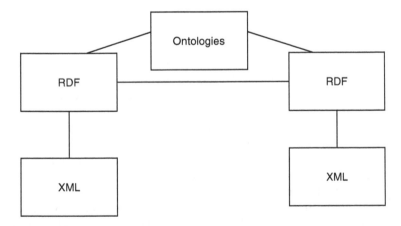

FIGURE 10.8 XML, RDF, and interoperability.

supports interoperability, as illustrated in Figure 10.9. XML and RDF are essential technologies for interoperability. Whether XML, RDF, or some other technology will predominate in the end is yet to be determined, but the Web community is moving in the right direction. What was thought to be almost impossible just 5 years ago is possible now. The community has more or less come to an agreement on common terminology and semantics. This was one of the major challenges faced by database researchers in the early 1990s.

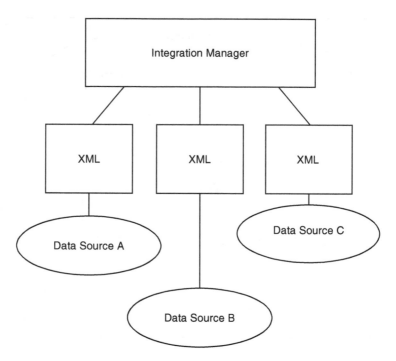

FIGURE 10.9 XML and database interoperability.

10.8 WEB VS. THE SEMANTIC WEB

There have been discussions regarding the differences between the Web and the semantic Web. Some say that the Web is a system where humans have to read the Web pages, whereas the semantic Web is a system where the machine reads and understands the Web pages. Others say that the Web today is the semantic Web of yesterday, and the Web tomorrow is the semantic Web of today. We are getting closer to machine-understandable Web pages, but we are still a long way from achieving this.

One cannot say that the semantic Web will end once we have a system with machine understandable Web pages. The enhancements will continue forever as new technologies emerge. That is, we cannot ever say that we have finished building the semantic Web because we believe that it will continue to evolve.

Figure 10.10 illustrates the evolution of the Web to the semantic Web. Yesterday we had HTML, today we have XML, tomorrow we will have RDF, and the day after we will have something else. The biggest challenge for us was to build the initial Web. This was accomplished by the pioneers like Tim Berners Lee. After that, there is no end in sight. The semantic Web is discussed again in Chapter 16, after applications of XML are covered.

10.9 SUMMARY

This chapter is devoted to a discussion of the semantic Web. I first provide an overview of the semantic Web and then show how it differs from the Web. Next, I

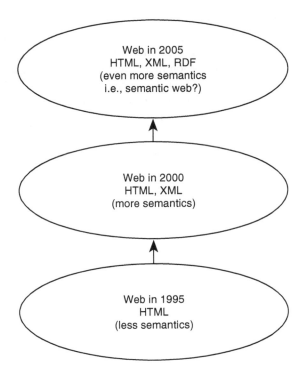

FIGURE 10.10 From the Web to the semantic Web.

discuss some technologies, RDF and ontologies, related to the semantic Web. An overview of agents and the DARPA DAML program follows. Then I discuss some issues on treating the semantic Web as a database and examine how the various database concepts could be reused to address the semantic Web. Finally, I cover interoperability issues and then provide a view of the Web vs. the semantic Web.

Although I have provided just a brief description of the semantic Web, many articles are written on the subject. The area is still relatively new and we expect significant developments to be made over the next few years. A good starting point to understanding the semantic Web is the article by Lee et al. [LEE01]. The book on weaving the Web by Lee is also a good introduction to how the Web has evolved (see, e.g., [LEE99], [LEE01]). The DAML program at DARPA has contributed significantly to the development of the semantic Web.

The last three chapters have introduced XML and showed how the various Web concepts have evolved into the semantic Web, but much work remains. As technologies emerge, the semantic Web will continue to expand, with no end to this technology. Almost all the services will be conducted on the Web. This would include not only conducting transactions but also having personal entries, diaries, appointment books, and everything there is to know. We can expect individuals to have their own spaces as well as shared spaces on the Web, conducting all their daily activities through the use of the Web. The goal is not only to push the information to the users' PDAs but also to pull the information from the Web and display it on the PDAs.

The next chapter in this part introduces semistructured databases. I decided to include this chapter in Part II partly because the initial development of XML was for semistructured databases, although XML has developed far beyond this stage and is now used for many information management technologies. In Part III, I take each of the data and information management technologies for XML that are addressed in Part I and show how XML can be applied to these technologies. These technologies include databases, information retrieval and information management systems, and electronic commerce (e-commerce).

11 Semistructured Databases

11.1 OVERVIEW

The previous chapters discuss XML and the semantic Web, providing an overview of the various constructs in XML as well as giving some idea of what the semantic Web is all about. Part I of this book mentions various technologies that have been influenced by, and have influenced, the development of XML. Most prominent among these technologies are databases. Although data management has affected the developments of XML a great deal, a special type of database systems, called semistructured database systems, inspired the development of XML in the beginning. XML was considered to be the model for semistructured databases. Therefore, I give a special place in this book to semistructured databases and cover it in Part II as an aspect of XML. Part III discusses applications of XML; many of the technologies discussed in Part I are examined again, including databases, e-commerce, information management, and information retrieval.

Semistructured databases are briefly discussed in Part I. Let us revisit this topic. Data could be completely unstructured such as a piece of text with no headings, paragraphs, or subtitles. On the other hand, data could be completely structured such as relational databases or even object databases. Something in between is called semistructured databases where data are partially structured. For example, this book could be considered to have semistructured data because it has definite sections such as front matter introduction, chapters, conclusion, references, appendices, and index. One could take unstructured data, then tag it, and get some structure out of it. One could convert unstructured data into semistructured data, essentially what XML provides for you. One could also take unstructured data, convert it into semistructured data, and finally use the tags to turn it into structured data. This transition is illustrated in Figure 11.1.

This chapter discusses various aspects for semistructured databases. A lot of overlap exists between the discussions for semistructured databases and multimedia databases as well as data management covered in Part I. Section 11.2 examines architectures; Section 11.3, data models; Section 11.4, functions; Section 11.5, interoperability and migration issues; Section 11.6, XML within the context of semistructured databases; and Section 11.7, various prototypes. The products and standards are explored later in Part III. Section 11.8 summarizes the chapter and also refers to a semistructured database management system (SS-DBMS), as well as a semistructured database (SS-database). Section 11.9 gives the conclusion to Part II.

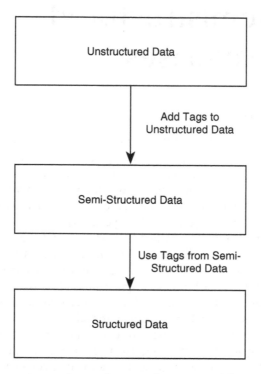

FIGURE 11.1 From unstructured to semistructured to structured data.

11.2 ARCHITECTURES FOR SEMISTRUCTURED DATABASES

Various architectures for the design and development of semistructured database systems are under examination. In one approach, the DBMS is used just to manage the metadata that give the structure, and a file manager is used to manage the unstructured data. In another approach, the DBMS is designed specifically to manage the semistructured data. The former approach is called the loose-coupling approach whereas the latter is called the tight-coupling approach. Both approaches are illustrated in Figures 11.2 and 11.3. One could also introduce an integration manager to manage all the data as is. This is illustrated in Figure 11.4. This figure depicts the three types of data. In summary, different combinations and different data managers can be used to manage SS-databases.

A database that stores XML documents is regarded as an SS-database. The corresponding data manager is a semistructured data manager. This is illustrated in Figure 11.5. In a way, this is the ideal management system that handles the SS-database. Furthermore, as in the case of databases and distributed databases, SS-databases can also be distributed. Every database manager is augmented by a semistructured distributed processor (SS-DP) as shown in Figure 11.6. (For background information on distributed databases, refer to Appendix B.)

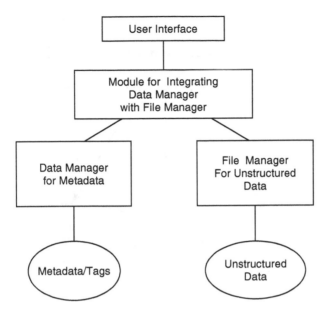

FIGURE 11.2 Loose-coupling integration architecture.

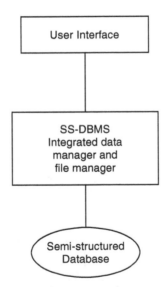

FIGURE 11.3 Tight-coupling architecture.

11.3 DATA MODELS FOR SEMISTRUCTURED DATABASES

As in the case of multimedia databases, when representing semistructured data, several features have to be supported. First, a way to capture the complex relationships between the different segments of a document, such as links, is mandatory.

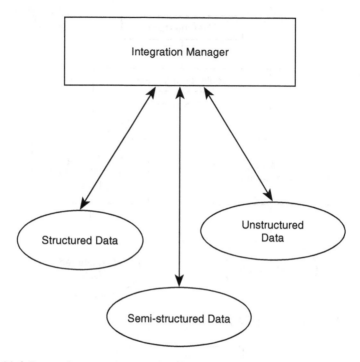

FIGURE 11.4 Integration manager.

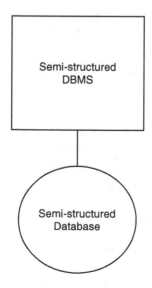

FIGURE 11.5 Semi-structured DBMS.

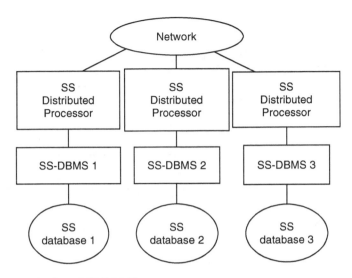

FIGURE 11.6 Distributed SS-DBMS.

Second, a document may have not just text, but also images, video, and audio segments. A way is needed for capturing the relationships such as to display portions of the document together or one after the other. Finally, a document may also have links to other documents.

Various data models are under examination to represent semistructured data. These include the traditional models such as relational and object, in addition to hypersemantic data and hypermedia. Models for information retrieval systems are also under development. This chapter includes illustrations of some of the models.

Figure 11.7 depicts a representation of an SS-database that is essentially a multimedia database. This example shows two objects: A and B. A consists of 2000 frames and B consists of 3000 frames. This database is semistructured because these documents have some structure such as objects A, B, and 2000 frames. Object A consists of a time interval between 4/95 and 8/95 and B consists of a time interval between 5/95 and 10/95.

In the example of Figure 11.7, with an object-oriented data model, each object in the figure corresponds to an object in the object model. The attributes of an object may be represented as instance variables and include time interval, frames, and content description. With the relational model, the object corresponds to an instance of a relation. With atomic values, however, it is difficult to capture the attributes of the instance. In the case of the object-relational model, the attribute value of an instance is an object. For the instance that represents, for example, object A, the attribute value time interval is the pair (4/95, 8/95). Representing object A with an object model is illustrated in Figure 11.8. Representing the same object with an object-relational model is illustrated in Figure 11.9.

Note that one could build extensions to an existing data model to support complex relationships for multimedia data. These relationships may include temporal relationships between objects such as play together, play before, and play after. These relationships are discussed in the next subsection.

Example:
Object
representation
Object A
2000 Frames
4/95
8/95
5/95
10/95
Object B
3000 Frames

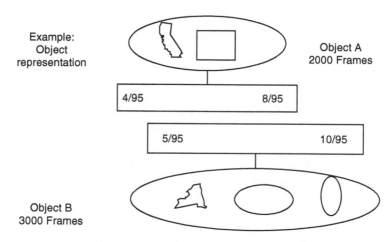

FIGURE 11.7 Data representation.

ID
XXX
Object A
interval (4/95, 8/95)
contents
Frames 2000

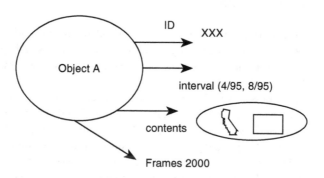

FIGURE 11.8 Data representation with object model.

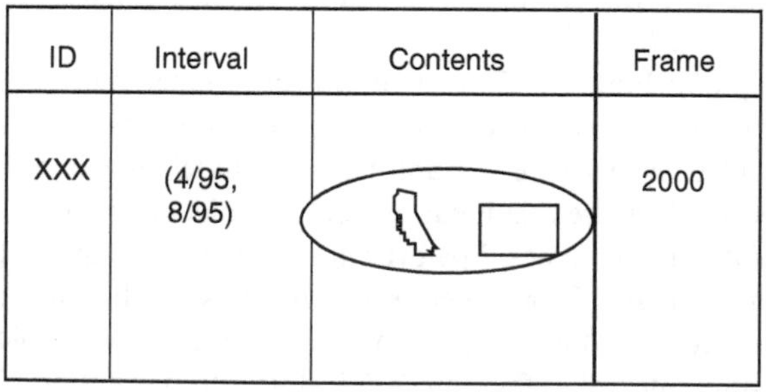

ID
Interval
Contents
Frame
XXX
(4/95,
8/95)
2000

FIGURE 11.9 Data representation with object-relational model.

Some argue that object models are better for multimedia databases whereas others argue that object-oriented models are better because they can represent complex data types. It appears that both types of models have to be extended to capture the temporal constructs and other special features. Associated with a data model is a query language. The language should support the constructs needed to manipulate the multimedia database. For example, one may need to query to play frames 500 to 1000 of a video script. Languages such as Structured Query Language (SQL) are extended for MM-DBMSs.

Both the object models and object-relational models use a rather coarse-grained representation of multimedia databases. With the models used, the fact that object A and object B have to be played together cannot be represented. One needs to augment the models with rules to represent the constraints. A discussion of rule representation in hypersemantic data models follows in the next subsection.

Hypersemantic data models are basically semantic data models with support for representing constraints and rules. They were studied in [TRUE88] and have been extended for various secure applications in [BINN94]. One can consider both object and object-relational data models to be semantic models, which capture the semantics of an application. As noted in the previous subsection, with both object and object-relational data models, one cannot represent constraints in a natural manner. Although one could enforce them as part of methods, it is better to express them in a more natural way such as rules. Hypersemantic models, for which no one standard is available, enable one to represent constraints also. One could extend any type of semantic model such as semantic nets as well as objects with rules in a hypersemantic data model.

Figure 11.10 illustrates an example of using a hypersemantic data model to represent the objects of Figure 11.7. In addition to representing the objects, we also have additional constraints such as object A has to be played before object B and object B has to be played before January 1, 2001. Temporal constraints are also enforced in this model.

One of the main concerns is where XML fits in. Remember that XML is not a data model, but a way of representing documents. One eventually needs a model to represent the information in the documents and that is what the data models provide. XML is somewhat of a metamodel and is a way to represent the document at a higher level. Then the contents of the XML document may be modeled using relational, object, object-relational, or hypersemantic models. These models are explored in this section. Figure 11.11 illustrates the relationship between an XML document and the models used to represent the contents of the document.

11.4 FUNCTIONS OF SEMISTRUCTURED DATABASES

11.4.1 OVERVIEW

Remember from Section 11.1, an SS-database system must support the basic DBMS functions. These include data manipulation functions such as query processing, transaction management, metadata management, storage management, data distribution, and security and integrity, described in sections 11.4.2, 11.4.3, 11.4.4, 11.4.5, 11.4.6, and 11.10, respectively. Figure 11.12 illustrates the functions of an SS-DBMS.

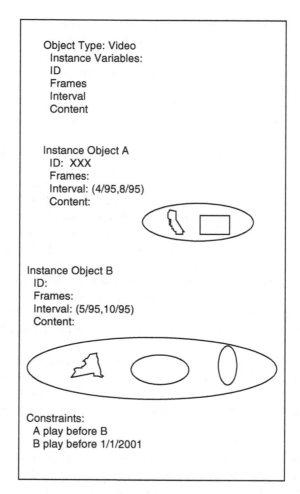

FIGURE 11.10 Data representation with hypersemantic data model.

11.4.2 DATA MANIPULATION AND QUERY PROCESSING

Data manipulation involves various aspects. Support for querying, browsing, and filtering the data is essential. Appropriate query languages are needed for this purpose. Recall that SQL extensions show much promise; however, with respect to XML documents, XMLSQL is one of the developments with the SQL standards group. The World Wide Web Consortium (W3C) has taken submissions similar to XMLQL and has developed XML Query Language (Xquery) (see [ACM01]). In addition to just querying the data, one also may want to edit the data. That is, two documents may be merged to form a third document. One could extract a piece of the document and display it. As an example, objects in Figure 11.7 may be merged based on time intervals and an object may be projected based on time intervals. Objects may also be updated in whole or in part.

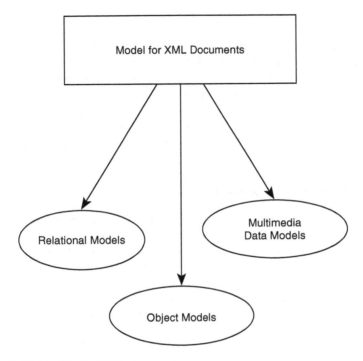

FIGURE 11.11 Models for XML documents.

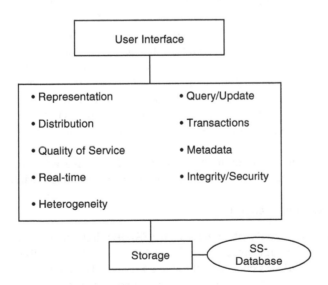

FIGURE 11.12 Functions of an SS-DBMS.

11.4.3 TRANSACTION MANAGEMENT

Some have discussed the issue of whether transaction management is needed in multimedia database systems [ACM94]. The concern is the same as to whether transactions may be executed on XML documents. That is, parts A and B of an XML document have to be updated or none of the parts are updated. Transaction management is important, because in many cases annotations may be associated with multimedia objects. For example, if one updates an image, then its annotation must also be updated. Therefore, the two operations have to be conducted as part of a transaction.

11.4.4 METADATA MANAGEMENT

Many of the metadata issues discussed for DBMSs also apply to SS-databases. What is a model for metadata? What are the techniques for metadata management?

With XML documents, metadata technology plays a key role, possibly capturing all the structure of a document; describing annotations and links; and including semantics and ontologies for RDF schema management, in the case of the semantic Web and ontologies. XML, RDF, ontologies, and the semantic Web all have to deal heavily with metadata. Metadata have to be extracted, captured, represented, and processed efficiently if the semantic Web is to become a reality.

11.4.5 STORAGE MANAGEMENT

The major issues in storage management include developing special index methods and accessing strategies for XML documents. These include developing strategies for multimedia data types. Content-based data access is important for many multimedia applications, although, efficient techniques for content-based data access are still a challenge. For example, in the case of an XML document, one may request to retrieve the part of the document that describes the story of the hare and the tortoise.

Other storage issues include caching data. How often should the data be cached? Are there any special considerations for multimedia data or special algorithms? Also, storage techniques for integrating different data types are needed. For example, a multimedia database may contain video, audio, and text databases instead of just one data type. The display of these different data types has to be synchronized. Appropriate storage mechanisms are needed so that continuous displays of the data are available.

Storage management for multimedia databases is also an area that has been given considerable attention. Several advances have been made [MDDS94].

11.4.6 DATA DISTRIBUTION

I have briefly discussed distribution issues for SS-DBMS. As illustrated in Figure 11.6, each SS-DBMS is augmented by an SS-DP. A distributed SS-DBMS is mainly a collection of SS-DBMSs connected through a network. The DP module is responsible for handling data distribution issues. As an example, how are the XML documents

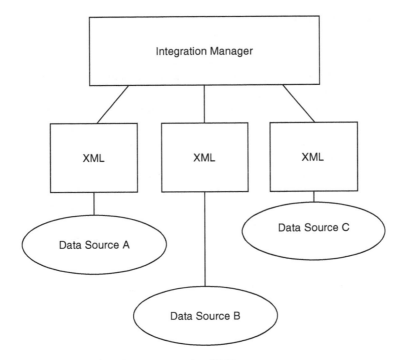

FIGURE 11.13 Integrating data sources using XML.

distributed? Are they distributed based on clusters or related topics? How can different documents be combined in query processing? Are there special mechanisms for distributed transaction management? How is the distributed metadata maintained? As an example, one could merge two documents at the two nodes to obtain the result to a query such as "retrieve all the contents of the distributed document A."

Although some efforts have been made on distributed multimedia DBMSs, distribution issues for XML documents have not been studied extensively. Bertino and Ferrari have done some work on distributed XML documents with respect to secure updates as well as queries (see, e.g., [BERT01]). Interoperability and migration of distributed XML documents are discussed later in this chapter.

11.4.7 QUALITY OF SERVICE

Not all applications require high-quality data to be displayed in a document. In some cases, breaks in display of video data may be tolerated, whereas in other cases, it may not. For example, low-quality data may be presented in a normal mode but higher-quality data, in a crisis mode.

The challenges with these applications include specifying quality of service primitives and implementing these primitives. Formal approaches may help in this area. One needs to develop a model and an associated language for quality of service. Quality of service for XML is a topic that has not received much attention, but is an area that needs work [ALLE01].

11.4.8 REAL-TIME PROCESSING

In a real-time database system, the queries and transactions have to meet timing constraints. A strong connection exists between real-time database management systems (RT-DBMSs) and multimedia database management systems (MM-DBMSs). For example, the audio and video data have to be synchronized. This means that certain timing constraints have to be imposed on the data and have to be met. If not, one could hear Jane's voice with Robert speaking on the video script.

The issue is whether the timing constraints are hard, soft, or firm. If they are hard, they have to be met. Otherwise there could be a catastrophic situation. If they are firm, they have to be met, but with no serious consequence. If they are soft, it will be good to meet the constraints. Once the type of constraints are determined for an application, techniques are needed to handle these constraints. Real-time scheduling techniques may help in this case.

The connection between real-time processing and XML documents is not clear. Of course, XML documents may have to be displayed in a timely manner and some documents may be more critical than others. Furthermore, some documents may have to be updated in a timely manner. The issues seem similar to those for real-time database systems.

11.4.9 USER INTERFACE

Research on user interfaces and database management has been proceeding almost independently. Only recently have visualization tools have integrated with database management systems. For multimedia database management, a variety of interfaces have to be provided. These include interfaces for communicating with video, audio, and text databases. In addition, interfaces to support SQL extensions for multimedia data as well as Object Database Management Group (ODMG) standards are needed. Similar issues need to be dealt with for SS-databases and XML document databases.

11.4.10 MAINTAINING DATA INTEGRITY AND SECURITY

Integrity — Maintaining data integrity includes support for data quality, integrity constraint processing, concurrency control and recovery for multiuser updates, and accuracy of the data on output. Enforcing integrity constraints for SS-databases remains a challenge. For example, what kinds of integrity constraints can be enforced on various portions of a text document? Little research has been done to address these issues.

Discretionary security — Security mechanisms include supporting access rights and authorization. Bertino et al. are conducting extensive work on security for XML documents (see [BERT00], [BERT02]). Researchers have additional concerns. For example, in the case of video data, should access control rules be enforced on entire scripts or frames? Interest in security for multimedia data systems is increasing (see [IEEE95]).

Multilevel security — This type of security is also needed for certain multimedia applications. Some work has been reported on multilevel security [THUR90]. For example, parts of a document can be classified whereas other parts may be unclassified. Multilevel security for XML documents and SS-databases is an area that remains to be investigated.

11.5 INTEROPERABILITY AND MIGRATION OF SEMISTRUCTURED DATABASES

Although Section 11.4 briefly addresses distribution issues for SS-databases as well as XML documents, in many cases the documents may be heterogeneous in nature. For example, one source may be unstructured, a second source may be semistructured, and a third source may be structured. One needs the ability to query the heterogeneous documents. Some efforts have been made on querying heterogeneous SS-databases. One of the efforts is mentioned in Section 11.7.

As illustrated in Figure 11.13, an integration manager is responsible for joining the heterogeneous data sources. In the case of legacy databases, however, one may extract the structure of the documents so that the legacy documents can be integrated with newer ones. XML is used to store the structure of the legacy documents so that interoperability is facilitated. This is illustrated in Figure 11.12.

11.6 REVISITING XML

Throughout this chapter, the relationships of SS-databases to XML have been discussed. Although relational databases are completely structured and unstructured databases have no structure, SS-databases have some structure. An SS-database can be represented as an XML document, however, various data models are being examined to represent the contents of an XML document. XML is somewhat of a metamodel, not a data model. It is used to represent the structure of a document at a higher level.

An unstructured database can be converted to an SS-database by incorporating tags. These tags can further be processed and the SS-databases converted to relational databases. Relational databases can be coded in XML. Furthermore, XML is extended with query languages so that XML documents may be queried. One example is XMLQL.

The functions of SS-databases and the impact of XML for each function have been examined. For example, in the case of security for SS-databases, we need to investigate security for XML documents. Some excellent work in this area has been reported by Bertino et al. ([BERT00], [BERT02]).

Mainly, an SS-database can be considered to be a collection of XML documents with various architectures for managing these documents. The challenge is to develop a complete data manager to effectively manage all the XML documents. That is, we need an SS-database management system. There are, however, debates as to whether to use a relational database system or an SS-DBMS for semistructured data [INF01].

11.7 SOME DEVELOPMENTS

Of the number of research and development efforts on SS-databases around the world, the most notable effort is the LORE project at Stanford University [WIDO98].

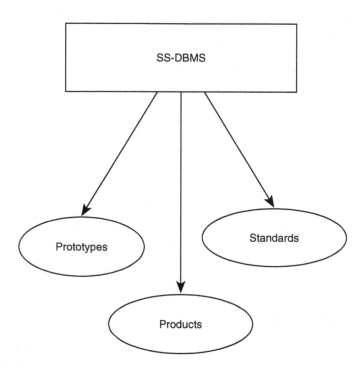

FIGURE 11.14 Developments with SS-DBMS.

This project initially developed techniques and tools for managing SS-databases, and then developed technology for essentially making LORE the database for XML documents.

Among the efforts in Europe, notable are those at INRIA on querying heterogeneous SS-databases. For this project, one gets the legacy information in XML and then uses XML to integrate the various databases. The project is called the Aquarelle project and is reported in [ERCIM].

Numerous uniform resources locators (URLs) exist on SS-databases including efforts on mining, graphical user interfaces, and integration. Although SS-databases were developed before XML, with the advent of XML they are mainly known as databases for storing XML documents.

Commercial products have also emerged. For example, many of the database system vendors such as Oracle, eXcelon, and other companies have provided support for storing and maintaining XML documents. These databases support semistructured data. Many of these databases also store multimedia data. Not only are several research efforts on SS-DBMSs under way but commercial products are also emerging. As XML standards become more advanced, we can expect better tools and techniques for managing semistructured data. Figure 11.14 illustrates the developments, which are discussed in Part III.

11.8 SUMMARY

The status and challenges for SS-databases from architectural, data modeling, and functional viewpoints are discussed throughout this chapter.

Topics include architectures for SS-databases; data models; functions such as query processing, editing, transaction management, metadata management, storage management, security, and integrity; the relationship to XML; and finally, some of the research efforts in progress.

As stressed, SS-databases and XML go hand in hand. SS-databases are really the databases for managing XML documents. Because each technology has influenced the development of the other in a great way, SS-databases are included in Part II, together with a discussion of XML and the semantic Web.

Conclusion to Part II

Part II, consisting of four chapters, described various aspects of XML. XML basics were covered in Chapter 8, including a discussion of elements, attributes, and namespaces. Chapter 9 discussed advanced concepts of XML, including semantics, data integration, and data types. The topics of Chapter 10 were the semantic Web and RDF (remembering that the future will be the semantic Web). The Part concluded with a discussion of SS-databases, or the essential databases for storing XML documents.

With this overview of XML technologies and fundamentals, we are now in a position to explore the applications in Part III.

Part III

Applications of XML

Part III, which consists of five chapters, describes the applications of XML. Chapter 12 covers applications of XML to electronic business (e-business), and Chapter 13, applications of XML to data management, particularly XML applications to metadata aspects, query management, interoperability, and migration. XML application to information management technologies including multimedia, training, collaborative computing, knowledge, decision support, and other areas such as agents are discussed in Chapter 14. XML-related products are described in Chapter 15. I have included this under applications because one can regard the products to have been developed as a result of the applications of XML. Finally, Chapter 16 examines issues on building the semantic Web. Whereas Chapter 16 is not strictly an application of XML, I have included this discussion in Part III after having discussed the technologies, constructs, and applications of XML. In a way, one can think of the semantic Web as a kind of XML application because XML plays a role in developing the semantic Web.

As Part III discusses applications, it attempts to combine the background information for XML given in Parts I and II.

12 XML Applications to E-Commerce

12.1 OVERVIEW

In Part I, I discussed various supporting technologies for XML, because these supporting technologies have helped with the development of XML. These supporting technologies include the Web, Web databases, information retrieval, metadata, information management, and electronic commerce (e-commerce). In each of the chapters in Part I, I also discussed the relationship of the technology to XML briefly. This gave the reader some idea about XML.

Then in Part II, I explored XML technologies, starting with some basic issues about XML and then advanced topics. Next to be covered is the semantic Web and finally an overview of semistructured databases.

This part combines the two previous parts and discusses applications of XML, particularly applications of XML in e-commerce, data management, and information management are examined. This chapter begins with the applications, particularly those of XML in e-businesses and e-commerce.

The organization of this chapter follows: Section 12.2, covers various areas where XML, could be applied to e-commerce, especially XML applications for e-commerce documents, interoperability, and information management issues. Although this chapter focuses only on aspects relating to e-commerce, a more general discussion of applications of XML in data and information management are discussed in the next two chapters. Section 12.3 provides an overview of some of the related efforts including the work on e-business XML (ebXML), Commerce One.Net, and RosettaNet. These are all efforts of various consortia promoting XML for e-commerce. A discussion of all the numerous other efforts under way is beyond the scope of this book. The chapter is summarized in Section 12.4.

12.2 DISCUSSION OF APPLICATIONS

In this section, I discuss various applications of XML to e-commerce including document representation, data and information management, and interoperability. Figure 12.1 illustrates the various areas under examination.

First let us consider document representation. When corporations have to conduct transactions, numerous documents have to be exchanged. These documents could be text documents, bills, contracts, legal papers, and many other such items. A uniform way to represent the documents is needed. That is, corporations A, B, and C have to be consistent in their representations. Each community is preparing its own XML specifications, for example, the legal community is developing specifications for legal documents, the tax community is developing specifications for tax

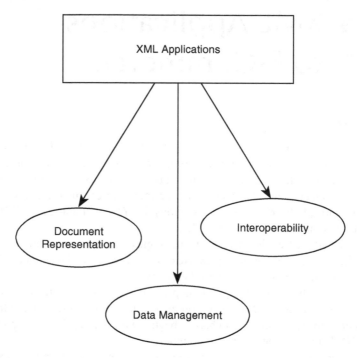

FIGURE 12.1 XML applications.

documents, and the business community is developing specificationss for business documents. Therefore, document representation is an area that is critical for e-commerce and XML provides the solution. A scenario is illustrated in Figure 12.2.

Next, look at data management for e-business. A lot of data may be in databases or elsewhere that may have to be used for various transactions. For example, the data may be in relational databases, flat files, semistructured databases, or object databases. The structure as well as the content of the data has to be captured. For example, consider a table EMP with attributes SS#, Ename, and Salary, with values "100, John, 50K." This information can be represented in XML as follows:

```
<table>
<tname> EMP</tname>
<attributes>
  <SS#> 100 </SS#>
  <Ename> John </Ename>
  <Salary> 50K </Salary>
</attributes>
</table>
```

Similarly, structure and data in object databases can be represented in XML also. The main issue is that with various organizations using all kinds of data to conduct e-commerce transactions, XML provides a facility to represent the data so that the different organizations can understand the data.

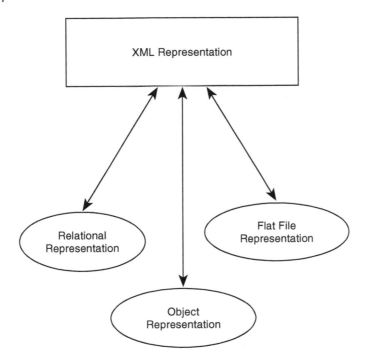

FIGURE 12.2 Document representation.

Other areas of data management include data mining. In this instance, the information in the XML documents has to be mined so that one can understand the data in the various databases. Another aspect is to mine the usage patterns also gathered in XML documents for business intelligence. Data mining for business intelligence is becoming an important aspect for many organizations whether they be commercial, government, or academic. Mining XML documents is a new area.

XML documents have to be stored efficiently. Therefore, we need access methods and index strategies for these documents. This topic is addressed in the next chapter where the entire chapter is devoted to data management and XML. XML applications for data management in e-commerce are illustrated in Figure 12.3.

Another area is interoperability. Again different organizations have to collaboratively work together. This is called collaborative commerce. For example, organization A places an order with organization B. Then B has to get the parts from organizations C and D. This means A, B, C, and D have to work together. XML is essential for communication between the different organizations. Many documents, contracts, and subcontracts will be exchanged between the organizations. Unless they are specified in some common language, it will be very difficult to make sense and, as a result, to conduct the transaction in a timely manner. Interoperability through XML is illustrated in Figure 12.4.

Although I could discuss numerous areas where XML can be applied for information management in e-commerce transactions, I have mentioned only some of the applications in this section. Further elaborations on XML for data management and information management appear in the next two chapters.

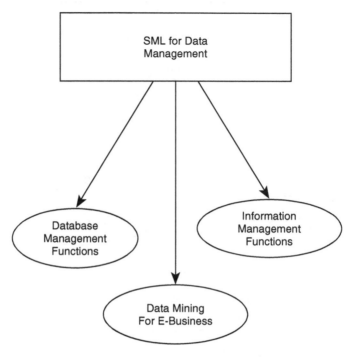

FIGURE 12.3 XML for data management.

12.3 SOME RELATED EFFORTS

12.3.1 OVERVIEW

Several efforts are under way on developing XML standards for e-commerce applications. For a fairly comprehensive overview of the various efforts, see [IEEE00]. In addition to the World Wide Web Consortium (W3C) effort, many industry consortia also are engaged in the development. In addition, the U.S. federal government is funding efforts on digital e-commerce.

An overview of just three of the efforts is given. The first one is ebXML, an effort by the United Nations. The second one is RosettaNet, a global business consortium. The third is *Commerce One.Net,* which is a business-to-business (B-to-B) e-marketplace.

The organization of this section is as follows: Section 12.3.2 covers ebXML; Section 12.3.3, RosettaNet; and Section 12.3.4, *Commerce One.Net.* The areas to be explored are illustrated in Figure 12.5.

12.3.2 ebXML

Electronic Business Extensible Markup Language, (ebXML) is an effort by the United Nations Center for Trade Facilitation and Electronic Business (UN/CEFACT) and Organization for the Advancement of Structured Information Standards (OASIS). The two organizations have formed an initiative with participation from

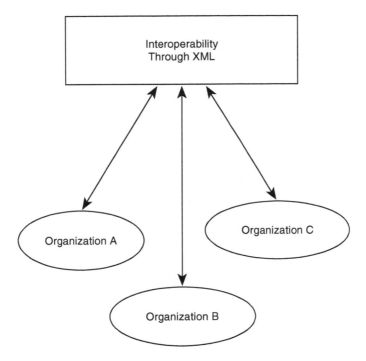

FIGURE 12.4 Interoperability through XML.

industry, academia, and businesses throughout the world to standardize XML for business specifications. The goal is to develop uniform standards so that there is no confusion when organizations across nations conduct businesses.

A number of working groups are focusing on different aspects, but all are coordinating their activities. One group is developing business processes. These processes include those for work flow, purchasing, order management, and other services. Another group focuses on core components, which are the core modules; a third group, on technical architecture requirements; a fourth group, on transport and routing and packaging; a fifth group, on registry and repository (essential for conflict resolution); and a sixth group, on technical coordination. A seventh group, focusing on technical architecture, already has developed architecture for managing XML documents in e-business. Finally, an eighth group focuses on marketing and education.

Like any consortia, the group brainstorms at the meetings and sends request for proposals for specific aspects such as architecture and business processes. Then the group evaluates the proposals and prepares the final specifications. Some of the technical developments include Universal Business Language (UBL), business process specification schema, ebXML architectures, and ebXML interoperability. Numerous other developments can be found under [EBXML]. Also in Chapter 15, I discuss some of the other standards and products that are not addressed here. These include Web Services Description Language (WSDL), Simple Object Access Protocol (SOAP), and some other developments.

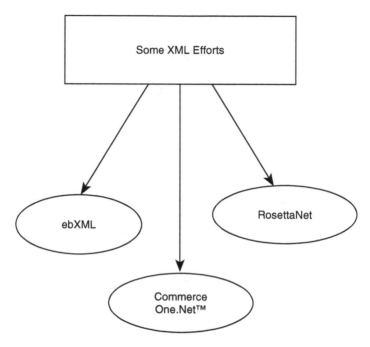

FIGURE 12.5 Some XML initiatives.

ebXML has been active for the past 2 years or so. The initial announcement was made around the latter part of 1999 and the group meets every few weeks, continually updating the Web pages with the latest information. I encourage the reader to keep up with these developments. Because this is an international effort, the results will be used by many around the world.

12.3.3 ROSETTANET

RosettaNet, a global consortium of several companies, is a nonprofit consortium that creates standards for supply chain management. The consortium developed business processes for supply chain management as well as architecture and framework. The key component of RosettaNet is a dictionary with all the information about resources, framework for supply chain management, partner interface processes (PIP), and various e-business processes. All these taken together are the main focus of RosettaNet.

Various business processes, the PIP, and the framework are specified in XML. Therefore, XML standardization for supply chain management is a major undertaking of RosettaNet. RosettaNet also supports the ebXML effort as well as standards for XML-based B2B integration. Commercial products such as the BEA *WebLogic* are conforming to the specifications of RosettaNet for B-to-B integration. Numerous discussions and notes on the efforts of RosettaNet can be found in [ROSET].

12.3.4 COMMERCE ONE.NET

Commerce One.Net is a B-to-B e-marketplace. Functioning mainly in North America, it provides services for maintenance, repair, and operations, as well as for trading. Descriptions of some of the services follow.

In one of the services using what Commerce One calls source tools, detailed information is available about trading partner products, services, and complete directory information. This also provides support for making use of the auction services. In the collaboration tools provided by Commerce One, one could collaborate and communicate with the trading partners, conduct meetings, share information, exchange data, and develop relationships. In the trade tools, the services provided include order management, auctions, and transaction management.

For all the services provided by Commerce One, XML is an essential component. Whether with source tools, collaboration tools, or trading tools, a uniform method is crucial for representing documents, processes, and contracts. Therefore, Commerce One is developing XML standards for its needs. It is also working with organizations like ebXML, W3C, and RosettaNet. This way, all the initiatives will be well coordinated, with each taking advantage of what the other has developed. For more details on Commerce One, refer to [COMM1].

12.4 SUMMARY

This chapter begins with a discussion of the applications of XML for e-commerce, particularly document representation, data management, and interoperability aspects. Then an overview is provided of the various efforts under way on XML and e-commerce. These include the efforts on ebXML, Commerce One, and RosettaNet, which are the various developments of XML-related efforts on e-commerce. Figure 12.6 illustrates the evolution of XML and e-business. They have now converged, resulting in efforts such as ebXML.

Several applications of XML to data and information management have not been addressed in this chapter, because I wanted to focus on e-commerce aspects only. The next two chapters elaborate on XML applications to data and information management, essentially continuing with the evolution of the Web as illustrated in Chapter 2.

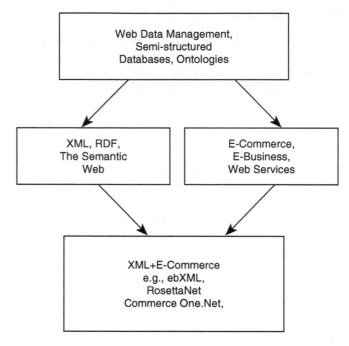

FIGURE 12.6 Evolution of XML and e-commerce.

13 Applications of XML to Data Management

13.1 OVERVIEW

Much of the focus in this book has been on databases and how XML relates to them. Part I covers Web databases; and Part II studies semistructured databases, which is a type of database system. Appendix B provides an overview of data management. This chapter examines various aspects of data management and their relationships to XML, although with some repetition because data management has been discussed earlier in many of the chapters. Data management, however, has been a key component to the development of XML and, therefore, without data management and the Web it is very likely that we may not have made such great progress with XML. Basically, this chapter consolidates much of the discussions in the previous chapters and focuses on all aspects of XML related to data management.

The organization of this chapter is as follows: XML and metadata are discussed in Section 13.2; XML and semistructured databases are covered again in Section 13.3, although already explored in Part II. Therefore, I will present a review in Section 13.3. Then Sections 13.4 to 13.7 examine XML and the various data management functions including query processing, transaction management, storage management, and security. Data distribution, interoperability, and migration issues are the topics of Sections 13.8 and 13.9; data warehousing and mining, of Section 13.10; XML and architectures, of Section 13.11; and the relationship to object technology, of Section 13.12. The chapter is concluded in Section 13.13. Figure 13.1 illustrates all the areas discussed in this chapter in relation to XML.

As mentioned in Chapter 11, one of the debates now is whether to use relational database technology for XML documents or develop data management technology especially for XML documents.

13.2 METADATA

Metadata describe the data, starting with data dictionaries and now evolving into ontologies and schemas. The main concern is what the connection is between XML and metadata. An XML document is mainly a document with tags. One can think of the domain-type definitions (DTDs), the schemas, and other information that describes the structure of the document to be the metadata. In describing resource description frameworks (RDF), I mention the models as well as the representation of semantics. The ontologies as well as the semantics and other information about the structure of the RDF documents are also part of the metadata.

Let us consider metadata for a particular database, which could be represented in XML. As discussed in previous chapters, this facilitates interoperability and migration

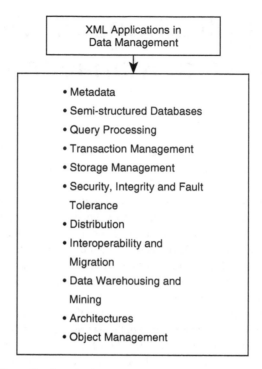

FIGURE 13.1 XML applications in data management.

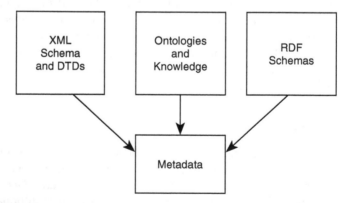

FIGURE 13.2 Metadata and XML.

because a common way to represent the metadata of heterogeneous databases now exists. In summary, because metadata are critical components of any database or information source, and XML is one of the best mechanisms to represent documents, metadata representation in XML is becoming popular. Furthermore, the evolution of XML from DTDs to schemas to RDF shows the importance of representing not only the syntax but also the semantics. Figure 13.2 illustrates metadata and XML.

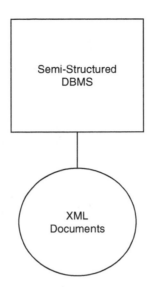

FIGURE 13.3 XML and semistructured databases.

13.3 SEMISTRUCTURED DATABASES

Although this topic is discussed in some detail in Chapter 11, for completeness it will be reviewed again. As stressed, semistructured databases and the Web essentially prompted the development of XML. At that time, structured as well as unstructured documents existed. Furthermore, many of the documents are also semistructured. For example, a document may have an introduction, a set of chapters, and a conclusion. The models for information retrieval systems as well as relational databases were not sufficient to represent semistructured databases. One needed efficient representation of semistructured databases, resulting in the development of Standard Generalized Markup Language (SGML); however, SGML was found to be inappropriate for Web documents. At that time, Hypertext Markup Language (HTML) was the language for developing Web pages, but it was too limiting. This resulted in the development of XML.

A semistructured database can be regarded as a collection of XML documents. Therefore, one needs efficient mechanisms for querying the documents, performing updates and possibly transactions on the documents, storing the documents, controlling access to ensure that the documents are protected, and distributing the documents. Many of these issues are examined in Chapter 11, but a lot of research has been conducted recently on managing XML documents. Much research in this area remains (see, e.g., [ICDE], [SIGM], [VLDB]). Figure 13.3 illustrates semistructured databases and XML.

There is debate as to whether to use relational databases for XML documents and build wrappers or to develop databases especially for XML documents. Specialized databases for managing XML documents are called Native XML Databases (NXDB). For a discussion of NXDB, we refer to [INFO01].

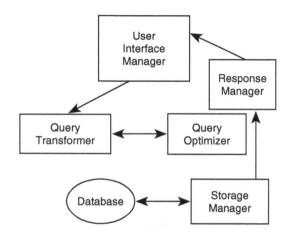

FIGURE 13.4 XML and query processing.

13.4 XML AND QUERY PROCESSING

Much of the data management related-work on XML has been with respect to query management. A few years ago, the World Wide Web Consortium (W3C) requested proposals for a query language for XML. Various efforts were reported at that time. Notable among those efforts is XML Query Language (XMLQL) from INRIA, AT&T, University of Pennsylvania, and University of Washington [XMLQL]. XMLQL has constructs that can query documents based on their DTDs. This effort also describes a data model with a graph structure for XML documents. This effort has influenced the W3C standardization effort of the Xquery effort (see [AMC01]).

Various commercial vendors have also developed Structued Query Language (SQL)-like constructs to query XML documents. For example, as stated in [XMLSQL], the Oracle XML SQL utility has developed techniques for transforming XML constructs to SQL constructs and vice versa. With this, one can use SQL to query XML documents. IBM has developed DB2 CXML extended to store and manipulate XML documents. Microsoft had extended SQL92 by developing OPENXML; and Sybase has developed its Adaptive Server, which introduced Result-SetXml Java class for processing XML documents.

Query processing is another issue for XML databases, for example, efficient query optimization techniques after being investigated for such databases. One can learn a lot from query optimization in relational databases as well as in text databases. Nevertheless, one needs techniques specifically designed for XML databases. Query processing is illustrated in Figure 13.4.

In summary, query language and query optimization are two of the major challenges for XML databases. Several research efforts are under way and we can expect much progress to be made in the near future. W3C efforts as well as the efforts of other groups such as electronic business XML (ebXML) and Organization for the Advancement of Structured Information Standards (OASIS) are also promising.

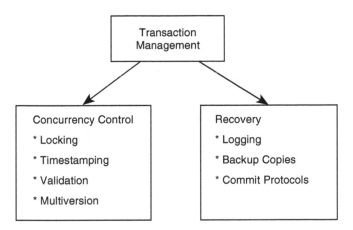

FIGURE 13.5 XML and transaction processing.

13.5 TRANSACTION PROCESSING

Only recently have transaction processing issues been examined for XML documents. For example, concurrency control models as well as recovery techniques are
under investigation. For example, what is a transaction for an XML document? In
some cases, two XML documents may have to be updated as a transaction. In this
case, are the issues different to the issues addressed for relational databases? What
are the differences between updating XML documents and, for example, documents
on object databases? If XML documents are represented as graph structures, then
do you have to lock the entire document or can parts of the document be updated?
How can the links such as XML Link Language (Xlink) and XML Pointer Language
(Xpointer) be updated? How can various parts of the document be recovered? What
happens if the document is distributed?

For many of the questions posed here, it appears that conventional solutions for
transaction processing such as concurrency control and recovery techniques for
relational databases may be sufficient for XML documents. Nevertheless, one needs
an active research program so that many of the issues can be investigated further.
In my previous book [THUR01], I discussed issues on transaction processing for
multimedia databases. These issues need to be reexamined for XML databases.
Issues in transaction processing are illustrated in Figure 13.5.

13.6 STORAGE MANAGEMENT

In the previous sections, I discuss query processing and transaction management.
Another data management function is storage management. The challenge with this
is what sorts of storage techniques are needed for XML documents. For example,
in the case of multimedia databases, I mention some storage mechanisms such as
disk striping. Are these methods appropriate for XML documents? Does one store
the DTDs with the document itself?

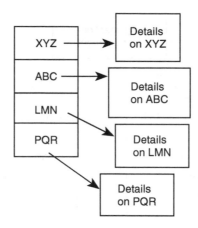

FIGURE 13.6 Keyword-based indexing.

Next, what are the index strategies for XML documents? The numerous indexing techniques for text documents include keyword indexing (see Figure 13.6) and attribute-based indexing. Can such techniques be used for XML documents? Some research has been conducted in this area and more progress can be expected in the next few years.

13.7 SECURITY, INTEGRITY, AND FAULT TOLERANCE

Security is critical for XML documents. That is, XML is becoming the common representation for documents on the Web and, therefore, it is essential that secure access be provided to these documents. Pioneering research on XML security has been conducted by Elisa Bertino and her team at the University of Milano (see, e.g., [BERT00], [BERT01], [BERT02]). Some other work has also been reported in [DAMI00]. The W3C and the OASIS groups are examining security for XML documents

Bertino et al. have developed an access control model for XML documents. For example, if one grants access to a particular node of a document, then does that access get propagated to the nodes and leaves that emanate from that particular node? Bertino et al. have also developed techniques for secure and distributed updates. They use encryption together with role-based access techniques. Access control in XML is illustrated in Figure 13.7.

Integrity and fault tolerance are also important aspects for XML. With respect to integrity, the main concern is how to ensure that the document is correct. What confidence do we have that the values are accurate? Note that the XML documents can come from anywhere in the Web and can be produced by anyone. Therefore, we need to have some measure to ensure the integrity of the document.

With respect to fault tolerance, we need recovery methods for documents that have lost content. Some aspects are discussed under transaction processing, but techniques such as checkpointing need to be examined for XML documents.

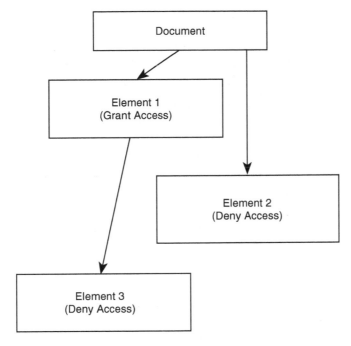

FIGURE 13.7 XML and access control.

13.8 DATA DISTRIBUTION

Although I discuss distributing XML documents in Chapter 11, for completeness I review some of the issues. Similar to relational databases and object databases, XML documents may also be distributed. For example, if a document is large, then part of it may be at one site and another part may be at another site. There could also be a situation where multiple authors work on portions of a document at different sites and therefore a document has to be distributed.

The challenges include distributed query processing, transaction management, metadata management, and security management. Chapter 11 discusses architecture for a distributed semistructured database that contains XML documents. The major modules of the architecture include a distributed query processor, transaction manager, metadata manager, and security and integrity manager. The approach followed is very similar to the one followed for distributed relational databases; however, much research remains to be conducted before we can determine that this is the right approach for distributing XML documents. Data distribution is illustrated in Figure 13.8.

13.9 INTEROPERABILITY AND MIGRATION

This is also a topic addressed in Chapters 11 and 12 when I discuss XML for business-to-business (B-to-B) exchange. Integrating heterogeneous databases has

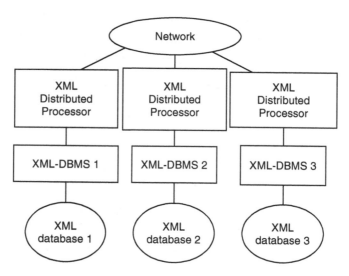

FIGURE 13.8 XML and distribution.

remained a challenge for the past 20 years; however, with the development of XML, we now have a way to specify the schemas in XML. This facilitates integration of the different database systems. That is, each database specifies its schemas in XML. One can also use this approach for federated databases where a collection of databases form a federation.

In the case of migrating legacy databases, we can encapsulate them in wrappers and make the schemas explicit in XML. This way, we can interoperate the legacy databases with the newer databases. In summary, XML has facilitated the migration of legacy databases a great deal, however, it is not the answer to all the problems. For example, XML still lacks semantic representation. Therefore, one cannot resolve semantic conflicts among the different databases. Hopefully, RDF and the semantic Web developments will help with these issues. Interoperability is illustrated in Figure 13.9.

13.10   DATA WAREHOUSING AND MINING

In my previous book, I discussed data warehousing and mining at length. A summary is given in Appendix B. With respect to data warehousing, there are two aspects concerning XML. One is that XML documents, semistructured databases, relational databases, and other data sources have to be integrated into a warehouse. Much of the work until now has been on integrating relational databases into a warehouse, also based on a relational model. When the databases are XML documents as well as semistructured databases, the concern is how to integrate them into a warehouse. What is an appropriate model for a warehouse? Because a mapping now exists between SQL and XML, can we still have an SQL-based model for the warehouse? The second aspect is representing the warehouse as a collection of XML documents. In this case, we need mapping between the data sources based on, for example,

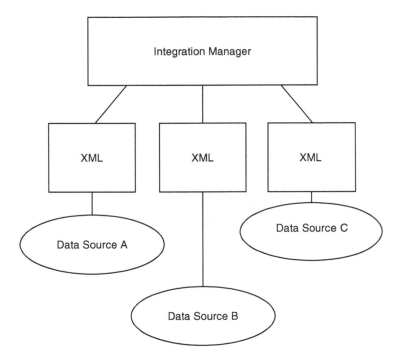

FIGURE 13.9 XML and interoperability.

relational and object models to XML data models. We also need to develop techniques for accessing, querying, and indexing the warehouse. Data warehousing is illustrated in Figure 13.10.

Recall that data mining is briefly discussed in Chapter 3. Mining XML documents is getting more attention. Two aspects must be considered. One is to mine the documents to extract useful information such as patterns and trends. For example, XML documents may be mined for business intelligence. One could mine these documents for customer relationship management. One could also mine the usage patterns so that we can advise the user about which links to follow in an XML document. Much work still remains on data mining.

13.11 ARCHITECTURES

As shown in Chapter 3, many aspects are included in architectures. One is an architecture for an XML database system including modules for query processing, transaction management, metadata management, storage management, and security management. Another is an architecture for distributed XML databases. Yet another architecture is for interoperability and migration. In this type, heterogeneous databases and legacy database have to be integrated through XML schemas. All these architectures are illustrated in the previous sections.

Three-tier architectures also exist, with the front-end ties as the presentation layer where XML documents are presented, the middle tier as the business object

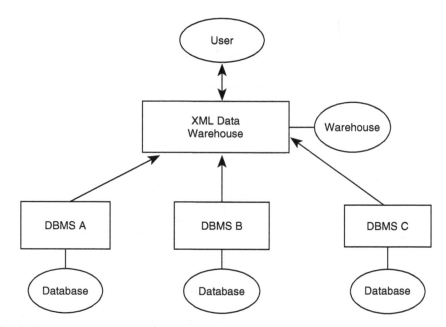

FIGURE 13.10 Warehousing and XML.

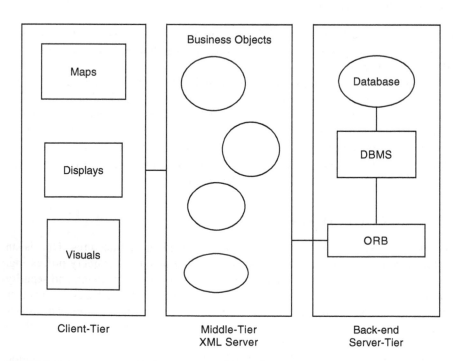

FIGURE 13.11 XML and three-tier computing.

layer that could have an XML-based Web server, and the back-end tier as the database layer consisting of relational databases. This architecture is illustrated in Figure 13.11. Really, no single architecture is applicable. Depending on what you want, whether it is centralized system or a distributed system, you can adopt different architectures. The challenge is to adapt these architectures for managing XML documents.

13.12 OBJECT TECHNOLOGY

See [THUR00] for a discussion of various aspects of object technology. A brief summary is given in Appendix B. Object technology includes object database management, distributed object management, object programming languages, object components and frameworks, and object-oriented design and analysis. The similarities between XML and object technology lie in the object model. The constructs in an object model include classes, attributes, and object instances. One can think of DTDs as document structures similar to classes whereas the documents are the instances; however, XML is not strongly typed. How types can be incorporated has been discussed. Also, XML is purely representational and does not have an execution model. Therefore, methods do not apply in this situation.

Concerning object-oriented design and analysis, the Uniform Modeling Language (UML) is extremely popular for representing both static as well as dynamic situations such as events and activities. Portions of UML could be used to be the data model for XML, although many aspects of UML represent the dynamic situations and are not applicable.

Distributed object management systems such as the Object Management Group's (OMG) object request broker (ORB)-based working groups are examining how XML could be used in conjunction with Interface Description Language (IDL). The schemas of the legacy databases are specified in XML, although calls to the methods are made in IDL. Some of the challenges and issues for interoperability are being examined by OMG [OMG]. Figure 13.12 illustrates the integration with ORBs.

13.13 SUMMARY

This chapter has presented a high-level overview of the relationship between data management and XML. Topics discussed include metadata issues, a review of semistructured databases, some of the key functions of database systems including query management, transaction processing, storage management, and security management; distribution, interoperability, and migration; warehousing and mining, and some general topics such as architectures and object technology. All these are explored with XML in mind, that is, how XML could be applied to various aspects of data management.

Some areas are more mature than others. For example, a lot of work has been conducted on querying XML databases as well as XML security. A lot of work is still needed on transaction management, data mining, and warehousing in relationship to XML. Nevertheless, this area is being investigated extensively, with much progress expected in the next few years.

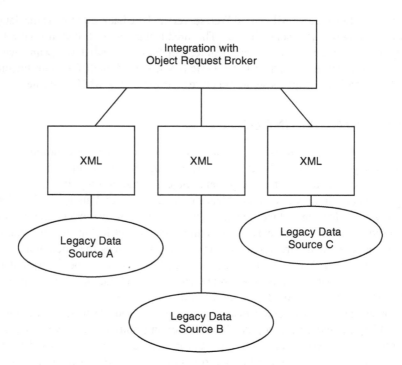

FIGURE 13.12 Integration with ORBs.

14 Applications of XML to Information Management

14.1 OVERVIEW

The last chapter described XML applications to data management. In Part I, in addition to data management technologies, information management technologies was discussed at length. No really clear-cut separation exists between data and information management. The assumption is that data management in general deals with database systems technologies whereas information management deals with a broader set of technologies including multimedia information systems, collaborative computing, knowledge management, intelligent agents, wireless information management, and decision support and related technologies.

This chapter discusses XML applications to information management technologies. Although XML applications to data management are somewhat more mature than XML applications to information management, some work has been reported in this area, especially with the advent of the semantic Web. Therefore, the discussion of the various topics is rather preliminary. Nevertheless, these will be important areas in the future.

The organization of this chapter follows: XML and multimedia is the subject of Section 14.2; collaborative computing and XML, of Section 14.3; XML related to knowledge management activities, of Section 14.4; decision support technologies and XML, of Section 14.5; agents and XML technologies, of Section 14.6; XML applications to wireless information management, of Section 14.7; and some other information technologies with respect to XML, of Section 14.8. The chapter is concluded in Section 14.9. Each of the technologies discussed in Chapter 5 are examined as how XML could be applied to them. Figure 14.1 illustrates the contents of this chapter.

14.2 MULTIMEDIA AND XML

Again, XML is a markup language for text data, evolving from Hypertext Markup Language (HTML) and Standard Generalized Markup Language (SGML). Whereas text is one type of media, multimedia implies a combination of data types. Efforts are under way to develop markup languages for multimedia data and also for individual data types such as images and video. One can also extract annotations for multimedia data and mark up the annotations with XML.

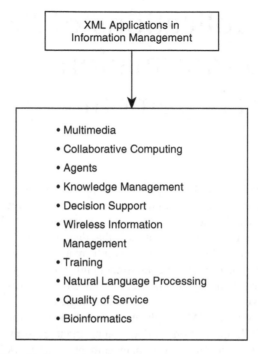

FIGURE 14.1 XML and information management.

This section examines markup languages for multimedia data. The popular markup language is Synchronized Multimedia Integration Language (SMIL) (see [SMIL1] and [SMIL2]). It is an XML-based language that combines the various pieces of media in the order we want them to appear and presents it to the user. A company called RealNetworks has developed SMIL for the Web. SMIL has many similarities to HTML, but with multimedia capabilities one can build complex presentations and use various scripts such as JavaScript programming. The World Wide Web Consortium (W3C) has also come up with specifications for SMIL. In addition, many discussions are available on presenting video, text, and other media with SMIL (see [SMIL1]). An excellent introduction to SMIL can be found in [SMIL3]. W3C has created SMIL as an XML application for multimedia presentations. It provides the ability to combine audio, video, and text, graphics, etc. in real time and display in Web pages. Authors essentially control what is to be presented and when. Figure 14.2 illustrates a graphical representation of the capability of SMIL.

14.3 COLLABORATIVE COMPUTING AND XML

Chapter 5 discusses collaborative computing where groups of individuals collectively work together on some common project. Recently, collaborative computing and electronic commerce (e-commerce) have been integrated to produce an area called collaborative commerce (c-commerce). C-commerce is about business-to-business

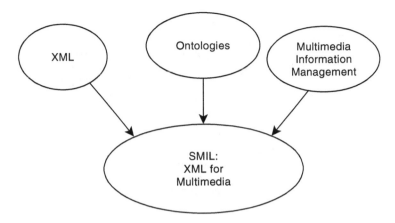

FIGURE 14.2 XML for multimedia.

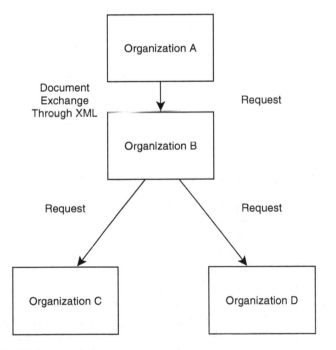

FIGURE 14.3 XML and c-commerce.

(B-to-B) exchange. That is, c-commerce is all about organizations collaboratively conducting transactions. For example, an organization A may request parts from an organization B. To conduct the transaction, B may request parts from C and D. Therefore, A to D have to work together — this is c-commerce. Figure 14.3 illustrates this.

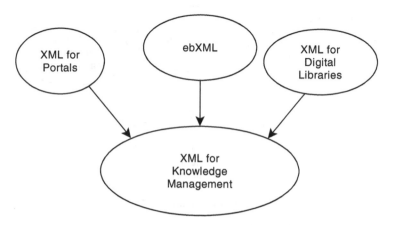

FIGURE 14.4 XML and knowledge management.

What is the role of XML in collaborative commerce? Because c-commerce is about B-to-B exchange, much of the discussion in Chapter 12 applies here. That is, consortia such as RosettaNet are developing XML standards for B-to-B exchange and as a result for c-commerce [XCC]. One can also apply the standards developed by *Commerce One.Net* and electronic business XML (ebXML) for c-commerce. That is, the standards that are being developed are applicable not just for e-commerce but also for c-commerce. For a discussion on c-commerce, refer to [GUPT01] in which c-commerce is viewed as an integration of knowledge management, e-commerce, and collaborative computing.

14.4 KNOWLEDGE MANAGEMENT AND XML

Knowledge management encompasses many areas, but basically it is about a corporation able to share and reuse knowledge. A corporate intranet is essential for effective knowledge management. A number of portals are emerging for various organizations both in government and in industry. There are products from corporations such as IBM, Oracle, and BEA Systems, among others that enable organizations to build portals. A portal is an example of a knowledge management tool. Furthermore, knowledge management is a component of c-commerce.

What is the role of XML in knowledge management? XML is a key technology for developing portals. It provides a mechanism for common document representation. Organizations can share documents efficiently with XML. The standards developed by consortia such as ebXML, RosettaNet, and Commerce One.Net are all applicable for knowledge management. These not only are standards for e-commerce and c-commerce but also provide standards for information sharing and exchange, therefore supporting knowledge management. Digital library efforts that involve intelligent searching and management of information are involved in XML standards. Figure 14.4 illustrates XML for knowledge management. For a discussion of some of the developments refer to [XKM].

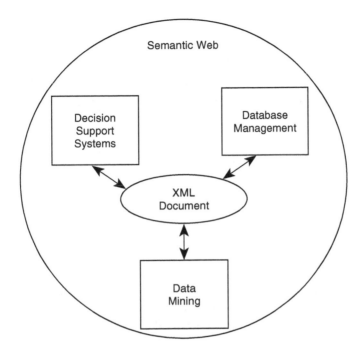

FIGURE 14.5 XML and decision support.

14.5 DECISION SUPPORT AND XML

Decision support systems are essentially systems that support managers to make effective decisions. Decision support is a combination of technologies including data management, data warehousing, and data mining. To make effective decisions, one needs a clear understanding of the content. This means that documents have to be well represented. In addition, we need to understand the semantics. That is, XML, resource description framework (RDF), and the semantic Web will become critical technologies for decision support.

I define the semantic Web to be a Web that can manage all activities for an individual. This means that the Web has to make decisions for the individuals. Therefore, the information has to be well represented. XML and RDF are necessary for managing the content of the documents.

Although it is clear that XML is essential for effective decision support, developing specific XML tools for decision support is just beginning; however, many of the efforts by consortia such as ebXML are also applicable to decision support. Figure 14.5 illustrates XML and decision support.

14.6 AGENTS AND XML

While XML was being developed in the late 1990s, many efforts were under way to develop mobile agent technology. Various industries, such as telecommunications,

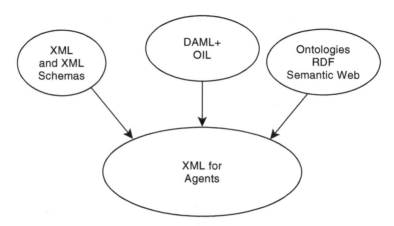

FIGURE 14.6 XML and agents.

investigated XML for agents, although this whole area received much prominence after the advent of the Defense Advanced Research Projects Agency (DARPA) Agent Markup Language (DAML). DAML developed a markup language for the semantic Web. The idea was conceived by Hendler, Lee, and others (see [LEE01]). Since then, a joint effort between the United States and Europe has resulted in the initiative called DAML + Ontology Interchange Language (OIL). Various efforts on DAML + OIL have been reported (see, e.g., [DOIL]).

The main contributions of DAML + OIL are to develop RDF, RDF schemas, XML, schemas and ontologies. The efforts also focus on developing the foundations for these technologies including axiomatic semantics. Although active work has gone on for about a year now, we have seen a lot of progress the last few months. Furthermore, W3C has also embraced the DAML + OIL effort. We can expect to see tremendous progress within the next year. Also joint workshops are conducted between the European Research Consortium for Informatics and Mathematics (ERCIM) and the National Science Foundation (NSF) in the United States. Figure 14.6 illustrates some of the developments.

14.7 WIRELESS COMPUTING

With the explosion of wireless communication, various information management technologies are being applied to widen computing and XML. One of the significant developments is the Wireless Application Protocol (WAP), an industry-wide standard for developing applications over wireless communication. WAP was the result of a consortium founded by corporations such as Nokia and Ericsson.

At about the same time, XML became very popular. Therefore, the corporations involved in wireless computing developed Wireless Markup Language (WML). WML is based on XML and is a markup language for Web pages to be displayed on mobile equipment such as cellular telephones and palm pilots. As stated in

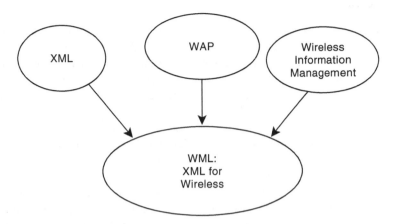

FIGURE 14.7 XML and wireless computing.

[WML], with WML one can specify content and user interfaces for narrowband devices. WML provides support for both text and images and has constructs for presenting documents on mobile devices. Associated with WML are many other standards including scripting languages and application specifications.

XML and WAP are two of the underlying technologies for WML. The consortium is continuing to make progress with WML. In the future, we can expect support for video and audio data as well as fully integrated multimedia data for wireless devices. Figure 14.7 illustrates XML applications to wireless communication.

14.8 OTHER INFORMATION TECHNOLOGIES AND XML

Some of the key information technologies have been discussed with respect to XML including multimedia, collaborative computing, wireless information management, decision support, and agents. Many other technologies are relevant to this discussion including training, natural language processing, speech processing, and bioinformatics. For example, training documents have to be presented in a consistent manner. Multimedia presentations are components of training technologies. As discussed earlier, SMIL is a markup language for multimedia data. Researchers working in training and instructional systems are investigating markup languages. Similarly, natural language processing, speech processing, and domain-specific information technologies (such as bioinformatics, financial information systems, and many others) have to exchange documents on the Web. Therefore, XML will be a key technology for many of these systems.

One area that needs investigation is quality of service for XML. That is, how do we reason with incomplete information? How can we ensure the quality of the documents? How can we ensure that secure access is provided? What kinds of trade-offs should we make? Some researchers are beginning to look into these areas. Also, some of the more recent applications of XML to Information Management are reported in [INFO01].

14.9 SUMMARY

This chapter discusses XML application to a number of areas including multimedia, collaborative computing, knowledge management, decision support, agents, and wireless computing. Some other areas such as training and instructional systems, natural language processing, and bioinformatics are also briefly mentioned. Many of these technologies have developed markup languages based on XML. These include SMIL, DAML, and WML, with a lot of overlap. For example, ebXML standards are applicable not only for e-commerce but also for knowledge management, decision support, and c-commerce. Perhaps as the technology matures, we may be able to clearly separate the applications of XML to, for example, knowledge management and c-commerce.

One aspect that is lacking is semantics for the various markup languages. This results partly from the fact that XML in its current form cannot represent semantics. Therefore, as we make progress with efforts such as DAML + OIL, XML schemas, and RDF, we can expect markup languages to represent not only the syntax, but also the semantics of the applications.

15 XML-Related Data and Information Management Tools for the Web

15.1 OVERVIEW

This chapter describes some example commercial Web data and information management products related to XML. They are grouped into various categories such as database systems, data mining, and knowledge management. Much of the information on the products is an update of what is provided in [THUR00]; however, some new details are added on recent breakthrough products and services such as *Simple Object Access Protocol (SOAP), Web Services Description Language (WSDL), DOTNET, Universal Description Discovery and Integration (UDDI),* and *Java 2 Enterprise Edition (J2EE).* These are the standards and technologies to be followed up. They are included as part of the products and tools chapter because technology is changing by the day, and the information that is current today may be outdated tomorrow. Therefore, it is very important to keep up with all the information that is available on the Web. Much of this information can be found in World Wide Web Consortium (W3C) white papers as well as under XML cover pages.

As stated earlier, all the information on these products has been obtained from published material as well as from vendor product literature. Also, the purpose in this text is to give an overview of what products are available, not the technical details of these products.

I discuss only some of the key features of the products, tools, and services. Various Web data management conferences including data management and mining magazines, books, and trade shows such as *Database Programming and Design* (Miller Freeman Publishers), *Data Management Handbook Series* (Auerbach Publications), and DCI Database Client Server Computing Conferences have several articles and presentations discussing the commercial products. I urge the reader to take advantage of the information presented in these magazines, books, and conferences and to keep up with the latest developments with the vendor products. Another excellent periodical is *Infoworld,* published weekly. This magazine not only describes technologies, but also provides in-depth alaysis of the usage. Furthermore, in areas relating to the Web, developments can be expected to change very rapidly. The various Web pages are also a useful source of information. In fact, some of the best material is now published on the Web and is continuously updated.

It should also be noted that I am not endorsing any of these products or prototypes. I have chosen a particular product or prototype only to explain a specific technology. I would have liked to have included discussions of many more products and prototypes, but such a discussion is beyond the scope of this book. In recent years various documents have provided a detailed survey of various Web data management products. As an example, for data mining, the Two Crows Corporation puts out a manual describing details of the products and compares them. I encourage the reader to take advantage of such up-to-date information.

The organization of this chapter follows: Section 15.2 discusses tools for the Web database system; Section 15.3, Web for data mining; Section 15.4, for Web application servers; Section 15.5, for Web knowledge management; and Section 15.6, Web metadata, particularly XML-based tools. An overview of some other tools, such as those for Web security, collaboration, and agents, is given in Section 15.7. The recent breakthrough products and services, such as SOAP, WSDL, UDDI, and DOTNET, are described in Section 15.8, with the chapter summarized in Section 15.9. Figure 15.1 provides an overview of the various Web data and information management tools. Figure 15.2 illustrates graphically the tools discussed in this chapter.

15.2 WEB DATABASE SYSTEM TOOLS

Web databases are a key part of Web data management. I discussed Web database systems in Chapter 3. Current trends include accessing relational databases on the Web though Java Database Connectivity (JDBC). Application servers and data servers (i.e., Web servers) also access database systems and format data in a way that can be understood by Web clients.

Almost every major database system vendor now has access to the Web. That is, relational, object-oriented, and object-relational systems have Web access. Web clients can now access these databases. XML is becoming a standard language for formatting the responses from database systems so that Web clients can understand the results. With XML, one can eliminate the various gateways discussed in Chapter 3.

This section describes a sample database system and discusses how it can be interfaced to the Web. The database system that we have selected is the recent Web database system product of Oracle Corporation. As mentioned earlier, I selected this product only because I am more familiar with it than some of the other products. This does not mean that this is the best product or that I am endorsing it. As stated, every major database system vendor including Oracle, Sybase, Informix, and Object Design has designed its products in such a way that it has Web interfaces. I am most familiar with Oracle's product and will therefore discuss it in this section. Other good products include, for example, the Sybase *ASE* product for the Web and enterprise information management. An excellent discussion of the various products can be found in the *Infoworld* magazines (see for example [INFO01]).

Let us examine the features of the Oracle products called *Oracle 8i* and *Oracle WebDB*. Oracle 8i (as described in [ORAC1]) combines Internet database capabilities with traditional warehousing and transaction processing capabilities. The internet file system feature of Oracle 8i enables users to move their data into the Oracle database. In addition, the intermedia module supports the management of multimedia data. WebDB (to be described later) is a tool to build Hypertext Markup Language

FIGURE 15.1 Data and information management tools for the Web.

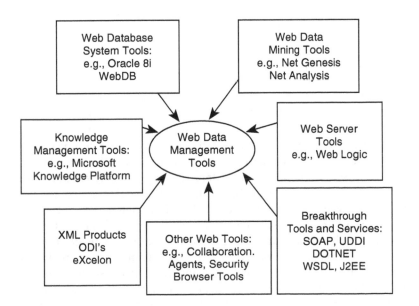

FIGURE 15.2 Tools discussed in this chapter.

(HTML)-based Web pages with data from Oracle databases. Oracle 8i integrates the Java Virtual Machine into its server and this way can deploy Java programs at various tiers (such as client and middle tiers).

In addition to supporting Web data management, Oracle 8i also supports various database management functions. It has enhanced features for transaction processing and warehouse management, database administration, indexing, parallel servers management, replication, caching, fine-grained access control, and support for objects. Oracle 8i also provides rich support for enterprise data management.

Oracle WebDB (see the description in [ORAC2]) is mainly a Web browser that builds Web pages from various types of data in the Oracle databases. For example, Oracle 8i supports the management of multimedia data such as video and text. With the Web browser, the multimedia data can be viewed efficiently. WebDB enables the visualization of the data in the database via the Web. The Web pages can be personalized and can provide multiple views of the same data. For example, some users may want to see graphs whereas others may want to see just numbers. WebDB provides the support for both views.

Many of the emerging products have support for managing XML documents. As stated in Chapter 13, the Oracle XML Structured Query Language (SQL) utility has developed techniques for transforming XML constructs to SQL constructs and vice versa. With this, one can use SQL to query XML documents. More recently, Oracle launched the 9i product that is highly scalable and has kept up with the latest developments on XML with W3C.

Oracle 8i as well as 9i, Oracle WebDB, and many of the other tools that are emerging make Web data management a reality. As stressed, I have chosen products in this book mainly due to my familiarity with them. Various database vendors such as IBM, Sybase, Microsoft, Informix, and Object Design (now eXcelon Corporation) have developed assorted Web database management products. This is one of the fastest growing areas in Web information management.

15.3 WEB MINING TOOLS

In the Web page of KDD Nuggets [KDDN], numerous resources to data mining are given. These include references to Web mining products. Some of the recent Web mining products include *Easy Miner* for Web by MINEit Software that carries out cross-section analysis, *HiLis* by Accrue Software that carries out server log analysis, *e.Analysis* by Genesis that carries out e-business intelligence analysis, and *NetTracker* by Sane Solutions that is an Internet usage tracking program. In addition to products, free software is available including AltavistaDiscovery, which one can attach to the browser to search the Web, and the Kensington Open Infrastructure for Enterprise Data Mining by Guo et al. at Imperil College in London (see [GUO00]).

Because this book has a strong emphasis on electronic commerce (e-commerce), I discuss the Net Genesis products. These products attempt to provide customer inelligence to the electronic business (e-business) enterprise so those customers can be retained. For example, different segments of shoppers are evaluated and analyzed so that the e-business organization can conduct customized marketing. These products also enable the enterprise to identify the key drivers of the business and how they can provide competitive advantage; and help the organization to understand the nature of the different shoppers and why they behave the way they do, and give reasons as to why they purchase certain products.

The Web mining products such that as the ones described in this chapter are still in their infancies, with many of them around less than a year. As we learn more about e-commerce and e-business we will see more and more tools applying data mining to e-business. Because XML is becoming the standard representation for Web documents, we will see many tools to mine XML documents for business intelligence and for other purposes emerging in the marketplace.

15.4 WEB APPLICATION SERVER TOOLS

Various server tools have emerged over the years since the mid-1990s. These server tools perform various functions including access to database management systems and legacy databases. As described in Chapter 3, the application servers are often based on Enterprise Java Beans (EJB) technology. Also, data servers exist that access the database systems.

Many application server tools are now on the market. The chapter illustrates some of the concepts with the tool called *WebLogic,* a product of BEA systems (see, e.g., [BEA]). BEA states that its e-commerce application server products include WebLogic and *BEA Tuxedo.* They are used to build rapid e-commerce applications and transactions, utilizing the latest distributed technologies including Enterprise Java and ORB. The *BEA eLink* integrates new and existing applications for office systems. The BEA products are based on multitier client–server computing with business logic for e-commerce applications in the middle tier.

The BEA WebLogic application server is essentially based on component technology. Its goals are to provide a complete set of tools for enterprise applications and to ensure scalability and security. It interfaces to Web applications on the one side and server technologies on the other side. Through products such as WebLogic, client applications to legacy databases are made less complex. Associated with WebLogic is the BEA WebLogic Enterprise, which provides support for manipulating business logic across to multiple servers and multiple heterogeneous databases. Also, the application server tools are being integrated with data servers that manage XML documents. Furthermore, these tools are also integrating heterogeneous databases that have used XML to specify their schemas.

15.5 WEB KNOWLEDGE MANAGEMENT TOOLS

Numerous tools for knowledge management are emerging. These include collaboration and decision support tools as well as Web information management tools. The term *knowledge management* is still rather vague and therefore various types of tools have been grouped together and called knowledge management tools.

I describe a suite of tools for knowledge management by Microsoft Corporation and its industry partners. These tools are called the *Knowledge Management Platform* (see, e.g., [MICR]. This platform has the following five components: knowledge desktop, knowledge services, system, connected devices, and partner solutions. All are briefly discussed next.

Knowledge desktop is a collection of tools to seamlessly access and use the Microsoft Corporation knowledge assets. Products such as *Office 2000* enable this. Knowledge services include collaboration services such as meeting facilities, content management services that capture and manage various experiences and ideas, analysis services that turn data into knowledge, and tracking and work flow services that capture best practices.

The system component mainly consists of a Microsoft server that provides a complete set of services to the user. Connected device components support knowledge workers through partnerships, for example, with telecommunications companies; and partner solution components enable Microsoft to team with industries partners to produce various tools such as digital dashboards.

Described in this chapter is a collection of tools by Microsoft to support the various knowledge management, collaboration, and decision support functions that have been described in earlier chapters. Also, several smaller companies exist that specialize entirely on knowledge management products. This is an area in which we can expect numerous products to be developed within the next few years. Furthermore, as definitions of knowledge management become clearer we can also decide which of these products really perform knowledge management. Chapter 14 covers the relationship between XML and knowledge management. The commercial portals and knowledge management tools are also supporting the exchange and management of XML documents.

15.6   WEB METADATA AND XML TOOLS

Various XML tools have emerged during the past year or so. One of the prominent tools is *eXcelon* by Object Design Inc. Much of the information about this tool is obtained from [ODI]. eXcelon is an application development environment for integrating structured, unstructured, and semistructured data. The goal of eXcelon is to support a variety of e-business Web information management activities for the enterprise. To achieve its goal, the company is providing a toolbox to support various XML tools.

One of the key components of this product is eXcelon Stylus, a visual Extensible Style Language (XSL) editor for XML. The eXcelon data server stores and manages XML documents. Therefore, Object Design provides a complete solution to XML, with the server to manage the data and the tools to edit and manipulate the XML data.

Object Design has discussed various applications for eXcelon. These include Web commerce, knowledge management, business-to-business (B-to-B), and enterprise application integration. Web e-commerce is about conducting transactions on the Web. Typically, one has to advertise the company's products. Object Design eXcelon enables the specification of the company's products that may be described as structured, unstructured, or semistructured. Knowledge management is enhanced by eXcelon through capturing the knowledge assets of the corporation in various data formats. B-to-B applications are enhanced by eXcelon by its support for XML extensions. Traditional Electronic Data Interchange (EDI)-type information exchange is rather limiting for such applications and one needs richer representation schemes. The data server component facilitates enterprise application integration. That is, one needs to efficiently integrate the data of the corporation and be able to query the data effectively for enterprise application management. The Object Design eXcelon provides this support.

In summary, XML tools such as eXcelon are becoming popular for B-to-B exchange. Products are also emerging from other corporations such as Siebel systems and Vitria to support B-to-B exchange. Although they provide many critical capabilities for e-business, much work remains. As progress is made on XML, we can expect these tools to advance also.

15.7 OTHER WEB INFORMATION MANAGEMENT TOOLS

I briefly discuss various Web data management tools in this chapter. Of the numerous other tools that have not been mentioned, some are now named.

Several tools for Web security have emerged. These tools include firewall products as well as *secure Java* and *Microsoft ActiveX*. In addition, various secure transaction systems have also emerged for the Web. These include the secure payment protocols. Encryption products are also a type of Web security products.

Other Web tools include tools for collaboration. I discuss knowledge management tools, which included collaboration. Corporations such as Lotus have developed various collaboration tools, and these tool enable users to share information and collaborate with one another. Another example of a prototype collaborative system is given in [JONE99]. I discuss Web browser tools such as Oracle's *WebDB*. This is only one such tool where database data is transformed into Web pages. Numerous other tools such as Netscape's browsers* also perform visualization. Web agent tools include the various types of Web crawlers and "knowbots" that locate resources and enable information sharing and collaboration.

Other Web tools include tools for distance learning, multimedia information processing, and decision support. Some of these functions arc already provided by the tools previously discussed. For example, Oracle 8i supports multimedia information management. The Microsoft knowledge platform provides support for collaboration, decision support, and training. In addition to these large corporations, many smaller corporations are specializing in collaboration, multimedia, decision support, and training. Distance learning and training will become key components of e-business; therefore, many tools can be expected to emerge in this area.

In addition to the data management tools for the Web, we can also envision various components and infrastructures for the Web. We can expect plug-and-play tool-based component technology as well as specialized framework and infrastructures to emerge. The Object Management Group (OMG) ORB-based tools are the first step toward such infrastructures.

---

* Netscape is now part of America Online (AOL).

In summary, during the past 2 years or so, the number of Web data management tools has grown almost exponentially. We cannot expect to see a slow down in the near future. In fact, this exponential growth will continue well into the 21st century.

15.8 BREAKTHOUGH STANDARDS, TOOLS, AND SERVICES

15.8.1 OVERVIEW

A number of breakthrough standards, tools, and services are now available. We are calling it "breakthrough" because they are providing support to a number of products for Web data and information management. The tools to be discussed next are SOAP, WSDL, UDDI, Microsoft DOTNET (also known as .NET), and J2EE. They are all related to XML in some way or another.

The organization of this section follows: Section 15.8.2 describes SOAP; Section 15.8.3, WSDL; Section 15.8.4, UDDI; and Section 15.8.5, DOTNET. Section 15.8.5 provides an overview of J2EE.

15.8.2 SOAP

SOAP is a lightweight protocol for exchanging messages using XML. It works in a distributed decentralized environment. The messages are structured and typed information. SOAP does not define application semantics, however, it provides a mechanism for expressing application semantics and also has encoding mechanisms for encoding application data. This way SOAP can be used in various messaging systems and remote procedure call-based system. For a complete discussion of SOAP version 1.2, refer to [SOAP].

As stated in [SOAP], SOAP has four parts: a way to define what a message is, encoding rules, remote procedure call representation, and binding. For example, SOAP messages can be carried in Hypertext Transfer Protocol (HTTP). XML is used to specify SOAP messages. Various example messages, the design goals, the message exchange model, and the bindings are described in [SOAP]. Similar to XML, SOAP specification is a W3C product.

15.8.3 WSDL

Although SOAP is a message protocol, and Web community is developing standards for messages and formats, some way is needed to describe the communication in a structured and organized way. WSDL does this by defining an XML grammar for describing network services. As described in [WSDL], the network services are described as a collection of communication end points capable of exchanging messages.

A WSDL document has various elements including:
Types, which is a container for data-type definition
Message, which is the data communicated
Operation, which is an action supported by the service
Port type, which is a subset of operations supported by the end points

Binding, which is a concrete protocol and data format specification for a
   particular port type
Port, which is an end point
Service, which is a collection of end points

WDSL also provides binding extensions to protocols such as SOAP. For a detailed
discussion we refer to [WSDL]. Similar to XML and SOAP, WSDL is also a W3C
product.

15.8.4 UDDI

As stated in [UDDI], e-commerce has essentially changed the way we do business.
Organizations are collaboratively working together to meet the needs of customers.
Various trading partnerships are being formed. Numerous resources are available on
the network and, in many cases, it is difficult to find the resources and potential
partners. That is, we need a way to effectively conduct B-to-B e-commerce.

   To address the previously mentioned need, organizations have come together to
develop UDDI (Universal Description, Discovery, and Integration) specification. As
mentioned in [UDDI], UDDI created a global platform-independent framework for
businesses to find each other, define how they can interact over the Internet, and
share information in a global registry. This way, participants in UDDI can effectively
conduct B-to-B e-commerce. UDDI takes advantage of the developments with W3C
including XML, SOAP, and HTTP.

15.8.5 DOTNET

In the latter part of the year 2000, Microsoft released a product strategy called
DOTNET (known as .Net). The goal was to produce a new application development
framework that can provide a fully integrated system for developing Web applications. It has also been stated that .Net is a revolutionary way to develop applications.

   As stated in [DOTNET], DOTNET has three parts. The first is .Net framework,
which is a new development environment for Web applications; the second is .Net
product, which includes applications such as Office and Visual Studio; and the third
is .Net services, which enables third-party developers to create various services on
the .Net platform. The .Net framework that is at the heart of the .Net strategy has a
run-time engine, a set of class libraries, and *arenas* for developing Web applications.
For more details on the framework as well as the other components of .Net, refer
to [DOTNET].

15.8.6 J2EE

Although DOTNET is the Microsoft strategy for developing integrated Web applications and services, the product that has been around for the last 2 years is J2EE
(Java 2 Enterprise Edition). As stated in [J2EE], developers want to write distributed
applications with all the features such as security and reliability for the enterprise.
J2EE provides a component-based approach to developing enterprise applications.

In general, multitiered applications are difficult to write because of the complexity of the system. J2EE is component-based and enables developers to write applications in a consistent and an organized way. J2EE uses EJB technology and has a security model, a transaction model, lookup services, and a remote connectivity model. For details of J2EE, refer to [J2EE]. Also, articles on the Web comparing J2EE with DOTNET are available.

15.9 SUMMARY

This chapter provides a brief overview of the various XML-related Web data and information management tools. In particular, it describes tools for Web database management, Web mining, Web server management, and knowledge management as well as some of the recent breakthrough products and services such as WSDL and SOAP. First, a general discussion of the tools is given, followed by the description of an example tool. Also mentioned are some other classes of tools. I have selected the tools only because of my knowledge about them (not an endorsement of any of the products). A description of all the tools are beyond the scope of the book. Furthermore, because of the rapid developments in the field, the information about these products may soon be outdated. Therefore, I urge the reader to take advantage of the various commercial and research material available on these products.

The developments in Web data and information management over the last few years have shown a lot of promise. Although some of the tools have been around for a while, for instance, database system products are now being integrated with the Web. We need the integration of multiple technologies to make Web data management work. Therefore, in the future, we will see increasing numbers of tools integrated with each other to provide effective Web data and information management.

16 Building the Semantic Web

16.1 OVERVIEW

Part I discussed technologies for XML and Part II discusses XML concepts as well as semantic Web concepts, with Part III covering applications of XML. Now that we have some idea on what the semantic Web will look like, let us examine some preliminary information on how one can go about building the semantic Web. Eventually, we have to build a semantic Web to see if the goals and objectives can be met. We may not realize, however, that the semantic Web could be well on its way to being built. This is mainly because no really clear definition of the semantic Web has been adopted. If we assume the definition of Lee et al. [LEE01], then we are far from building the semantic Web; however, if we assume that the semantic Web is the Web of yesterday with more intelligence, then we have it. That is, the semantic Web will never be complete, but it will continually evolve. The Web of today will be the semantic Web of yesterday, and the Web of tomorrow will be the semantic Web of today.

This chapter discusses some of my ideas on how to go about building the semantic Web. The concepts about the semantic Web are discussed in Chapter 10, but a discussion of the issues on building the Web follows the discussion on technologies, constructs, and applications of XML. The chapter is organized as follows: the Web vs. the semantic Web is described in Section 16.2, a repeat of the material in Chapter 10. Issues on the incremental evoluton of the Web are covered in Section 16.3. This is in many ways similar to migrating legacy applications to new architectures and systems. Architectural aspects are also the subject of Section 16.3. Data and information management aspects are examined in Section 16.4; interoperability issues as well as XML and resource description framework (RDF), in Section 16.5; Web services, in Section 16.6; and putting everything together, in Section 16.7. Finally, the chapter is summarized in Section 16.8. For more information on some of the recent developments about the semantic Web, refer to the recent workshops on this topic (see [WORK1] and [WORK2]). Section 16.9 gives a conclusion to Part III.

16.2 REVISITING WEB VS. THE SEMANTIC WEB

Much of the information in this section about ideas on the Web vs. the semantic Web has been obtained from Chapter 10. The difference between the Web and the semantic Web have been studied. Some say that the Web is a system where the human has to read the Web pages, whereas the semantic Web is a system where the

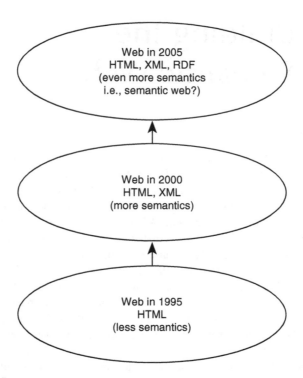

FIGURE 16.1 From the Web to the semantic Web.

machine reads and understands the Web pages. Others say that the Web today is the semantic Web of yesterday, and the Web tomorrow is the semantic Web of today. Although we are getting closer machine understandable Web pages, we are still a long way from achieving this.

We cannot say that the semantic Web will end once we have a system with machine understandable Web pages. The enhancements will continue as new technologies emerge.

Figure 16.1 illustrates the evolution of the Web to the semantic Web. Yesterday we had Hypertext Markup Language (HTML), today we have XML, tomorrow we will have RDF, and the day after we will have something else. The biggest challenge was to build the Web, with no end in sight.

16.3 INCREMENTAL EVOLUTION AND ARCHITECTURAL ASPECTS

In many ways, we can think of incrementally building and evolving the Web. For example, many of the pieces of the Web are already in place. What we do not have are the components for understanding the information on the Web. The semantic Web is intended to provide the tools for understanding the information on the Web, not simply reading them.

For example, what do we do with a module that simply reads the Web pages and the human directs it regarding what actions to take? What happens when this

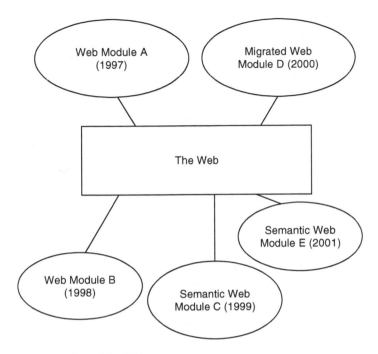

FIGURE 16.2 Evolution of the Web.

module becomes obsolete and we now have tools for understanding the information on the Web? Then we need to migrate the legacy tools and systems to new tools and systems. Perhaps we can use the migration technology discussed in Chapter 3 to help with this task. We are already using XML to specify schemas of legacy databases. These XML schemas facilitate migration. At a later time, we may have RDF schemas to facilitate migration. RDF may also handle semantic heterogeneity, however, the tools that may become obsolete are also covered. For example, we may have a tool that informs users about their appointments. Tomorrow we may have a tool that also gives advice to users about what actions to take. This means that we need to migrate from the existing tool to the new tool or to replace the existing tool with the new tools.

We can envisage objects to play a major role. That is, the Web is viewed as a collection of objects. We replace the objects as new objects become available, as illustrated in Figure 16.2. An incremental evolution to building the semantic Web is envisioned. That is, the semantic Web will never be complete.

Next, let us examine the architectural aspects for the semantic Web. In Chapter 3, federated architectures, three-tier client–server architectures for the Web, and architectures for electronic commerce (e-commerce) and collaborative commerce (c-commerce) are covered. Objects are a key part of the incremental evolution. Furthermore, business objects will become increasingly sophisticated as Web understanding develops. That is, the business objects will have the facility to read the Web pages, understand the Web pages, and give advice to the user, for example, through the client interface. The three-tier architecture discussed in Part I and duplicated in

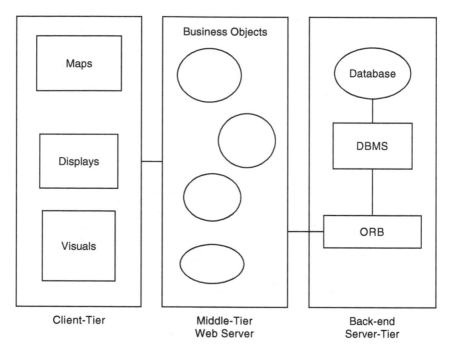

Client-Tier   Middle-Tier   Back-end
                               Web Server   Server-Tier

FIGURE 16.3 An architecture for the semantic Web.

Figure 16.3 will likely remain the same. It could be extended to N-tier architecture, although the capability of the business objects will vastly improve as we migrate from the Web to the semantic Web.

16.4 DATA AND INFORMATION MANAGEMENT ASPECTS

All the technologies for the Web data and information management discussed in Part I are critical for developing the semantic Web. All these technologies need to work well together to make the semantic Web a reality. One of the main concerns is what technologies constitute the Web and the semantic Web because no real cut-off point between the two exists. The semantic Web is really an intelligent Web that can understand the information and make decisions. This means that the data and information management technologies have to be effective and work as they were intended to make the semantic Web a reality.

As examples, agents are key to the semantic Web and researchers have examined the use of agents for the semantic Web. When agent technologies become mature and we can fully exploit their capabilities, then we can say that we now have a semantic Web. Various data management technologies are being used for the Web. When we can effectively mine the data on the Web and make sense out of the data, we can say with some confidence that we are migrating toward the semantic Web. When we can handle semantic heterogeneity, then we can migrate from the Web to the semantic Web. All the Web technologies discussed have to work effectively together; only then can we achieve the objectives of the semantic Web. Figure 16.4

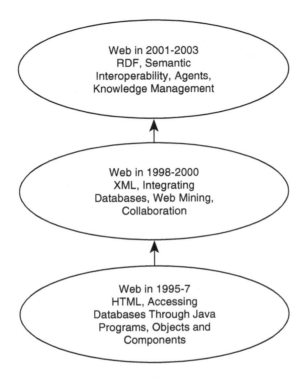

FIGURE 16.4 An architecture for the semantic Web.

illustrates how the technologies have evolved over the years to make the Web successful.

16.5 INTEROPERABILITY ISSUES, XML, AND RDF

The interoperability issues discussed in Chapter 10 are revisited, along with the roles of XML and RDF (resource description framework) as the Web continues to evolve. What do we mean by interoperability? We could have interoperability with respect to heterogeneous platforms such as databases, applications, and architectures. Object technology is key to interoperability. The three-tier architecture with business objects for supporting a variety of Web applications is one aspect of interoperability. Because the main interest in this text is about databases, database interoperability is the focus.

Chapter 3 (as well as in Appendix B) describes database interoperability. The challenge is not just syntactic interoperability, but also semantic interoperability.

Discussions on XML supporting interoperability in common representation of documents show how it is possible for different systems to interpret the document the same say. Common representation is key to interoperability, however, XML does not support semantics. Therefore, various aspects such as semantic heterogeneity cannot be handled by XML. One proposal is to use RDF to facilitate semantic heterogeneity, as illustrated in Figure 16.5. That is, RDF with the use of ontologies supports semantics. This way, one can handle syntactic as well as semantic heterogeneity.

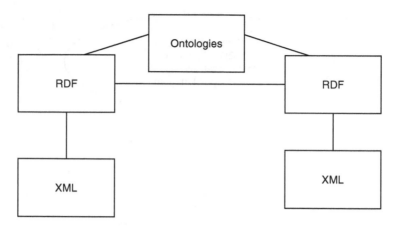

FIGURE 16.5 XML, RDF, and interoperablity.

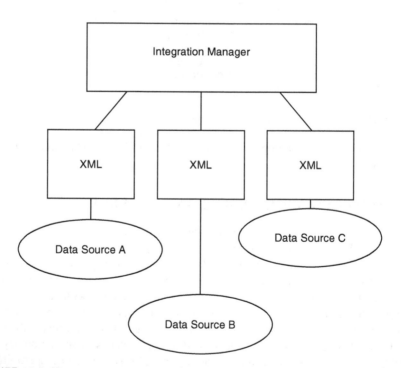

FIGURE 16.6 XML and integrating databases.

In the case of database interoperability, with both XML and RDF one can represent the schemas of various databases including legacy databases. This in turn supports interoperability as illustrated in Figure 16.6. That is, XML and RDF are essential technologies for interoperability. Whether XML, RDF, or some other technology will be used in the end is yet to be determined; however, the Web community

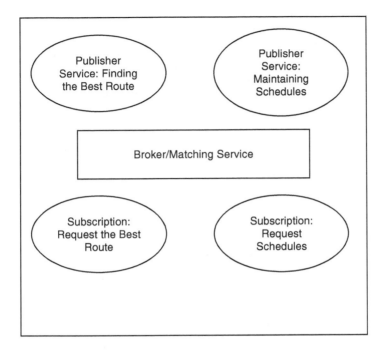

FIGURE 16.7 Example of Web services.

is moving in the right direction. What was thought to be almost impossible just 5 years ago is possible now. The community has more or less come to an agreement on common terminology and semantics. This was one of the major challenges faced by database researchers in the early 1990s.

16.6 WEB SERVICES

The discussion of Web Services Description Language (WDSL) in Chapter 15 is repeated here, followed by a brief discussion of Web services. Because some way to describe the communication on the Web in a structured and organized way is needed, WSDL does this by defining an XML grammar for describing network services. As described in [WDSL], the network services are described as a collection of communication end points capable of exchanging messages. For a review of WSDL document elements, see Chapter 15, Section 15.8.3.

What are Web services? These are services provided by the Web to its users. These could be publishing services, data management services, information management services, directory services, etc. Any service that the Web provides is a Web service and WSDL provides the means to specify the service. Web services is an area that will expand a great deal in the coming years. These services will form the essence of the semantic Web. Figure 16.7 shows the publisher and subscriber services that the Web provides. This is an example of a Web service and duplicates information provided in Chapter 10.

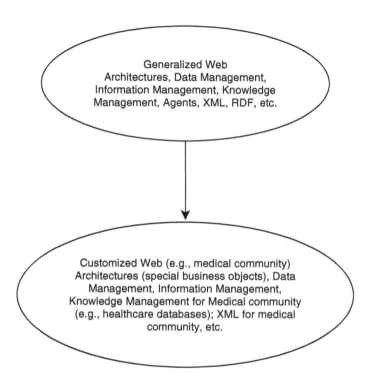

FIGURE 16.8 Building the semantic Web.

16.7 PUTTING IT TOGETHER

Now the challenge is how to build the Web, keeping in mind that the technologies will continue to evolve. Therefore, I propose an incremental evolution, ensuring that the new technologies are introduced without disrupting any existing Web access and support. That is, a seamless integration of the old and new technologies is needed. XML and RDF as well as data, information, and knowledge management technologies will be inserted as the Web evolves. The task is to develop technologies, to enhance the existing technologies, and also to insert them so that researchers can develop the semantic Web. Different communities, for example, medical and financial, have different needs. That is, the Web has to be customized. This means a single general-purpose Web cannot support all classes of users, but instead specialized Web is needed to build all the technologies and then to customize them to suit those needs.

Researchers are already on the right path. Recall that different domain groups are developing customized XML specifications. Some examples are the e-commerce group, the wireless group, and the multimedia group. The geographic information systems community is coming up with its own markup languages (e.g., Geographic Markup Language [GML]), whereas the medical community is coming up with its own XML specifications. That is, XML is getting customized. Other technologies can be expected to become customized also. Figure 16.8 illustrates some general trends toward building the Web. For example, we can expect to see a semantic Web for biotechnology application and another semantic Web for financial applications. They should both be built from the same foundations, but customized for different communities.

16.8 SUMMARY

This chapter reviews and provides directions for building the semantic Web. At no point will the semantic Web be complete. As new technologies are introduced, the Web will continue to be enhanced.

Then I discuss architectural and data and information management aspects for the Web. With respect to Web architectures, the current architectures may suffice; however, sophisticated business objects are needed. I also show how data and information management technologies have been integrated into the Web. The chapter also covers interoperability aspects, Web services, and suggestions as to how to put all of the concepts together to build the semantic Web.

Note that the discussions in this chapter are preliminary, just some suggestions and ideas. They are by no means concrete suggestions. The technologies are still not mature. The reader should keep up with all the information, especially following the developments with the World Wide Web Consortium (W3C) and examining www.w3c.org periodically. Only then can readers be current with the developments of the semantic Web.

Conclusion to Part III

This brings us to the end of Part III, which was all about XML and its applications to data and information management technologies. Chapter 12 described XML applications to e-commerce. Chapter 13 provided an overview of XML applications to databases, particularly modeling, metadata management, query processing, integration, migration, and many other aspects. Chapter 14 covered XML applications to information technologies such as multimedia, collaboration, and wireless computing. Chapter 15 examined XML-related tools for data and information management on the Web. Finally, Chapter 16 explored preliminary ideas on building the semantic Web.

Writing good XML documents is only one aspect of the problem. We need a good understanding of how applications can use and process XML documents. This part attempts to give a brief overview of the latter aspects. This means that business specialists have to work with technologists to effectively use XML. Progress in Web technologies will enhance the use of XML.

17 Summary and Directions

17.1 ABOUT THIS CHAPTER

This chapter brings us to a close of *XML Databases and the Semantic Web.* Various Web data and information management technologies with XML in mind, XML and semantic Web concepts, and finally an overview of the various applications of XML have been provided. This chapter summarizes the contents of this book and then provides an overview of the challenges and directions in XML, Web databases, and the semantic Web. I also give the reader some suggestions on where to go from here.

The organization of this chapter follows: Section 17.2 summarizes the contents of this book. The summaries from Chapters 2 to 16 are now put together to form an overall summary. Section 17.3 mentions the challenges and directions for XML, databases, and the semantic Web. Some of the challenges and directions for Web data management discussed in [THUR00] are reviewed because XML and Web databases go hand in hand. Then I add some new directions with respect to XML and the semantic Web. Finally, Section 17.4 gives suggestions to the reader as to where to go from here. Some of the key points in this book are reiterated, and then the reader is encouraged to take advantage of XML and the semantic Web.

17.2 SUMMARY OF THIS BOOK

Figure 17.1 duplicates Figure 1.5 to recap what I have described throughout this book. The three parts to this book include Part I, which described supporting technologies for XML in Chapters 2 to 7. Part II, consisting of Chapters 8 to 11, described XML; and Part III, consisting of Chapters 12 to 16, described XML applications. Each chapter is again summarized in this section.

Chapter 2 provided an overview of the World Wide Web (WWW), starting with a discussion of the evolution of the Web and then showing how corporations are taking advantage of the Web. Some supporting technologies for the Web including a discussion of Java, hypermedia, and Hypertext Markup Language (HTML) are examined. Finally, overviews of the World Wide Web Consortium (W3C) and the origins of XML are given. That is, the previous sections describe the evolution of the Web and some of the main ideas behind the Web. The remaining parts of this book describe XML, particularly the supporting technologies for XML such as data management and information retrieval, details of XML, and applications of XML to various areas including electronic business (e-business).

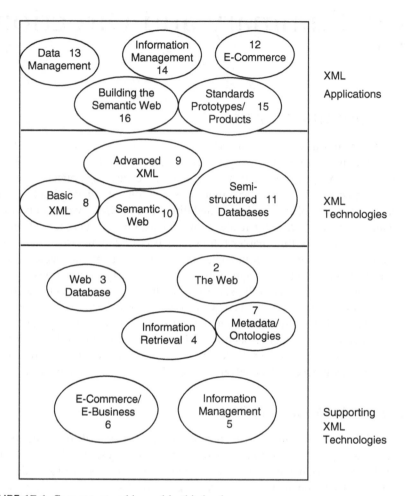

FIGURE 17.1 Components addressed in this book.

Chapter 3 provided a broad overview of the developments and challenges on Web database management and the relationship to XML. Beginning with an introduction to Java issues and a discussion of digital libraries, the chapter next discusses issues on accessing databases on the Web. In particular, an overview of Java Database Connectivity (JDBC) and an examination of data modeling for the Web are included, followed by a discussion of database functions. The next focus is on Web mining as well as privacy and security aspects. Finally, architectural aspects including architecture for database access, three-tier computing, interoperability, migration, client–server paradigm, push and pull computing, and the federated model are addressed. This chapter ends with a discussion of the relationship of XML to all the technologies considered including Web databases, data mining, security, and interoperability.

Chapter 4 described information retrieval systems and mining individual data types. Mining is introduced to show the importance of extracting entities from, for example, text through tagging. This requires the use of markup languages such as Standard Generalized Markup Language (SGML). Following a discussion of SGML, the chapter ends with an examination of the relationship of XML to information retrieval systems.

Chapter 5 provided an overview of a number of information management technologies, including collaboration, multimedia, knowledge management, decision support, training, agents, and visualization. The relationships of these technologies to XML also are briefly explored.

Chapter 6 gave a broad overview of e-commerce, starting with a discussion of the e-commerce process and explaining the differences between e-business and e-commerce. Models, architectures, and functions for e-commerce, the application of Java; and the communications for e-commerce are described. After an overview of information technologies for e-commerce, the chapter ends with a discussion of the relevant relationship to XML.

Chapter 7 was devoted to exploring Web metadata management and mining. An overview of the various types of metadata and a discussion of metadata management on the Web are included. Because mining metadata is critical for Web data management so that one can extract, for example, usage patterns, this topic is then covered. Metadata are the central component to many kinds of information systems such as decision support systems, database systems, and machine learning systems. The chapter concluded with a discussion of ontologies. A flavor for XML was given in Chapter 7.

Chapter 8 introduced some of the basic concepts of XML, starting with a definition of an example XML document with components such as prolog, root, and other information. Prolog has the declarations part of the document and the root has essentially the key elements and attributes of the document. The optional end part has comments and other information. Next containers, elements, and attributes, all the key components of an XML document, are examined. Namespaces to resolve conflicts are explored. That is, different groups have different notations and some way is needed to resolve conflicts. Finally, the chapter provides an overview of data typing in XML; for example, the XML domain-type definitions (DTDs) can be extended with data types so that there is more structure to XML documents.

Chapter 9 introduced some of advanced concepts in XML, including a discussion of semantic issues; a review of DTDs; and XML Link Language (Xlink) and related technologies such as XML Pointer Language (Xpointer) and XML Path Language (Xpath). These latter technologies enable documents to be linked. The chapter closes with discussions of XML schemas and their use, querying XML documents, data integration aspects, and internationalization.

Chapter 10 was devoted to a discussion of the semantic Web, providing an overview of the semantic Web and showing how it differs from the Web. Some technologies related to the semantic Web such as resource description framework (RDF) and ontologies are studied, followed by an overview of agents and the Defense Advanced Research Projects Agency (DARPA) Agents Markup Language (DAML) program. Some issues on treating the semantic Web as databases and how the various database concepts could be reused to address the semantic Web are examined. Finally, interoperability issues and also the differences between the Web and the semantic Web are described.

Chapter 11 started with a discussion of architectures for semistructured databases and data models, followed by a discussion of functions including query processing, editing, transaction management, metadata management, storage management, security, and integrity. Next, I discuss the relationship to XML and some of the development efforts under way.

Chapter 12 began with a discussion of the applications of XML for e-commerce, particularly document representation, data management, and interoperability aspects. Then an overview of the various efforts under way on XML and e-commerce is provided, including the efforts on E-business Extensible Markup Language (ebXML), Commerce One.Net, and RosettaNet.

Chapter 13 presented a high-level overview of the relationship between data management and XML. First, I discussed metadata issues, followed by a review of semistructured databases. Then I focus on some of the key functions of database systems including query management, transaction processing, storage management, and security management, followed by distribution, interoperability, migration, warehousing, and mining. Finally, I discussed some general topics such as architectures and object technology. In covering all these topics I had XML in mind, especially how XML could be applied to various aspects of data management.

Chapter 14 discussed XML application to a number of areas including multimedia, collaborative computing, decision support, wireless computing, agents, decision support, and knowledge management. Also briefly mentioned are some other areas such as training and instructional systems, natural language processing, and bioinformatics. Many of these technologies have developed markup languages based on XML, including Synchronized Multimedia Integration Language (SMIL), DAML, and Wireless Markup Language (WML). As we have seen, a lot of overlap exists, for example, ebXML standards are applicable not only for e-commerce but also for knowledge management decision support, and collaborative commerce. Perhaps as the technology matures we may be able to clearly separate the applications of XML, for example, to knowledge management and to c-commerce.

Chapter 15 provided a brief overview of the various XML related Web data and information management tools. In particular, tools for Web database management, Web mining, Web server management, and knowledge management tools as well as some of the recent breakthrough products and services as Web Services Description Language (WSDL) and Simple Object Access Protocol (SOAP) are discussed. A general discussion of the tools was given, followed by the description of an example tool. Some other classes of tools are also described. I have selected the tools only because of my knowledge about them and am not endorsing any of the products. A description of all the tools are beyond the scope of this book. Furthermore, due to the rapid developments in the field, the information about these products may soon be outdated. Therefore, I urge the reader to take advantage of the various commercial and research materials available on these products.

Finally, Chapter 16 provided some directions for building the semantic Web. This chapter, even though it repeats some of the information in previous chapters, provided directions for building the semantic Web. The chapter started by saying that there is no point where we can say that we have built the semantic Web. The Web will continue to evolve and will never be complete. As new technologies are introduced, the Web will continue to be enhanced. Architectural aspects as well as data and information management aspects for the Web are also covered. With respect to architectures, the current architectures may suffice, although sophisticated business objects are needed. The chapter also shows how data and information management technologies have been integrated into the Web, discusses interoperability aspects, and finally, gives some suggestions as to how to put all the concepts together to build the Web.

As stressed throughout, the concept of the semantic Web is rather vague. That is, one cannot say that what constitutes the Web and what constitutes the semantic Web. In fact, some argue that there should be no difference between the two. The semantic Web of today may not be the semantic Web of tomorrow. In any case, I distinguish between what a Web is today and what a semantic Web is today, and discuss some issues for building the semantic Web. Although Chapter 16 did not fit entirely within the theme of Part III, applications of XML, I revisited semantic Web issues after describing concepts, technologies, and applications of XML. That is, I chose to address issues on building the semantic Web until the end of this book.

17.3 CHALLENGES AND DIRECTIONS FOR XML, DATABASES, AND THE SEMANTIC WEB

17.3.1 OVERVIEW

This book focuses on XML, the semantic Web, Web data management, and electronic commerce (e-commerce). In particular, technologies, techniques tools, and trends are discussed. Although XML is the underlying theme, Web databases and e-commerce are mentioned as well. Therefore, in this section, I first review some of the directions discussed in [THUR00] and then provide an overview of the directions and challenges for XML and the semantic Web.

The organization of this section follows: Section 17.3.2 discusses Web data management directions; Section 17.3.2, e-commerce directions; and Section 17.3.3, XML directions.

17.3.2 CHALLENGES AND DIRECTIONS FOR WEB DATABASE MANAGEMENT

This section covers future directions in Web data management. In this area, one of the major challenges is scalability, or how to efficiently access large quantities of data on the Web. Other challenges include enhancing the traditional database technologies for the Web such as query strategies, transaction management, indexing, security, and integrity. We need novel architectures for the Web. The Object Management Group (OMG) ORB-based infrastructures are just one aspect. Component-based plug-and-play technologies as well as integration of ORB-based middleware with, for example, transaction monitors and message-oriented middleware, may be the directions.

Two aspects should be taken into consideration in the area of Web mining. The first is how to mine all the available data and extract useful information, and the second is mining to help the e-business. We need better mining tools to work with the Web. Mining for the e-business is one of the major directions in information technology. Security and privacy aspects for Web mining should also be given some consideration in the future.

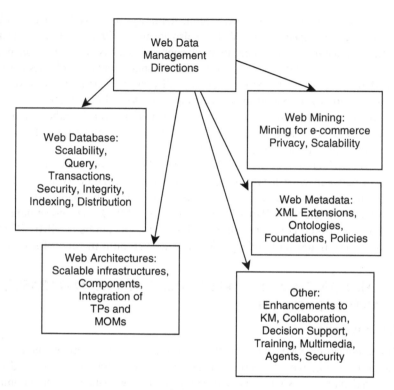

FIGURE 17.2 Web data management directions.

XML and ontology technologies will continue to explode. Numerous extensions to XML have been proposed, and although some type of XML-like language will endure, we could expect to see a radical change when various extensions are combined. The support or complex data structures in XML will be important. In addition to XML and ontologies, various other aspects of metadata management will be given prominence. The definition of metadata will continue to evolve. Further directions for XML are explored in Section 17.3.4.

Other directions in Web data management include better tools for knowledge management, collaboration, decision support, and training. Currently, these terms are rather vague. We can expect to see the emergence of standard definitions, tools for enterprise data management, and enterprise application integration. Finally, support for organizations to share and collaborate with each other as well as form partnerships will be critical.

Figure 17.2 illustrates some of the directions for Web data and information management. In addition to all these above areas, it is time to focus on the foundational aspects. Is there some sort of theory upon which Web-based systems can be built? For example, XML has origins in areas such as the lambda calculus, and theoreticians are continuing to pursue in this direction. Query processing and transaction management is built on various theories, in general. Do these theories apply for the Web also? Extensive research is needed in this area.

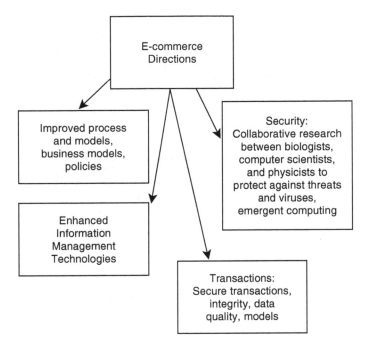

FIGURE 17.3 E-commerce directions.

17.3.3 CHALLENGES AND DIRECTIONS FOR E-COMMERCE

Each of the Web data management technologies discussed in this book and their future developments will have a significant impact on e-commerce. Some organizations will increasingly become involved in e-commerce. Other organizations will become involved in e-business. We can expect clearer definitions for e-commerce and e-business to emerge.

To provide better support for commerce we need developments in Web database management, Web mining, knowledge management, collaboration, metadata management, multimedia information management, and many of the other technologies discussed in this book. Now that we have entered the new millennium and much of our fear of the year 2000 problem is over, we can expect to see many developments in e-commerce security. Various research programs are under way in the United States and in Western Europe. We need more than information technology. Physicists, biologists, mathematicians, and computer scientists will have to work together to produce security solutions for the Web.

The e-commerce transaction area will continue to evolve. In addition to technological advances, we also need organizational advances. E-commerce is a new way of doing business. Therefore, many of the business schools have yet to address e-commerce. We can expect to see major programs mainly in business schools combined with information technology to teach e-commerce. Policies and procedures for credit card transactions have to be established. Then these procedures have to be implemented. Figure 17.3 illustrates directions for e-commerce.

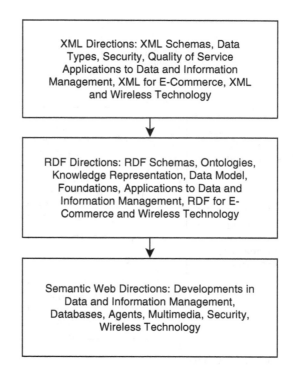

FIGURE 17.4 XML, RDF, and semantic Web directions.

17.3.4 CHALLENGES AND DIRECTIONS FOR XML AND THE SEMANTIC WEB

This section describes challenges and directions for XML and the semantic Web. With respect to XML, the work on standards will continue to evolve. In addition to XML schemas and data types, an increased interest in security, integrity, and quality of service will continue. We also need techniques for querying and storing XML documents. Much progress will be made on RDF. In addition to ontology research, work will continue also on knowledge representation, RDF schemas, and data model and foundations.

Both XML as well as RDF will continue to contribute to the semantic Web. No one technology is appropriate for the semantic Web. All technologies discussed in this text — including data, information, and knowledge management — will contribute to the semantic Web. In particular, database management, multimedia information management, security and agent technologies will be critical components. Figure 17.4 illustrates the directions for XML, RDF, and the semantic Web. Developments in XML will contribute to the developments in RDF. Furthermore, developments in RDF will contribute to developments of technologies for the semantic Web.

17.4 WHERE TO GO FROM HERE

This text provides a broad overview of XML and related technologies, and also gives many references should the reader need in-depth coverage of a particular topic. All the reading, however, is not going to give the reader a better appreciation for what XML and the semantic Web are all about. It is certainly useful to have a good knowledge in XML technologies and to be able to speak intelligently about them. If you want to know what the details are, however, you need hands-on experience with the tools. As in the case of many technologies, XML and Web data management get better with practice; the reader is urged to work with practical applications in using the tools and, if possible, with developing the tools. It is important for readers to be able to write good XML documents if they are to make effective use of XML. Again, this book provides directions and gives references where the reader can get more information on detailed syntax of XML, RDF, and related technologies such as Simple Object Access Protocol (SOAP) and Universal Description, Discovery, and Integration (UDDI).

Another point to note is that when you want to develop a Web application or an e-commerce project, especially with XML and related technologies, you need management buy-in. This is partly because many of the technologies discussed here are rather new. This means financial and personnel resources. Furthermore, you need to decide whether to contract the work or to have it done in-house. If you are using a commercial tool, then you need to have frequent communication with the developer. The customer, the e-commerce tool or solutions developer, the data mining tools or solutions developer, and those who conduct e-commerce and Web data management have to work very closely together for success of the project.

This book also gives some brief information about various XML-related data and information management tools. As stressed, I have selected these products only because of my familiarity with them and am not endorsing any of the products. Furthermore, due to the rapid developments in the field, the information about these products may soon be outdated. Therefore, I urge the reader to take advantage of the various commercial and research materials available on these products.

Many exciting opportunities are available in Web databases, XML, the semantic Web, and e-commerce. Furthermore, technology integration, such as integration of data management, data mining, objects, and security, is making a lot of progress. As the user gets flooded with increasing amounts of multimedia data and information, the need to analyze this information, to give only the information the user needs, and to extract previously unknown information to help the user in the decision-making process will become urgent. Also, various laws and policies will be clearer with e-commerce, with corporations and consumers soon becoming familiar with the process of e-commerce. We can also expect universities to offer special courses and specialization certificates on e-commerce, semantic Web, and related technologies. The vast interest in the United States, Europe, and the rest of the world and the amount of work being done in industry and in academia will promote the semantic Web a great deal. The opportunities and challenges in Web technologies, in general, and e-commerce, in particular, will be endless.

Some of the key points discussed in this book follow (as we make progress, we will understand the issues much better):

- The Web will be the integration platform for all types of multimedia data, information, and knowledge management technologies. XML will play a key role.

- The various multimedia data, information, and knowledge management technologies have to work with the Web. This will include database access through the Web and collaboration on the Web.
- We need infrastructures for the Web to support the various data, information, and knowledge management technologies.
- E-commerce and e-business will thrive only if we successfully establish the Web as the integration platform.
- We need research and development programs to enable the Web to be the integration platform. This means that whenever we conduct research on data, information, and knowledge management technologies, we cannot ignore the Web.
- Ontologies and adding semantics will continue to play a major role in the development of XML. Interest and research dealing with the semantic Web will increase, although many of the technologies under development have to work together to make the semantic Web a reality.

References

[ACM90] Special issue on federated databases, *ACM Comput. Surv.,* 1990.

[ACM91] Special issue on computer supported cooperative work, *Commun. ACM,* December 1991.

[ACM94] Proceedings of the ACM Multimedia Database System Workshop, October 1994.

[ACM95] Special issue on digital libraries, *Commun. ACM,* May 1995.

[ACM96] Special issue on electronic commerce, *Commun. ACM,* June 1996.

[ACM99] *Commun. ACM,* May 1999.

[ACM01] *ACM SOGMOD Rec.,* September 2001.

[AIPA95] Proceedings of the Symposium on Advanced Information Processing and Analysis, Tysons Corner, VA, March 1995.

[AIPA96] Proceedings of the Symposium on Advanced Information Processing and Analysis, Tysons Corner, VA, March 1996.

[ALLE01] Allen, D., private communication, Bedford, MA, 2001.

[BEA] www.beasys.com/products/weblogic/

[BERT00] Bertino, E. et al., XML Security, Proceedings of the IFIP Database Security Conference, Amsterdam, The Netherlands, August 2000.

[BERT01] Bertino, E. et al., Distributed Updates for XML Documents, University of Milan, Milan, Italy, report, July 2001.

[BERT02] Bertino, E. et al., *XML Security,* Addison-Wesley, London, 2002.

[BINN94] Binns, L. et al., Secure Hypersemantic Data Model, Proc. of the International Federation for Information Processing (IFIP) Database Security Conference, Hildesheim, Germany, August 1994.

[BUSH45] Bush, V., As We May Think, *The Atlantic Monthly,* July 1945.

[CACM99] Communications of Association for Computing Machinery, October 1999.

[CHES94] Cheswick, W. and Bellovin, S., *Firewalls and Internet Security: Repelling the Wily Hacker,* Addison-Wesley, Reading, MA, 1994.

[CHOR94] Chorafas, D., *Intelligent Multimedia Databases,* Prentice Hall, Englewood Cliffs, NJ, 1994.

[CLIF96] Clifton, C., Text Mining, private communication, Bedford, MA, January 1996.

[CLIF97] Clifton C., Privacy Issues for Data Mining, private communication, Bedford, MA, April 1998.

[CLIF98] Clifton, C., Image Mining, private communication, Bedford, MA, July 1998.

[CLIF99a] Clifton C., Data Mining and Security, Proceedings of the IFIP Conference on Database Security, Seattle, July 1999.

[CLIF99b] Clifton, C., Data Mining for Intrusion Detection, IFIP 1999 Database Security Conference Panel, Seattle, July 1999.

[CODD70] Codd, E. F., A relational model of data for large shared data banks, *Commun. ACM,* 1970.

[COMM1] www.commerceone.net

[COOL98] Cooley, R., Taxonomy for Web Mining, private communication, Bedford, MA, August 1998.

[CORR99] Corradi, A., Montanari, R., and Stefanelli, C., Security Issues in Mobile Agent Technology, Proceedings of IEEE FTDCS, Cape Town, Republic of South Africa, December 1999.

[DAMI00] Damiani, S. et al., Component Based Approach to XML Security, Proceedings of the IFIP Database Security Conference, Amsterdam, The Netherlands, August 2000.

[DAML] www.daml.org/

[DATE90] Date, C.J., *An Introduction to Database Management Systems,* Addison-Wesley, Reading, MA, 1990 (6th ed. published in 1995 by Addison-Wesley).

[DAVE97] Davenport, T., *Working Knowledge: How Organizations Manage What They Know,* Harvard Business School Press, Cambridge, MA, 1997.

[DECI00] *Decision Support Journal,* Elsevier/North Holland, Amsterdam, October 2000.

[DEUT99] Deutch, A. et al., XMLQL: A Query Language for XML, w3c1.inria.fr/TR/1998/NOTE-xml-ql-19980819/.

[DIGI95] Adam, N. et al., Eds., Proceedings of the Advances in Digital Libraries Conference, McLean, VA, May 1995.

[DIPI99] DiPippo, L., Hodys, E., and Thuraisingham, B., Towards a Real-Time Agent Architecture: A White Paper, Proceedings of IEEE WORDS, Monterey, CA, 1999.

[DOIL] xml.coverpages.org/ni2001-03-28-a.html

[DOTNET] www.halcyonsoft.com/news/javadotnet.asp

[EBXML] xml.coverpages.org/ebXML.html

[ERCIM] Vassilis, C., Scholl, M., and Vercoustre, A.-M., Querying Heterogeneous Semi-structured Databases, www.ercim.org/publication/Ercim_News/enw33/scholl.html.

[FELD95] Feldman, R. and Dagan, I., Knowledge Discovery in Textual Databases (KDT), Proceedings of the 1995 Knowledge Discovery in Databases Conference, Montreal, Canada, August 1995.

[FIKE96] Fikes, R., Ontologies: what are they, and where's the research?, *Knowledge Rep. J.,* Sept. 1996.

[FIRE] Chapman, B., Building Internet Firewalls Tutorial, www.greatcircle.com/tutorials/bif.html

[FOWL97] Fowler, M. et al., *UML Distilled: Applying the Standard Object Modeling Language,* Addison-Wesley, Reading, MA, 1997.

[FROS86] Frost, R., *On Knowledge Base Management Systems,* Collins Publishers, United Kingdom, 1986.

[GHOS98] Ghosh, A., *E-Commerce Security, Weak Links and Strong Defenses,* John Wiley & Sons, New York, 1998.

[GRIN95] Grinstein, G. and Thuraisingham, B., Data Mining and Visualization: A Position Paper, Proceedings of the Workshop on Databases in Visualization, Atlanta, GA, October 1995.

[GUO00] Yike, G., Kensington Data Mining System, Technical Report, Imperial College, University of London, January 2000.

[GUPT01] Gupta, A. et al., Collaborative Commerce and Knowledge Management, MIT report, Cambridge, MA, June 2001.

[HARV96] Harvard Business School Articles on Knowledge Management, Harvard Business School, Cambridge, MA, 1996.

[HTML] www.cwru.edu/help/introHTML/toc.html

[ICDE] Proceedings of the IEEE Data Engineering Conference, series, Los Alamitos, CA, 1998–2001.

[ICTA97] Panel on Web Mining, International Conference on Tools for Artificial Intelligence, Newport Beach, CA, November 1997.

[IEEE95] IEEE Multimedia Database Systems Workshop, Blue Mountain Lake, NY, August 1995.

[IEEE98] *IEEE Data Eng. Bull.,* March 1998.

[IEEE99] Special issue on collaborative computing, *IEEE Comput.,* September 1999.

[IEEE00] Special issue on e-business, *IEEE Comput.*, October 2000.

[IFIP97] Proceedings of the IFIP Database Security Conference, Lake Tahoe, CA, 1997.

[IMIE92] Imielinski, T. et al. Distributed Databases for Mobile Computing, Proceedings of the Very Large Database Conference, Vancouver, BC, Canada, August 1992.

[INFO01] *Informationworld,* December 2001.

[JAVA] Java Programming Language, www.javasoft.com/

[JDBC] Java Database Connectivity, java.sun.com/products/jdbc/index.html

[JONE99] Jones, S., Collaborative computing workspace, *Linux J.,* September, 1999.

[J2EE] java.sun.com/j2ee/tutorial/doc/Overview.html

[JUNG98] Prasad, K., and Rajaraman, R., Junglee Corporation, Virtual database technology, XML, and the evolution of the Web, *IEEE Data Eng. Bull.,* June 1998.

[KDD] Proceedings of the Knowledge Discovery in Databases Conference series, New York, 1998–2001.

[KDD98] Panel Presentation, Knowledge Discovery in Database Conference, New York, August 1998.

[KDDN] www.kdnuggets.com/

[LAUR00] St. Laurent, S., *XML: A Primer,* Power Books Publishing, 2000.

[LEE99] Lee, T.B., *Weaving the Web,* HarperCollins, San Francisco, CA, 1999.

[LEE01] Lee, T.B., et al., The semantic Web, Sci. Am., May 2001.

[MDDS94] Proceedings of the Massive Digital Data Systems Initiative Workshop, CMS Report, Washington, D.C., February 1994.

[MERL97] Merlino, A. et al., Broadcast News Navigation Using Story Segments, Proceedings of the 1997 ACM Multimedia Conference, Seattle, WA, November 1998.

[META96] Proceedings of the First IEEE Metadata Conference, Silver Spring, MD, April 1996 (originally published on the Web, Musick, R., Ed., Lawrence Livermore National Laboratory).

[MICR] www.microsoft.com/COMMERCE/km/

[MORE98a] Morey, D., Web Mining, private communication, Bedford, MA, June 1998.

[MORE98b] Morey, D., Knowledge Management Architecture, *Handbook of Data Management,* Thuraisingham, B., Ed., Auerbach Publications, New York, 1998.

[MORE01] Morey, D., Maybury, M., and Thuraisingham, B., Eds., *Knowledge Management,* MIT Press, Cambridge, MA, January 2001.

[NETG] www.netgen.com/

[NSF95] Proceedings of the Database Systems Workshop, Report published by the National Science Foundation, 1995 (also in *ACM SIGMOD Rec.,* March 1996).

[ODBC] Open Database Connectivity, www.microsoft.com/data/odbc/default.htm

[ODI] www.odi.com/excelon/main.htm

[OMG] www.omg.org

[OMG95] *Common Object Request Broker Architecture and Specification,* OMG Publications, John Wiley & Sons, New York, 1995.

[ONTO] www-db.stanford.edu/LIC/HPKBtalk/sld002.htm

[ORAC1] www.oracle.com/database/oracle8i/

[ORAC2] www.oracle.com/tools/webdb/

[ROSE99] Rosenthal, A., XML Presentation, Bedford, MA, February 1999.

[ROSET] xml.coverpages.org/rosettaNet.html

[RDF] www.w3.org/TR/REC-rdf-syntax/

[SGML] www.uic.edu/orgs/tei/sgml/teip3sg/ and www.uic.edu/orgs/tei/sgml/teip3sg/

[SIGM] Proceedings of the ACM SIGMOD Conference Series, New York, 1998–2001.

[SMIL1] hotwired.lycos.com/webmonkey/00/41/index4a.html

[SMIL2] www.w3.org/TR/REC smil/

238   XML Databases and the Semantic Web

[SMIL3] www.w3.org/AudioVideo/Activity
[SOAP] www.w3.org/TR/2001/WD-soap12-20010709/
[THUR90] Thuraisingham, B., Multilevel Security for Multimedia Database Systems, Proceedings of the IFIP Database Security Conference, Halifax, United Kingdom, September 1990.
[THUR93] Thuraisingham, B., Object Technology for Medical Applications, *MITRE Information Systems Journal,* October 1999.
[THUR96a] Thuraisingham, B., *Internet Database Management,* Database Management, Auerbach Publications, New York, 1996.
[THUR96b] Thuraisingham, B., Data Mining and Visualization, Proceedings of the Compugraphics Conference, Paris, December 1996.
[THUR97] Thuraisingham, B., *Data Management Systems Evolution and Interoperation,* CRC Press, Boca Raton, FL, 1997.
[THUR98] Thuraisingham, B., *Data Mining: Technologies, Techniques, Tools, and Trends,* CRC Press, Boca Raton, FL, 1998.
[THUR00] Thuraisingham, B., *Web Data Management and Electronic Commerce,* CRC Press, Boca Raton, FL, 2000.
[THUR01] Thuraisingham, B., *Managing and Mining Multimedia Databases for the Electronic Enterprise,* CRC Press, Boca Raton, FL, 2001.
[TRUE88] Trueblood, W. and Potter, R., Hypersemantic data model, *Data and Knowledge Eng. J.,* April 1985.
[TSUR98] Tsur, D. et al., Query Flocks: A Generalization of Association Rule Mining, Proceedings of the 1998 ACM SIGMOD Conference, Seattle, WA, June 1998.
[TURB97] Turban, E. and Aronson, J., Decision Support Systems and Intelligent Systems, Prentice Hall, Englewood Cliffs, NJ, 1997.
[UDDI] www.uddi.org/whitepapers.html
[VIS95] Grinstein, G., Ed., Proceedings of the IEEE Workshop on Visualization and Databases, Atlanta, GA, October 1995.
[VLDB] Proceedings of the Very Large Database Conference Series, San Francisco, 1998–2001.
[XCC] www.itpapers.com/cgi/PSummaryIT.pl? paperid=5085&scid=177
[XKM] www.dmreview.com/master.cfm?
NavID = 198&EdID = 1454
[XML1] www.W3c.org
[XML2] www.xml.org/
[XMLQL] www.w3.org/TR/NOTE-xml-ql/
[XMLSQL] www.xml.com/pub/a/2001/06/20/databases.html
[WDM99]
[WIDO98] Widom, J., Lore DBMS, Stanford Database Workshop, Palo Alto, CA, September 1998.
[WML] www.oasis-open.org/cover/wap-wml.html
[LEE01] Lee T.B. et al., The semantic Web, *Sci. Am.,* May 2001.
[WOEL86] Woelk, D. et al., An Object-Oriented Approach to Multimedia Databases, Proceedings of the ACM SIGMOD Conference, Washington, D.C., June 1986.
[WORK1] Semantic Web Workshop, Stanford University, Palo Alto, CA, July 2001.
[WORK2] NSG-EU Semantic Web Workshop, Sophia Antipolis, France, October 2001.
[WSDL] www.w3.org/TR/wsdl
[WWW] Proceedings of the World Wide Web Conference Series, Cambridge, MA, 1998–2001.

Appendix A
Data Management Systems: Developments and Trends

A.1 OVERVIEW

In this appendix, I provide an overview of the developments and trends in data management as discussed in my previous book *Data Management Systems Evolution and Interoperation* [THUR97]. Because data play a major role in Web data management, a good understanding of data management is essential for Web data management.

Recent developments in information systems technologies have resulted in computerizing many applications in various business areas. Data have become critical resources in many organizations; therefore, efficient access to data, sharing the data, extracting information from the data, and making use of the information have become urgent needs. As a result, several efforts have been made to integrate the various data sources scattered across several sites. These data sources may be databases managed by database management systems or they may simply be files. To provide the interoperability between the multiple data sources and systems, various tools are under development. These tools enable users of one system to access other systems in an efficient and transparent manner.

I define data management systems to be systems that manage the data, extract meaningful information from the data, and make use of the information extracted. Therefore, data management systems include database systems, data warehouses, and data mining systems. Data could be structured (such as those found in relational databases) or unstructured (such as text, voice, imagery, and video). Numerous discussions have taken place in the past to distinguish between data, information, and knowledge.* I do not attempt to clarify these terms. For the purposes of this text, data could be just bits and bytes or could convey some meaningful information to the user. I will, however, distinguish between database systems and database management systems. A database management system is the component that manages the database containing persistent data. A database system consists of both the database and the database management system.

A key component to the evolution and interoperation of data management systems is the interoperability of heterogeneous database systems. Efforts on the interoperability between database systems have been reported since the late 1970s.

---

* More recently, the area of knowledge management is receiving a lot of attention. I address knowledge management in Chapter 5. More details are given in [MORE98].

Only recently, however, have commercial developments in heterogeneous database systems emerged. Major database system vendors are now providing interoperability between their products and other systems. Furthermore, many of the database system vendors are migrating toward an architecture called the client–server architecture that facilitates distributed data management capabilities. In addition to efforts on the interoperability between different database systems and client–server environments, work is also directed toward handling autonomous and federated environments.

The organization of this appendix follows. Because database systems are key components of data management systems, I first provide an overview of the developments in database systems. These developments are discussed in Section A.2. Then I provide a vision for data management systems in Section A.3. My framework for data management systems including data mining, warehousing, and Web data management components is discussed in Section A.4. Building information systems from my framework with special instantiations is discussed in Section A.5. The relationship between the various texts that I have written (or am writing) for CRC Press is discussed in Section A.6. This appendix is summarized in Section A.7, with references given in Section A.8.

A.2 DEVELOPMENTS IN DATABASE SYSTEMS

Figure A.1 provides an overview of the developments in database systems technology. Although the early work in the 1960s focused on developing products based on the network and hierarchical data models, much of the developments in database systems took place after the seminal paper by Codd describing the relational model [CODD70] (see also [DATE90]). Research and development work on relational database systems was conducted during the early 1970s and several prototypes were developed throughout the 1970s. Notable efforts include International Business Machine Corporation (IBM) System R and the University of California at Berkeley Ingres. During the 1980s, many relational database system products were being marketed (notable among these products are those of Oracle Corporation, Sybase Inc., Informix Corporation, Ingres Corporation, IBM Corporation, Digital Equipment Corporation, and Hewlett Packard Company). During the 1990s, products from other vendors have emerged (e.g., Microsoft Corporation). In fact, to date numerous relational database system products have been marketed; however, Codd has stated that many of the systems that are marketed as relational systems are not really relational (see, e.g., the discussion in [DATE90]). He then discussed various criteria that a system must satisfy to be qualified as a relational database system. Although the early work focused on issues such as data model, normalization theory, query processing and optimization strategies, query languages, and access strategies and indexes, later the focus shifted toward supporting a multiuser environment, particularly concurrency control and recovery techniques were developed. Support for transaction processing was also provided.

Research on relational database systems as well as on transaction management was followed by research on distributed database systems around the mid-1970s. Several distributed database system prototype development efforts also began around

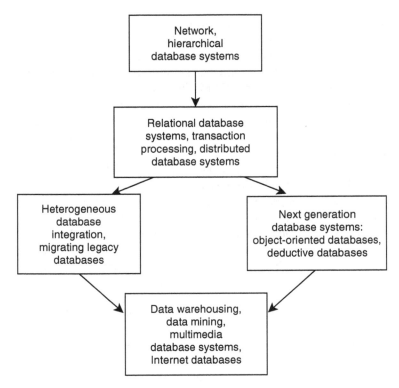

FIGURE A.1 Developments in database systems technology.

the late 1970s. Notable among these efforts include System R☆ by IBM, Distributed Database Testbed System (DDTS) by Honeywell Inc., SDD-I and Multibase by Computer Corporation of America (CCA), and Mermaid by System Development Corporation (SDC). Furthermore, many of these systems (e.g., DDTS, Multibase, Mermaid) function in a heterogeneous environment. During the early 1990s, several database system vendors (such as Oracle Corporation, Sybase Inc., Informix Corporation) provided data distribution capabilities for their systems. Most of the distributed relational database system products are based on client–server architectures. The idea is to have the client of vendor A communicate with the server database system of vendor B. In other words, the client–server computing paradigm facilitates a heterogeneous computing environment.

Interoperability between relational and nonrelational commercial database system is also possible. The database systems community is also involved in standardization efforts. Notable among the standardization efforts are the American Standards Institute (ANSI) and Systems Planning and Requirement Committee (SPARC) three-level schema architecture, the Information Resource Dictionary System (IRDS) standard for Data Dictionary Systems, the relational Structured Query Language (SQL), and the Remote Database Access (RDA) protocol for remote database access.

Another significant development in database technology is the advent of object-oriented database management systems. Active work on developing such systems began in the mid-1980s and they are now commercially available (notable among them include the products of Object Design Inc., Ontos Inc., Gemstone Systems Inc., and Versant Object Technology). It was believed that new generation applications such as multimedia, office information systems, computer-aided design (CAD), and computer-aided manufacturing (CAM), process control, and software engineering have different requirements. Such applications utilize complex data structures. Tighter integration between the programming language and the data model is also desired. Object-oriented database systems satisfy most of the requirements of these new generation applications [CATT91].

According to the Lagunita report published as a result of a National Science Foundation (NSF) workshop in 1990 (see [NSF90] and [SIGM90]), relational database systems, transaction processing, and distributed (relational) database systems are stated as mature technologies. Furthermore, vendors are marketing object-oriented database systems and demonstrating the interoperability between different database systems. The report goes on to state that as applications are getting increasingly complex, more sophisticated database systems are needed. Furthermore, because many organizations now use database systems, in many cases of different types, the database systems need to be integrated. Although work has begun to address these issues and commercial products are available, several issues still need to be resolved. Therefore, challenges faced by the database systems researchers in the early 1990s were in two areas. One was next-generation database systems and the other was heterogeneous database systems.

Next-generation database systems include those that are object-oriented and functional; that have special parallel architectures to enhance the performance of database system functions; that are high-performance, real-time, scientific, and temporal; that handle incomplete and uncertain information; and that are intelligent (also sometimes called logic or deductive database systems).* Ideally, a database system should provide the support for high-performance transaction processing and model complex applications, represent new kinds of data, and make intelligent deductions. Although significant progress has been made during the late 1980s and early 1990s, there is much to be done before such a database system can be developed.

Heterogeneous database systems have been receiving considerable attention during the past decade [ACM90]. The major issues include handling different data models, query processing strategies, transaction processing algorithms, and query languages. Should a uniform view be provided to the entire system or should the users of the individual systems maintain their own views of the entire system? These questions that have yet to be answered satisfactorily. Also envisaged is that a complete solution to heterogeneous database management systems is a generation away. Although research should be directed toward finding such a solution, work should also be carried out to handle limited forms of heterogeneity to satisfy the customer needs. Another type of database system that has received some attention lately is a federated database system. Some have used the terms *heterogeneous database system*

---

* For a discussion of the next-generation database systems, refer to [SIGM90].

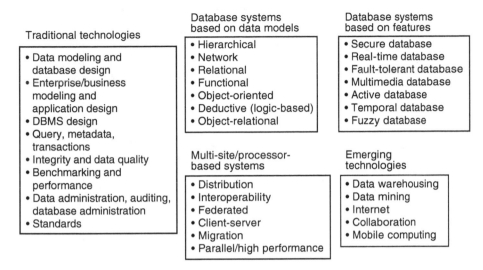

FIGURE A.2 Comprehensive view of data management systems.

and *federated database system* interchangeably. Although heterogeneous database systems can be part of a federation, a federation can also include homogeneous database systems.

The explosion of users on the Internet and the Web as well as developments in interface technologies has resulted in even more challenges for data management researchers. A second workshop was sponsored by NSF in 1995, and several emerging technologies have been identified to be important as we go into the twenty-first century [NSF95]. These include digital libraries, managing very large databases, data administration issues, multimedia databases, data warehousing, data mining, data management for collaborative computing environments, and security and privacy. Other significant developments from the 1990s are object-relational systems. Such systems combine the advantages of both object-oriented and relational database systems. Also, many corporations are now focusing on integrating their data management products with Internet technologies. Many organizations have an increasing need to migrate some of the legacy databases and applications to newer architectures and systems such as client–server architectures and relational database systems. There is no end to data management systems. As new technologies are developed, new opportunities will emerge for data management research and development.

A comprehensive view of all data management technologies is illustrated in Figure A.2. As shown, traditional technologies include database design, transaction processing, and benchmarking. Database systems based on, for example, relational and object-oriented models are also available. Database systems may depend on features they provide such as security and real time. Also in existence are database systems based on multiple sites or processors such as distributed and heterogeneous, parallel, and migrated systems. Finally, technologies such as data warehousing and mining, collaboration, and the Internet are emerging. Any comprehensive text on

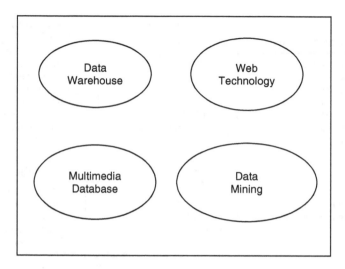

FIGURE A.3 Stand-alone systems.

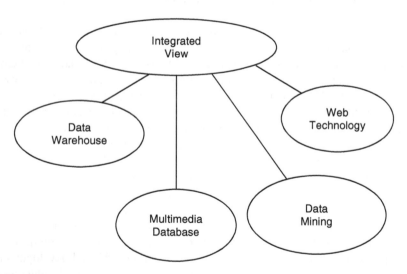

FIGURE A.4 Vision.

data management systems should address all these technologies. I have selected some of the relevant technologies and put them in a framework. This framework is described in Section A.5.*

---

* In my previous book, *Data Management Systems Evolution and Interoperation,* I selected certain topics in data management and explained the various concepts.

A.3 STATUS, VISION, AND ISSUES

Significant progress has been made on data management systems, although many of the technologies are still stand-alone technologies, as illustrated in Figure A.3. For example, multimedia systems are yet to be successfully integrated with warehousing and mining technologies. The ultimate goal is to integrate multiple technologies so that accurate data, as well as information, are produced at the right time and distributed to the user in a timely manner. My vision for data and information management is illustrated in Figure A.4.

The work discussed in [THUR97] addressed many of the challenges necessary to accomplish this vision, particularly integration of heterogeneous databases, as well as the use of distributed object technology for interoperability, was discussed. Although much progress has been made on the system aspects of interoperability, semantic issues still are challenges. Different databases have different representations. Furthermore, the same data entity may be interpreted differently at different sites. Addressing these semantic differences and extracting useful information from the heterogeneous and possibly multimedia data sources are major challenges. This book attempts to address some of the challenges through the use of data mining.

A.4 DATA MANAGEMENT SYSTEMS FRAMEWORK

For the successful development of evolvable interoperable data management systems, heterogeneous database system integration is a major component; however, other technologies have to be successfully integrated with each other to develop techniques for efficient access and sharing of data as well as for extraction of information from the data. To facilitate the development of data management systems to meet the requirements of various applications in fields such as medical, financial, manufacturing, and military, I have proposed a framework, which can be regarded as a reference model, for data management systems. Various components from this framework have to be integrated to develop data management systems to support the assorted applications.

Figure A.5 illustrates this framework, which can be regarded as a model, for data management systems.* This framework consists of three layers. One can think of the component technologies, which I also refer to as components, belonging to a particular layer to be more or less built on the technologies provided by the lower layer. Layer 1 is the database technology and distribution layer. This layer consists of database systems and distributed database systems technologies. Layer 2 is the interoperability and migration layer, consisting of technologies such as heterogeneous database integration, client–server databases, and multimedia database systems to handle heterogeneous data types; and migrating legacy databases.** Layer

---

* Note that this three-layer model is subjective and is not a standard. This model has helped me in organizing my views on data management.
** I have placed multimedia database systems in layer 2, because I consider them to be a special type of heterogeneous database system. A multimedia database system handles heterogeneous data types such as text, audio, and video.

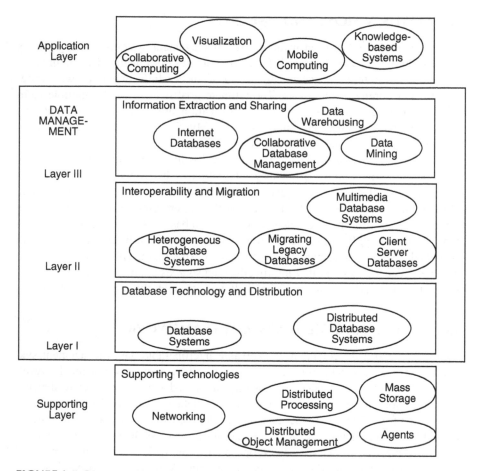

FIGURE A.5 Data management systems framework.

3 is the information extraction and sharing layer, mainly consisting of technologies for some of the newer services supported by data management systems. These include data warehousing, data mining [THUR98], Internet databases, and database support for collaborative applications.*,** Data management systems may utilize lower level technologies such as networking, distributed processing, and mass storage. I have grouped these technologies into a layer called the supporting technologies layer. This supporting layer does not belong to the data management system frame-

---

* Note that I could also argue whether database support for collaborative applications should be discussed here. This is because collaborative computing is not part of the data management framework, although such applications do need database support, and the focus has been on this support.

** Although Internet database management is an integration of various technologies, I have placed it in layer 3 because it still deals with information extraction. The data management framework consists of technologies for managing data as well as for extracting information from the data; however, what one does with the information, such as collaborative computing, sophisticated human computer interaction, natural language processing, and knowledge-based processing, does not belong to this framework. These types of information belong to the application technologies layer.

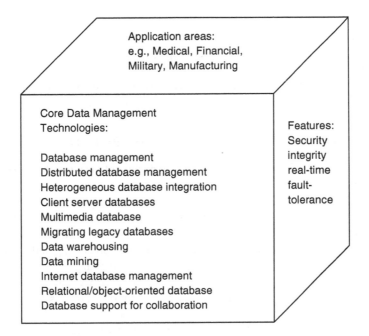

FIGURE A.6 A three-dimensional view of data management.

work. This supporting layer also consists of some higher level technologies such as distributed object management and agents.* Also shown in Figure A.5 is the application technologies layer, including collaborative computing systems and knowledge-based systems that belong to the application technologies layer and may utilize data management systems. The application technologies layer is also outside of the data management systems framework.

The technologies that constitute the data management systems framework can be regarded to be some of the core technologies in data management; however, features such as security, integrity, real-time processing, fault tolerance, and high-performance computing are needed for many applications utilizing data management technologies. Applications utilizing data management technologies may be medical, financial, or military, among others. I illustrate this in Figure A.6, where a three-dimensional view relating data management technologies with features and applications is given. For example, one could develop a secure distributed database management system for medical applications or a fault tolerant multimedia database management system for financial applications. **

Integrating the components belonging to the various layers is important to developing efficient data management systems. In addition, data management technologies have to be integrated with the application technologies to develop successful

---

* Note that technologies such as distributed object management enable interoperation and migration.
** In some cases, one could also consider multimedia data processing and reengineering, which is an essential part of system migration, to be at the same level as features like security and integrity. One could also regard them to be emerging technologies.

information systems. However, at present, there is limited integration between these various components. My previous book, *Data Management Systems Evolution and Interoperation,* focused mainly on the concepts, developments, and trends belonging to each of the components shown in the framework. Furthermore, my current book on Web data management, which I also refer to as Internet data management, focuses on the Internet database component of layer 3 of the framework in Figure A.5.

A.5 BUILDING INFORMATION SYSTEMS FROM THE FRAMEWORK

Figure A.5 illustrates a framework for data management systems. As shown in that figure, the technologies for data management include database systems, distributed database systems, heterogeneous database systems, migrating legacy databases, multimedia database systems, data warehousing, data mining, Internet databases, and database support for collaboration. Furthermore, data management systems take advantage of supporting technologies such as distributed processing and agents. Similarly, application technologies such as collaborative computing, visualization, expert systems, and mobile computing take advantage of data management systems.*

Many of us have heard the term *information systems* on numerous occasions. These systems terminology have sometimes been used interchangeably with data management systems. In the terminology of this text, information systems are much broader than data management systems, but they do include data management systems. In fact, a framework for information systems includes not only the data management system layers but also both the supporting and application technologies layers. That is, information systems encompass all kinds of computing systems. They can be regarded as the finished product that can be used for various applications. Whereas hardware is at the lowest end of the spectrum, applications are at the highest end.

A combination of the technologies of Figure A.5 can put together information systems. For example, at the application technology level, one may need collaboration and visualization technologies so that analysts can collaboratively carry out some tasks. At the data management level, one may need both multimedia and distributed database technologies. At the supporting level, one may need mass storage as well as some distributed processing capability. This special framework is illustrated in Figure A.7. Another example is a special framework for interoperability. One may need some visualization technology to display the integrated information from the heterogeneous databases. At the data management level is heterogeneous database system technology. At the supporting technology level, one may use distributed object management technology to encapsulate the heterogeneous databases. This special framework is illustrated in Figure A.8.

Finally, I illustrate the concepts described earlier by using a specific example. Suppose a group of physicians or surgeons want a system where they can collaborate and make decisions about various patients. This could be a medical video teleconferencing application, at the highest level. At the application technology level, one needs a variety of technologies including collaboration and teleconferencing. These applications will make use of data management technologies such as distributed and

---

* Note that databases could also support expert systems as in the case of collaborative applications.

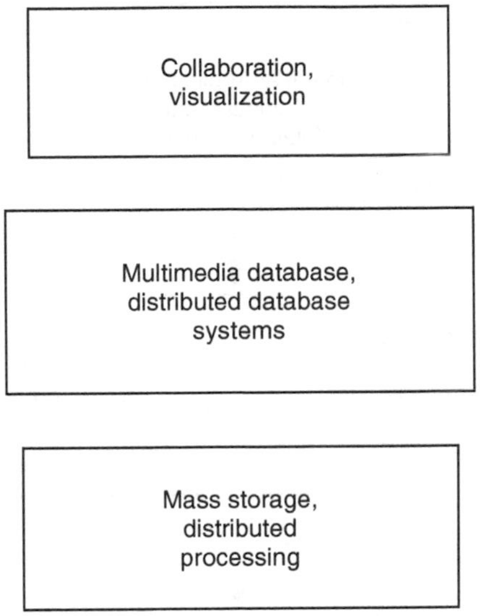

FIGURE A.7 Framework for multimedia data management for collaboration.

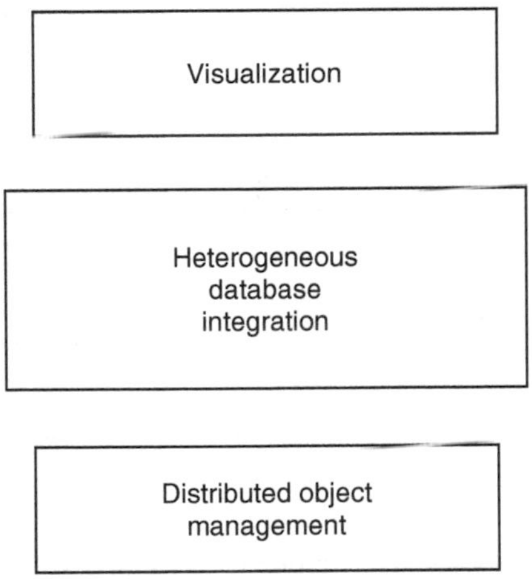

FIGURE A.8 Framework for heterogeneous database interoperability.

multimedia database systems. That is, support for multimedia data, such as audio and video, may be needed. The data management technologies in turn draw on lower level technologies such as distributed processing and networking. Figure A.9 illustrates this.

In summary, information systems include data management systems as well as application layer systems such as collaborative computing systems and supporting layer systems such as distributed object management systems.

Although application technologies make use of data management technologies and data management technologies make use of supporting technologies, the ultimate

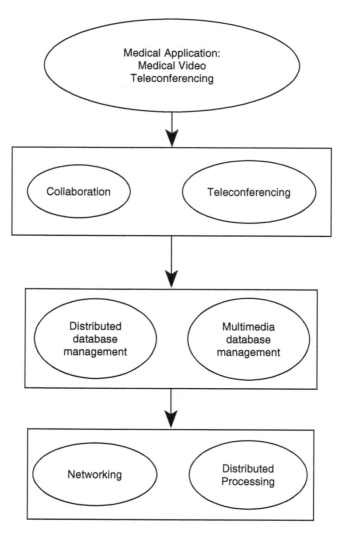

FIGURE A.9 Specific example.

user of the information system is the application itself. Today, numerous applications make use of information systems. These applications are from multiple domains such as medical, financial, manufacturing, telecommunications, and defense. Specific applications include signal processing, electronic commerce, patient monitoring, and situation assessment. Figure A.10 illustrates the relationship between the application and the information system.

A.6 RELATIONSHIP BETWEEN THE TEXTS

I have published four books on data management and mining in addition to this text (*XML, Databases, and the Semantic Web*). These books are *Data Management Systems Evolution and Interoperation* [THUR97], *Data Mining Technologies, Techniques,*

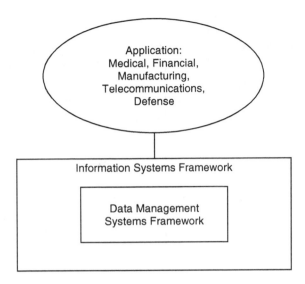

FIGURE A.10 Application-framework relationship.

Tools, and Trends [THUR98], *Web Data Management and Electronic Commerce* [THUR00], and *Managing and Mining Multimedia Databases for the Electronic Enterprise* [THUR01]. All these publications have evolved from the framework illustrated in this appendix and address different parts of the framework. The connection between these texts is illustrated in Figure A.11.

A.7 SUMMARY

In this appendix, I provide an overview of data management, first discussing the developments in data management and then providing a vision for data management. Then I illustrate a framework for data management. This framework consists of three layers: database systems, interoperability, and information extraction. Web data management belongs to layer 3. Finally, I show how information systems can be built from the technologies of the framework.

The chapters in this book not only discuss XML and Web databases, they also show how the technologies can be applied to the various applications such as electronic commerce (e-commerce). Many of the technologies shown in the framework of Figure A.5 have been useful in the discussion of Web databases and XML. These include database systems, distributed database systems, data warehousing, and data mining. In addition, some other features for data management such as metadata and security also play a role in various chapters of this book. For example, metadata for the Web is the subject of Chapter 7. Security and privacy issues are discussed both with respect to the Web and to multimedia data management and mining in Chapter 3.

Data management is essential to many information technologies including data mining, multimedia information processing, interoperability, and collaboration and knowledge management. This appendix stresses data management. The next appendix

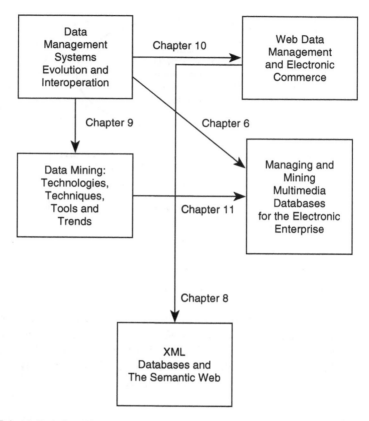

FIGURE A.11 Relationship between texts.

focuses on various other key technologies for XML including database systems, data mining, object technology, and security.

A.8 REFERENCES

[ACM90] Special issue on heterogeneous database systems, *ACM Comput. Surv.,* September 1990.

[CATT91] Cattell, R., *Object Data Management Systems,* Addison-Wesley, Reading MA, 1991.

[CODD70] Codd, E.F., A relational model of data for large shared data banks, *Commun. ACM,* 13, (6), June 1970.

[DATE90] Date, C.J., *An Introduction to Database Management Systems,* Addison-Wesley, Reading, MA, 1990 (6th ed. published in 1995 by Addison-Wesley).

[MORE98] Morey, D., Knowledge Management Architecture, *Handbook of Data Management,* Thuraisingham, B., Ed., Auerbach Publications, New York, 1998.

[NSF90] Proceedings of the Database Systems Workshop, Report published by the National Science Foundation, 1990 (also in *ACM SIGMOD Rec.,* December 1990).

[NSF95] Proceedings of the Database Systems Workshop, Report published by the National Science Foundation, 1995 (also in *ACM SIGMOD Rec.,* March 1996).

[SIGM90] Next generation database systems, *ACM SIGMOD Rec.,* December 1990.

[THUR97] Thuraisingham, B., *Data Management Systems Evolution and Interoperation,* CRC Press, Boca Raton, FL, 1997.

[THUR98] Thuraisingham, B., *Data Mining: Technologies, Techniques, Tools, and Trends,* CRC Press, Boca Raton, FL, 1998.

[THUR00] Thuraisingham, B., *Web Data Management and Electronic Commerce,* CRC Press, Boca Raton, FL, 2000.

[THUR01] Thuraisingham, B., *Managing and Mining Multimedia Databases for the Electronic Enterprise,* CRC Press, Boca Raton, FL, 2001.

Appendix B
Database Systems and
Related Technologies

B.1 OVERVIEW

Database systems play a key role in Web data management. Having good data is key to effective Web data management, and, therefore, considerable attention is given to database systems in this book. It should be noted that this text takes quite a data-oriented perspective to the Web.

Database system technology has advanced a great deal during the past four decades from the legacy systems based on network and hierarchical models to relational and object-oriented database systems based on client–server architectures. This appendix provides an overview of the important developments in database systems relevant to the contents of this book. Much of the discussion in the this book builds on the information presented in this appendix.

As stated in Appendix A, I consider a database system to include both the database management system (DBMS) and the database (see also the discussion in [DATE90]). The DBMS component of the database system manages the database. The database contains persistent data. That is, the data are permanent even if the application programs go away.

The organization of this appendix follows: Section B.2 covers relational data models, as well as entity-relationship (ER) models. Section B.3 describes various types of architectures for database systems, including centralized database system, schema, and functional architectures. Database design issues are discussed in Section B.4; database administration issues, in Section B.5; and database management system functions, in Section B.6. These functions include query processing, transaction management, metadata management, storage management, maintainance of integrity and security, and fault tolerance. Although the previous sections discuss database functions for a centralized database system, the remaining sections address distribution, interoperability, and migration. For example, distributed database systems is the subject of Section B.7; heterogeneous database integration aspects, of Section B.8; managing federated databases, of Section B.9; client–server database management, of Section B.10; and migrating legacy databases, of Section B.11. Data warehousing is discussed in Section B.12 whereas data mining will be the subject of Section B.13. A brief overview of object technology is given in Section B.14, with the appendix summary in Section B.15.

EMP

SS#	Ename	Salary	D#
1	John	20K	10
2	Paul	30K	20
3	Mary	40K	20

DEPT

D#	Dname	Mgr
10	Math	Smith
20	Physics	Jones

FIGURE B.1 Relational database.

B.2 RELATIONAL AND ENTITY-RELATIONSHIP DATA MODELS

B.2.1 OVERVIEW

It is widely accepted among the data modeling community that the purpose of a data model is to capture the universe that it is representing as accurately, completely, and naturally as possible [TSIC82]. Various data models have been proposed and I have provided an overview in my previous book [THUR97]. In this section, I discuss the essential points of the relational data model because it is the most widely used today. In addition, I also examine the ER data model because some of the ideas have been used in object models and, furthermore, ER models are in use extensively for database design. Many other models exist such as logic-based, hypersemantic, and functional models. Discussion of all these models is beyond the scope of this book, but I provide an overview of an object model in Section B.14 because object technology is essential for the Web and some of the ideas in XML have been influenced by object models.

B.2.2 RELATIONAL DATA MODEL

With the relational model [CODD70], the database is viewed as a collection of relations. Each relation has attributes and rows. For example, Figure B.1 illustrates a database with two relations EMP and DEPT. EMP has four attributes: SS#, Ename, Salary, and D#. DEPT has three attributes: D#, Dname, and Mgr. EMP has three rows, also called tuples, and DEPT has two rows. Each row is uniquely identified by its primary key. For example, SS# could be the primary key for EMP and D#, for DEPT. Another key feature of the relational model is that each element in the relation is an atomic value such as an integer or a string. That is, complex values such as lists are not supported.

Various operations are performed on relations. The Select operation selects a subset of rows satisfying certain conditions. For example, in the relation EMP, one may select tuples where the salary is more than 20K. The Project operation projects the relation onto some attributes. For example, in the relation EMP one may project onto the attributes Ename and Salary. The Join operation joins two relations over

FIGURE B.2 Entity-relationship representation.

some common attributes. A detailed discussion of these operations is given in [DATE90] and [ULLM88].

Various languages to manipulate the relations have been proposed. Notable among these languages is the American National Standards Institute (ANSI) Standard Structured Query Language (SQL). This language is used to access and manipulate data in relational databases [SQL3]. This standard is widely accepted among database management system vendors and users. It supports schema definition, retrieval, data manipulation, schema manipulation, transaction management, integrity, and security. Other languages include the relational calculus first proposed in the Ingres project at the University of California at Berkeley [DATE90]. Another important concept in relational databases is the notion of a view. A view is a virtual relation formed from the relations in the database. For further details, refer to [DATE90].

B.2.3 ENTITY-RELATIONSHIP DATA MODEL

One of the major drawbacks of the relational data model is its lack of support for capturing the semantics of an application. This resulted in the development of semantic data models. The ER data model developed by Chen [CHEN76] can be regarded as the earliest semantic data model. In this model, the world is viewed as a collection of entities and relationships between entities. Figure B.2 illustrates two entities, EMP and DEPT. The relationship between them is WORKS.

Relationships can be either one–one, many–one, or many–many. If it is assumed that each employee works in one department and each department has one employee, then WORKS is a one–one relationship. If it is assumed that an employee works in one department and each department can have many employees, then WORKS is a many–one relationship. If it is assumed that an employee works in many departments, and each department has many employees, then WORKS is a many–many relationship.

Several extensions to the ER model have been proposed. One is the ER-attribute model where attributes are associated with entities as well as relationships, and another has introduced the notion of categories into the model (see, e.g., the discussions in [ELMA85] and [YANG88]). ER models are used mainly to design databases, that is, most database computer-aided software engineering (CASE) tools are based on the ER model, where the application is represented using such a model and subsequently the database (possibly relational) is generated. Current database management systems are not based on the ER model. Unlike the relational model, ER models did not gain wide acceptance in the development of database management systems.

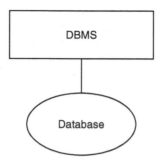

FIGURE B.3 Centralized architecture.

B.3 ARCHITECTURAL ISSUES

This section describes various types of architectures for a database system. First, I illustrate a very high level centralized architecture for a database system. Then I describe a functional architecture for a database system, particularly the functions of the DBMS component of the database system are illustrated in this architecture. Then I discuss the ANSI and Systems Planning and Requirements Committee (SPARC) three-schema architecture, which has been more or less accepted by the database community [DATE90]. Finally, I mention extensible architectures.

Figure B.3 is an example of a centralized architecture, in which the DBMS is a monolithic entity and manages a centralized database. Functional architecture illustrates the functional modules of a DBMS. The major modules of a DBMS include the query processor, transaction processor, metadata manager, storage manager, integrity manager, and security manager. The functional architecture of the DBMS component of the centralized database system architecture (of Figure B.3) is illustrated in Figure B.4.

Schema describes the data in the database. It has also been referred to as the data dictionary or contents of the metadatabase. Three-schema architecture, proposed for a centralized database system in the 1960s, is illustrated in Figure B.5. The levels are the external schema, which provides an external view; the conceptual schema, which provides a conceptual view; and the internal schema, which provides an internal view. Mappings between the different schemas must be provided to transform one representation into another. For example, at the external level, one could use ER representation. At the logical or conceptual level, one could use relational representation. At the physical level, one could use a representation based on B-trees.*

Another aspect to architectures is that of the extensible database. For example, for many applications, a DBMS may have to be extended with a layer to support objects, to process rules, to handle multimedia data types, or even to mine. Such an extensible architecture is illustrated in Figure B.6.

---

* Note that a B-tree is a representation scheme used to physically represent the data. However, it is at a higher level than the bits and bytes level. For a discussion on physical structures and models, refer to [DATE90].

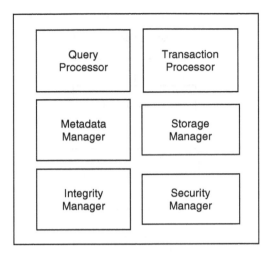

FIGURE B.4 Functional architecture for a DBMS.

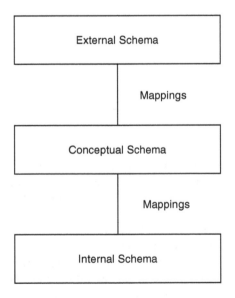

FIGURE B.5 Three-schema architecture.

B.4 DATABASE DESIGN

Designing a database is a complex process. Much of the work has been on designing relational databases. The three steps are illustrated in Figure B.7. The first step is to capture the entities of the application and the relationships between the entities. One could use a model such as the ER model for this purpose. Object-oriented data models, which are part of object-oriented design and analysis methodologies, are becoming popular to represent the application.

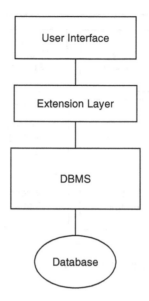

FIGURE B.6 Extensible DBMS.

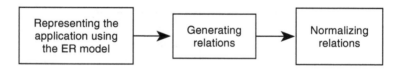

FIGURE B.7 Database design process.

The second step is to generate the relations from the representations. For example, from the ER diagram of Figure B.2, one could generate the relations EMP, DEPT, and WORKS. The relation WORKS will capture the relationship between employees and departments.

The third step is to design good relations. This is the normalization process. Various normal forms have been defined in the literature (see, e.g., [MAIE83] and [DATE90]). For many applications, relations in third normal form would suffice. With this normal form, redundancies, complex values, and other situations that could cause potential anomalies are eliminated.

B.5 DATABASE ADMINISTRATION

A database has a database administrator (DBA). It is the responsibility of the DBA to define the various schemas and mappings. In addition, the functions of the administrator include auditing the database as well as implementing appropriate backup and recovery procedures.

The DBA could also be responsible for maintaining the security of the system. In some cases, the system security officer (SSO) maintains security. The administrator

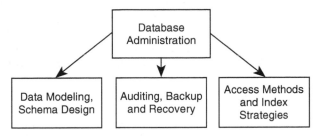

FIGURE B.8 Some database administration issues.

should determine the granularity of the data for auditing. For example, in some cases there is tuple (or row) level auditing whereas, in other cases, there is table (or relation) level auditing. It is also the administrator's responsibility to analyze the audit data.

A difference exists between database administration and data administration functions. Database administration assumes there is an installed database system, with the DBA managing this system. Data administration functions include conducting data analysis, determining how a corporation handles its data, and enforcing appropriate policies and procedures for managing the data of a corporation. Data administration functions are conducted by the data administrator. For a discussion of data administration, refer to [DMH94], [DMH95], [DMH96], [DMH98], [DOD94], and [DOD95]. Figure B.8 illustrates various database administration issues.

B.6 DATABASE MANAGEMENT SYSTEM FUNCTIONS

B.6.1 OVERVIEW

The functional architecture of a DBMS is illustrated in Figure B.4. The functions of a DBMS carry out its operations. A DBMS essentially manages a database, and it provides support to users by enabling them to query and update the database. Therefore, the basic functions of a DBMS are query processing and update processing. In some applications such as banking, queries and updates are issued as part of transactions. Therefore, transaction management is also another function of a DBMS. To execute these functions, information about the database, or metadata, have to be maintained. The function that is associated with managing the metadata is metadata management. Special techniques are needed to manage the data stores that actually house the data. The function that is associated with managing these techniques is storage management. To ensure that the preceding functions are conducted properly and that the user gets accurate data, some additional functions exist, including security management, integrity management, and fault management (i.e., fault tolerance).

The preceding functions are some of those essential for a DBMS. More recently, however, the emphasis is on extracting information from the data. Therefore, other functions of a DBMS may include providing support for data mining, data warehousing, and collaboration.

This section focuses only on the essential functions of a DBMS, query process-ing, transaction management, metadata management, storage management, main-taining integrity, security control, and fault tolerance. Note that I do not have a special section for update processing, because it can be handled as part of transaction management. Each of the essential functions are discussed in Sections B.6.2 to B.6.7.

B.6.2 QUERY PROCESSING

Query operation is the most commonly used function in a DBMS. It should be possible for users to query the database and obtain answers to their queries. The first of several aspects to query processing is the need of a good query language. Languages such as SQL are popular for relational databases. Such languages are extending to other types of databases. The second aspect is techniques for query processing. Numerous algorithms have been proposed for query processing in gen-eral and for the join operation, in particular (see also [KIM85]). Also, different strategies are possible to execute a particular query. The costs for the various strategies are computed, and the one with the least cost is usually selected for processing. This process is called query optimization. Cost is generally determined by the disk access. The goal is to minimize disk access in processing a query.

As stated earlier, users pose a query using a language. The constructs of the language have to be transformed into the constructs understood by the database system. This process is called query transformation, which is carried out in stages based on various schemas. For example, a query based on the external schema is transformed into a query on the conceptual schema. This is then transformed into a query on the physical schema. In general, rules used in the transformation process include the factoring of common subexpressions and pushing selections and projec-tions down in the query tree as much as possible. If selections and projections are performed before the joins, then the cost of the joins can be reduced by a considerable amount.

Figure B.9 illustrates the modules in query processing. The user interface man-ager accepts queries, parses the queries, and then gives them to the query transformer. The query transformer and query optimizer communicate with each other to produce an execution strategy. The database is accessed through the storage manager. The response manager gives responses to the user.

B.6.3 TRANSACTION MANAGEMENT

A transaction is a program unit that must be executed in its entirety or not executed at all. If transactions are executed serially, then a performance bottleneck occurs. Therefore, transactions are executed concurrently. Appropriate techniques must ensure that the database is consistent when multiple transactions update the database. That is, transactions must satisfy the atomicity, consistency, isolation, and durability (ACID) properties. Major aspects of transaction management are serializability, concurrency control, and recovery. They are discussed briefly in this section, but for a detailed discussion of transaction management, refer to [DATE90] and [ULLM88]. A good theoretical treatment of this topic is given in [BERN87].

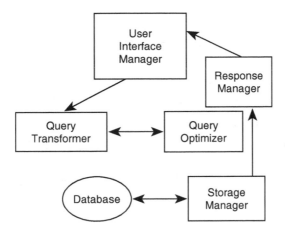

FIGURE B.9 Query processor.

Serializability — A schedule is a sequence of operations performed by multiple transactions. Two schedules are equivalent if their outcomes are the same. A serial schedule is a schedule where no two transactions execute concurrently. An objective in transaction management is to ensure that any schedule is equivalent to a serial schedule. Such a schedule is called a serializable schedule. Various conditions for testing the serializability of a schedule have been formulated for a DBMS.

Concurrency control — Concurrency control techniques ensure that the database is in a consistent state when multiple transactions update the database. Three popular concurrency control techniques that ensure the serializability of schedules are locking, time-stamping, and validation.

Recovery — If a transaction aborts due to some failure, then the database must be brought to a consistent state. This is transaction recovery. One solution to handling transaction failure is to maintain log files. The transaction actions are recorded in the log file. Thus, if a transaction aborts, then the database is brought back to a consistent state by undoing the actions of the transaction. The information for the undo operation is found in the log file. Another solution is to record the actions of a transaction but not make any changes to the database. Only if a transaction commits should the database be updated. Some issues remain; for example, the log files have to be kept in stable storage. Various modifications to the preceding techniques have been proposed to handle the different situations. When transactions are executed at multiple data sources, then a protocol called *two-phase commit* is used to ensure that the multiple data sources are consistent. Figure B.10 illustrates the various aspects of transaction management.

B.6.4 STORAGE MANAGEMENT

The storage manager is responsible for accessing the database. To improve the efficiency of query and update algorithms, appropriate access methods and index strategies have to be enforced. That is, in generating strategies for executing query and update requests, the access methods and index strategies that are used need to

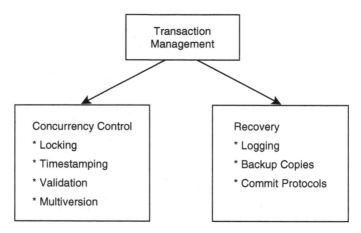

FIGURE B.10 Some aspects of transaction management.

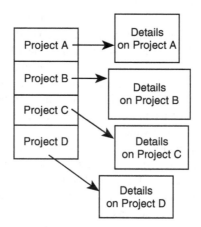

FIGURE B.11 An sample index on projects.

be taken into consideration. The access methods used to access the database would depend on the indexing methods. Therefore, creating and maintaining an appropriate index file are major issues in database management systems. By using an appropriate indexing mechanism, the query processing algorithms may not have to search the entire database. Instead, the data to be retrieved could be accessed directly. Consequently, the retrieval algorithms are more efficient. Figure B.11 illustrates a sample of an indexing strategy where the database is indexed by projects.

Much research has been conducted on developing appropriate access methods and index strategies for relational database systems. Some examples of index strategies are B-trees and hashing [DATE90]. Current research is focusing on developing such mechanisms for object-oriented database systems with support for multimedia data.

Relation REL

Relation	Attribute
EMP	SS#
EMP	Ename
EMP	Salary
EMP	D#
DEPT	D#
DEPT	Dname
DEPT	Mgr

FIGURE B.12 Metadata relation.

B.6.5 METADATA MANAGEMENT

Metadata describe the data in the database. For example, in the case of the relational database illustrated in Figure B.1, metadata would include the following information: the database has two relations, EMP and DEPT; EMP has four attributes; and DEPT has three attributes, etc. One of the main issues is developing a data model for metadata. In this example, one could use a relational model to model the metadata also. The metadata relation REL shown in Figure B.12 consists of information about relations and attributes.

In addition to information about the data in the database, metadata also include information on access methods, index strategies, security constraints, and integrity constraints. One could also include policies and procedures as part of the metadata. In other words, there is no standard definition for metadata, although efforts are under way to standardize metadata [META96]. Metadata becomes a major issue with some of the recent developments in data management such as digital libraries. Some of the issues are discussed in Part II of this book.

Once the metadata are defined, the issues include managing the metadata. What are the techniques for querying and updating the metadata? Because all the other DBMS components need to access the metadata for processing, what are the interfaces between the metadata manager and the other components? Metadata management is fairly well understood for relational database systems. The current challenge is in managing the metadata for more complex systems such as digital libraries and Internet database systems.

B.6.6 DATABASE INTEGRITY

Concurrency control and recovery techniques maintain the integrity of the database. In addition, another type of database integrity is enforcing integrity constraints. The two types of integrity constraints enforced in database systems are application-independent integrity constraints and application-specific integrity constraints. Integrity

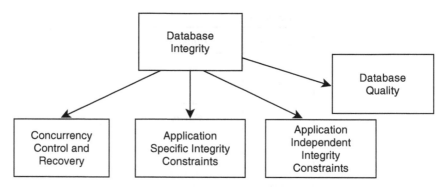

FIGURE B.13 Some aspects of database integrity.

mechanisms also include techniques for determining the quality of the data. For example, what is the accuracy of the data and of the source? What are the mechanisms for maintaining the quality of the data? How accurate is the data on output? [AFSB83] only discussed the enforcement of application-independent and application-specific integrity constraints, with the focus was on the relational data model. For a discussion of integrity based on data quality, refer to [MIT]. Note that data quality is very important for mining and warehousing. If the data that is mined is not good, then one cannot rely on the results.

Application-independent integrity constraints include the primary key constraint, entity integrity rule, referential integrity constraint, and various functional dependencies involved in the normalization process (see the discussion in [DATE90]).

Application-specific integrity constraints are those constraints that are specific to an application. Examples include "an employee's salary cannot decrease" and "no manager can manage more than two departments." Various techniques have been proposed to enforce application-specific integrity constraints. For example, when the database is updated, these constraints are checked and the data are validated. Aspects of database integrity are illustrated in Figure B.13.

B.6.7 DATABASE SECURITY

In this section, the focus is on discretionary security because this is the area of interest with respect to warehousing and mining.* The major issues in security are authentication, identification, and enforcement of appropriate access controls. For example, what are the mechanisms for identifying and authenticating the user? Will simple password mechanisms suffice? With respect to access control rules, languages such as SQL have incorporated grant and revoke statements to grant and revoke access to users. For many applications simple grant and revoke statements are not sufficient. More complex authorizations may be based on database content. Negative authorizations may also be needed. Access to data based on the roles of the user is also under investigation.

---

* Note that multilevel security issues for database systems are addressed in [AFSB83].

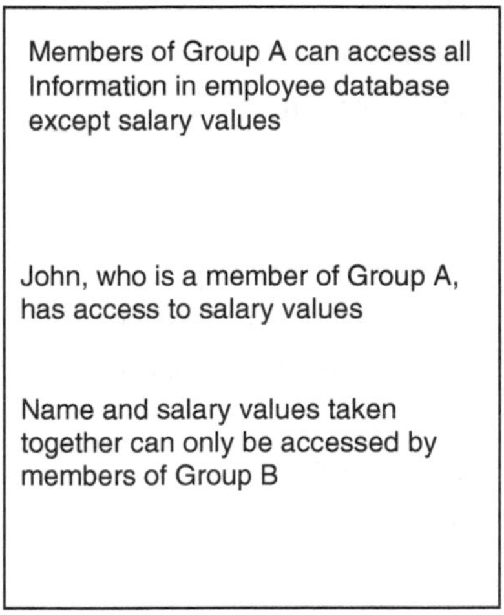

Members of Group A can access all
Information in employee database
except salary values

John, who is a member of Group A,
has access to salary values

Name and salary values taken
together can only be accessed by
members of Group B

FIGURE B.14 Access control rules.

Numerous articles have been published on discretionary security in databases. These can be found in various security-related journals and conference proceedings (see, e.g., [IFIP]). Some aspects of database security are illustrated in Figure B.14.

B.6.8 FAULT TOLERANCE

The previous two sections discuss database integrity and security. A closely related feature is fault tolerance. It is almost impossible to guarantee that the database will function as planned. In reality, various faults could occur. These could be hardware faults or software faults. Recall that one of the major issues in transaction management is to ensure that the database is brought back to a consistent state in the presence of faults. The solutions proposed include maintaining appropriate log files to record the actions of a transaction in case its actions have to be retraced.

Another approach to handling faults is checkpointing. Various checkpoints are placed during the course of database processing. At each checkpoint, the consistent state of the database is ensured. Therefore, if a fault occurs during processing, then the database must be brought back to the last checkpoint. This way it can be guaranteed that the database is consistent. Closely associated with checkpointing are acceptance tests. After various processing steps, the acceptance tests are checked. If the techniques pass the tests, then they can proceed further. Some aspects of fault tolerance are illustrated in Figure B.15.

B.7 DISTRIBUTED DATABASES

Although many definitions of a distributed database system have been given, no standard definition exists. The discussion of distributed database system concepts and issues has been influenced by [CERI84]. A distributed database system includes a distributed database management system (DDBMS), a distributed database, and a

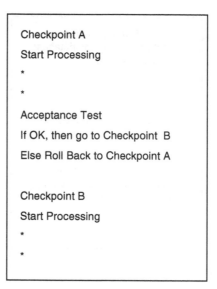

```
Checkpoint A
Start Processing
*

*

Acceptance Test
If OK, then go to Checkpoint  B
Else Roll Back to Checkpoint A

Checkpoint B
Start Processing
*

*
```

FIGURE B.15 Some aspects of fault tolerance.

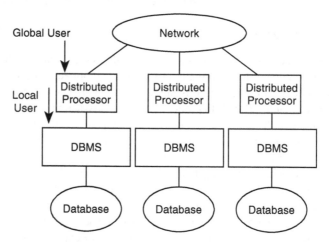

FIGURE B.16 An architecture for a DDBMS.

network for interconnection. The DDBMS manages the distributed database. A distributed database includes data that are distributed across multiple databases. My choice architecture for a distributed database system is a multidatabase architecture, which is tightly coupled. This architecture is illustrated in Figure B.16. I have chosen such an architecture, because I can explain the concepts for both homogeneous and heterogeneous systems based on this approach. In this architecture, the nodes are connected via a communication subsystem and local applications are handled by the local DBMS. In addition, each node is also involved in at least one global application, so there is no centralized control in this architecture. The DBMSs are

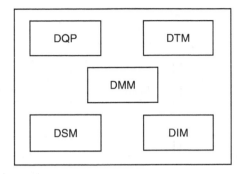

FIGURE B.17 Modules of DP.

connected through a component called the distributed processor (DP). In a homogeneous environment, the local DBMSs are homogeneous whereas in a heterogeneous environment, the local DBMSs may be heterogeneous.

Distributed database system functions include distributed query processing, distributed transaction management, distributed metadata management, and security and integrity enforcement across the multiple nodes [BELL92]. The DP is a critical component of the DDBMS. This module connects the different local DBMSs. That is, each local DBMS is augmented by a DP. The modules of the DP are illustrated in Figure B.17. The components are the distributed metadata manager (DMM), the distributed query processor (DQP), the distributed transaction manager (DTM), the distributed security manager (DSP), and the distributed integrity manager (DIM). DMM manages the global metadata, which include information on the schemas that describe the relations in the distributed database, the way the relations are fragmented, the locations of the fragments, and the constraints enforced. DQP is responsible for distributed query processing; DTM, for distributed transaction management; DSM, for enforcing global security constraints; and DIM, for maintaining integrity at the global level. The modules of DP communicate with their peers at the remote nodes. For example, the DQP at node 1 communicates with the DQP at node 2 for handling distributed queries.

B.8 HETEROGENEOUS DATABASE INTEGRATION

Figure B.18 illustrates an example of interoperability between heterogeneous database systems. The goal is to provide transparent access, both for users and application programs, for querying and executing transactions (see, e.g., [IEEE91], [ACM90], and [WIED92]). Note that in a heterogeneous environment, the local DBMSs may be heterogeneous. Furthermore, the modules of the DP have both local DBMS-specific processing as well as local DBMS-independent processing. Such a DP is called a heterogeneous distributed processor (HDP). Some of these issues are discussed in more detail in [THUR97].

Several technical issues need to be resolved for the successful interoperation between these diverse database systems. Heterogeneity could exist with respect to different data models, schemas, query processing techniques, query languages,

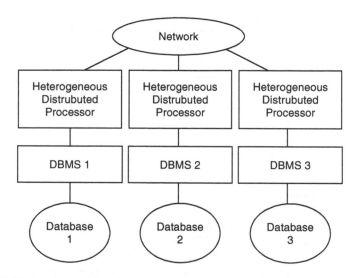

FIGURE B.18 Interoperability of heterogeneous database systems.

transaction management techniques, semantics, integrity, and security. Of the two approaches to interoperability, one is the federated database management approach where a collection of cooperating, autonomous, and possibly heterogeneous component database systems, each belonging to one or more federations, communicates with one another. The other is the client–server approach where the goal is for multiple clients to communicate with multiple servers in a transparent manner.

B.9 FEDERATED DATABASES

As stated by Sheth and Larson [SHET90], a federated database system is a collection of cooperating but autonomous database systems belonging to a federation. The goal is for the database management systems that belong to a federation to cooperate with one another and yet maintain some degree of autonomy. To be consistent with the terminology, distinguish between a federated database management system and a federated database system. A federated database system includes a federated database management system, the local DBMSs, and the databases. The federated database management system is that component that manages the different databases in a federated environment.

Figure B.19 illustrates federated database management; and B.20, the architecture for a federated database system. In the former, database systems A and B belong to federation F1 whereas database systems B and C belong to federation F2. I can use the architecture illustrated in Figure B.18 for a federated database system. In addition to handling heterogeneity, the HDP also has to handle the federated environment (see Figure B.20). That is, techniques have to be adapted to handle cooperation and autonomy. I have called such an HDP a federated distributed processor (FDP).

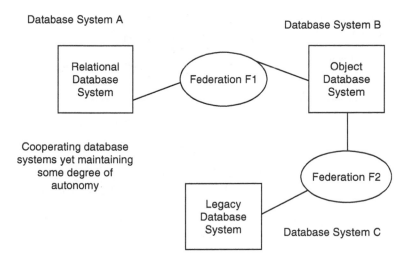

FIGURE B.19 Federated database management.

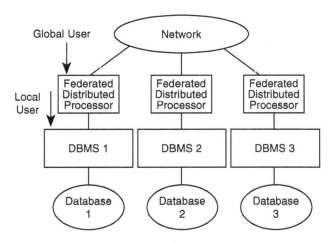

FIGURE B.20 Architecture for a federated database system.

Figure B.21 illustrates an example of an autonomous environment, in which communication occurs between components A and B and between B and C. Because of autonomy, it is assumed that components A and C do not wish to communicate with each other. Component A may receive requests from its own user or from component B. In this case, it has to decide which request to honor first. Also, there is a possibility for component C to get information from component A through component B. In such a situation, component A may have to negotiate with component B before it gives a reply to component B. The developments to deal with autonomy are still in the research stages. The challenges are the handling of transactions in an autonomous environment and transitioning of research into commercial products.

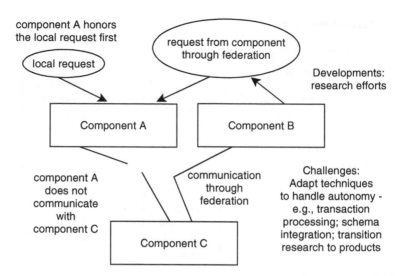

FIGURE B.21 Autonomy.

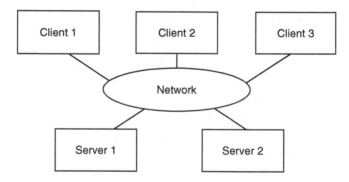

FIGURE B.22 Client–server architecture-based interoperability.

B.10 CLIENT–SERVER DATABASES

Earlier sections describe interoperability between heterogeneous database systems and focus on the federated database systems approach. In this approach, different database systems cooperatively interoperate with each other. This section describes another aspect of interoperability that is based on the client–server paradigm. Major database system vendors have migrated to an architecture called the client–server architecture. With this approach, multiple clients access the various database servers through some network. A high-level view of client–server communication is illustrated in Figure B.22. The ultimate goal is for multivendor clients to communicate with multi-vendor servers in a transparent manner. A specific example of client–server communication is illustrated in Figure B.23.

   One of the major challenges in client–server technology is to determine the modules of the distributed database system that need to be placed at the client and

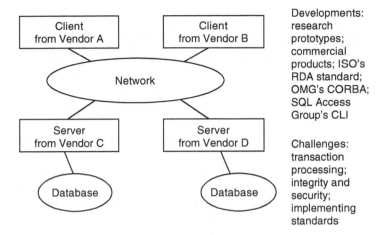

Developments: research prototypes; commercial products; ISO's RDA standard; OMG's CORBA; SQL Access Group's CLI

Challenges: transaction processing; integrity and security; implementing standards

FIGURE B.23 Example of client–server architecture.

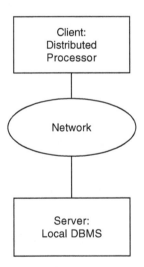

FIGURE B.24 An approach to place the modules.

server sides. Figure B.24 shows an approach where all the modules of the distributed processor of Figure B.17 are placed at the client side, whereas the modules of the local DBMS are placed at the server side. With this approach the client does a lot of processing, called the "fat client" approach. Other options are available; for example, some of the modules of the distributed processor could be part of the server in which case the client would be "thinner."

To facilitate the communication between multiple clients and servers, various standards are proposed. One example is the International Standards Organization (ISO) remote database access (RDA) standard. This standard provides a generic interface for communication between a client and a server. The Microsoft Corporation Open

Database Connectivity (ODBC) is also becoming an increasingly popular way for clients to communicate with the servers. The Object Management Group (OMG) Common Object Request Broker Architecture (CORBA) provides specifications for client–server communication based on object technology (see [OMG95]). With CORBA, one possibility is to encapsulate the database servers as objects and the clients to issue appropriate requests and access the servers through an object request broker (ORB). Other standards include the IBM Distributed Relational Database Access (DRDA) and the SQL Access Group Call Level Interface (CLI).* Although many of the developments have been in query processing, the challenges are in transaction processing, semantic heterogeneity, integrity, and security.

In my previous book [THUR97], I described various aspects of client–server interoperability, particularly technical issues for client–server interoperability; architectural approaches; three of the standards proposed for communication between clients and servers such as RDA, ODBC, and CORBA; and metadata aspects. A good reference is [ORFA94] and [ORFA96].

B.11 MIGRATING LEGACY DATABASES AND APPLICATIONS

Many database systems developed some 20 to 30 years ago are becoming obsolete. These systems use older hardware and software. Between now and the next few decades, many of today's information systems and applications will also become obsolete. Due to resource and, in certain cases, budgetary constraints, new developments of next-generation systems may not be possible in many areas (see, e.g., [BENS95]). Therefore, current systems need to become easier, faster, and less costly to upgrade and less difficult to support. Legacy database system and application migration is a complex problem, and many of the efforts under way are still not mature. Although a good book has been published on this subject [BROD95], no uniform approach for migration has been established. Because migrating legacy databases and applications are becoming necessary for most organizations, both government and commercial, one could expect a considerable amount of resources to be expended in this area in the near future. The research issues are also not well understood.

Migrating legacy applications and databases also have an impact on heterogeneous database integration. Typically, a heterogeneous database environment may include legacy databases as well as some of the next-generation databases. In many cases, an organization may want to migrate the legacy database system to an architecture like the client–server architecture and still want the migrated system to be part of the heterogeneous environment. This means that the functions of the heterogeneous database system may be impacted due to this migration process.

Two candidate approaches have been proposed for migrating legacy systems. One is execute to the migration all at once. The other is incremental migration. That is, as the legacy system gets migrated, the new parts have to interoperate with the old parts. Various issues and challenges to migration are discussed in [THUR97].

---

* It is now part of the Open Group. Note that the products and standards have evolved over the years and are continually changing. I encourage the reader to keep up with the developments. Much of the information can be obtained on the Web.

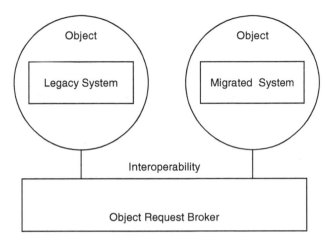

FIGURE B.25 Migrating legacy databases.

Figure B.25 illustrates an incremental approach to migrating legacy databases through the use of ORBs.

B.12 DATA WAREHOUSING

Data warehousing is one of the key data management technologies to support data mining and data analysis. Several organizations are building their own warehouses. Commercial database system vendors are marketing warehousing products. In addition, some companies are specializing only in developing data warehouses. What is a data warehouse? The idea behind this is that it is often cumbersome to access data from the heterogeneous databases. Several processing modules need to cooperate with one another to process a query in a heterogeneous environment. Therefore, a data warehouse will bring together the essential data from the heterogeneous databases. This way the users need to query only the warehouse.

As stated by Inmon [INMO93], data warehouses are subject oriented, their design depends to a great extent on the application utilizing them, they integrate diverse and possibly heterogeneous data sources, and they are persistent. That is, the warehouse is very much like a database: it varies with time. This is because as the data sources from which the warehouse is built get updated, the changes have to be reflected in the warehouse. Essentially, data warehouses provide support to decision support functions of an enterprise or an organization. For example, whereas the data sources may have the raw data, the data warehouse may have correlated data, summary reports, and aggregate functions applied to the raw data.

Figure B.26 illustrates a data warehouse. The data sources are managed by database systems A, B, and C. The information in these databases is merged and put into a warehouse. One of the various ways to merge the information is to simply replicate the databases. This does not have any advantages over accessing the heterogeneous databases. A second way is to replicate the information, but to remove any inconsistencies and redundancies. This has some advantages, because it is

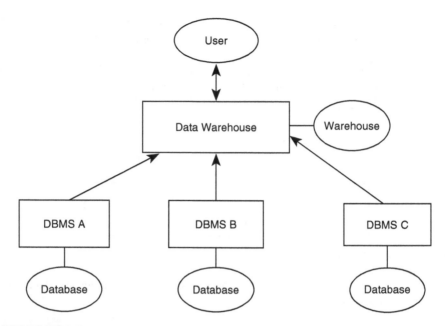

FIGURE B.26 Data warehouse example.

important to provide a consistent picture of the databases. The third approach is to select a subset of the information from the databases and place it in the warehouse. Several issues are involved in this approach. How are the subsets selected? Are they selected at random or is some method used to select the data? For example, one could take every other row in a relation (assuming it is a relational database) and store these rows in the warehouse. The fourth approach, which is a slight variation of the third approach, is to determine the types of queries that users would pose, then analyze the data, and store only the data that are required by the user. This is called online analytical processing (OLAP) as opposed to online transaction processing (OLTP).

With a data warehouse, data may often be viewed differently by different applications. That is, data are multidimensional. For example, the payroll department may want data to be in a certain format whereas the project department may want data to be in a different format. The warehouse must provide support for such multidimensional data.

In integrating the data sources to form the warehouse, challenges involve analyzing the application and selecting appropriate data to be placed in the warehouse. At times, some computations may have to be performed so that only summaries and averages are stored in the data warehouse. It is not always the case that the warehouse has all the information for a query. In this case, the warehouse may have to get the data from the heterogeneous data sources to complete the execution of the query. Another concern is what happens to the warehouse when the individual databases are updated. How are the updates propagated to the warehouse? How can security be maintained? These are some of the issues that are under investigation.

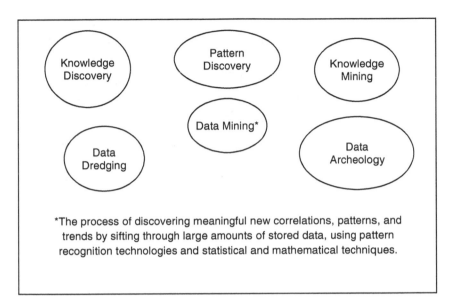

FIGURE B.27 Different definitions of data mining.

B.13 DATA MINING

B.13.1 OVERVIEW

Data mining is the process of posing various queries and extracting useful information, patterns, and trends (often previously unknown) from large quantities of data possibly stored in databases. For many organizations, the goals of data mining include improving marketing capabilities, detecting abnormal patterns, and predicting the future based on past experiences and current trends. There is clearly a need for this technology. Large amounts of current and historical data are stored. Therefore, as databases become larger, it becomes increasingly difficult to support decision making. In addition, the data could be from multiple sources and multiple domains. Analyzing the data to support planning and other functions of an enterprise is necessary.

Various terms have been used to refer to data mining, as shown in Figure B.27. These include knowledge, data, and information discovery as well as knowledge, data, and information extraction. Note that some define data mining to be the process of extracting previously unknown information whereas knowledge discovery is defined as the process of making sense out of the extracted information. In this book, I do not differentiate between data mining and knowledge discovery. It is difficult to determine whether a particular technique is a data mining technique. For example, some argue that statistical analysis techniques are data mining techniques. Others argue they are not and that data mining techniques should uncover relationships that are not straightforward. For example, with data mining, a medical supplies company could increase sales by targeting certain physicians in its advertising who are likely to buy the products, or a credit bureau may limit its losses by selecting candidates

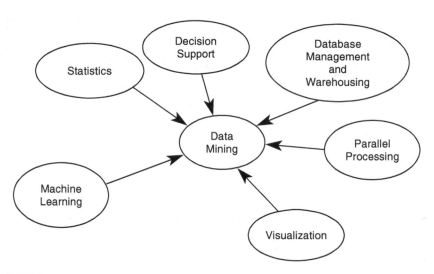

FIGURE B.28 Data mining technologies.

who are not likely to default on their payments. Such real-world experiences have been reported in various articles (see, e.g., [GRUP98]). In addition, data mining could also be used to detect abnormal behavior. For example, by using this technology, an intelligence agency could determine abnormal behavior of its employees.

Some of the data mining techniques include those based on rough sets, inductive logic programming, machine learning, and neural networks, among others. The data mining problems include classification (finding rules to partition data into groups), association (finding rules to make associations between data), and sequencing (finding rules to order data). One arrives at some hypothesis, which is the information extracted, from examples and patterns observed. These patterns are observed from posing a series of queries; each query may depend on the responses obtained to the previous queries posed. The several developments in data mining include tools by corporations such as Lockheed Martin Corporation. (see, e.g., [SIMO95]).

The remainder of this section is organized as follows: Section B.13.2 covers technologies that contribute to data mining; Section B.13.3, concepts in data mining including techniques; and Section B.13.4, trends in data mining. For a detailed discussion of data mining, refer to [THUR98].

B.13.2 DATA MINING TECHNOLOGIES

Data mining is an integration of multiple technologies, as illustrated in Figure B.28. These include data management such as database management, data warehousing, statistics, machine learning, decision support, and others such as visualization and parallel computing.* I briefly discuss the role of each of these technologies. It should, however, be noted that although many of these technologies, such as statistical

---

* I have distinguished between data management and database management, and also among data, information, and knowledge. These definitions are given in Appendix A as well as in [THUR97].

packages and machine learning algorithms, have existed for many decades, the ability to manage and organize the data has played a major role in making data mining a reality.

Data mining research is under way by various disciplines. Database management researchers are taking advantage of the work on deductive and intelligent query processing for data mining. One of the areas of interest is to extend query processing techniques to facilitate data mining. Data warehousing is another key data management technology for integrating the various data sources and organizing the data so that it can be effectively mined.

Researchers in statistical analysis are integrating their techniques with machine learning techniques to develop more statistical sophistication in data mining. Various statistical analysis packages are now being marketed as data mining tools, but with some dispute. Nevertheless, statistics is a major area contributing to data mining.

Machine learning has been around for a while. The idea is for the machine to learn various rules from the patterns observed and then apply these rules to solve the problems. Although the principles used in machine learning and data mining are similar, with data mining one usually considers the large quantities of data to be mined. Therefore, integration of database management and machine learning techniques are needed.

Researchers from the computer visualization field are approaching data mining from another perspective. One of their areas of focus is to use visualization techniques to aid the data mining process. In other words, interactive data mining is a goal of the visualization community.

Decision support systems are a collection of tools and processes to help managers make decisions and guide them in management. For example, tools for scheduling meetings, organizing events, preparing spreadsheets, viewing graphs, and evaluationing performance are examples of decision support systems. Decision support has theoretical underpinnings in decision theory.

Finally, researchers in the high-performance computing area are also working on developing appropriate techniques so that the data mining algorithms are scalable. Interaction with the hardware researchers is taking place so that appropriate hardware can be developed for high-performance data mining.

Several other technologies are beginning to have an impact on data mining including collaboration, agents, and distributed object management. A discussion of all these technologies is beyond the scope of this book, but I mention some of the key technologies in this appendix. Furthermore, I emphasize that having good data is the key to good mining.

B.13.3 Concepts and Techniques for Data Mining

A series of steps involved in data mining include getting the data organized for mining, determining the desired outcomes to mining, selecting tools for mining, carrying out the mining, pruning the results so that only the useful ones are considered further, taking actions from the mining, and evaluating the actions to determine benefits. Although these steps are discussed in detail throughout this book, I again briefly review some of the outcomes and techniques.

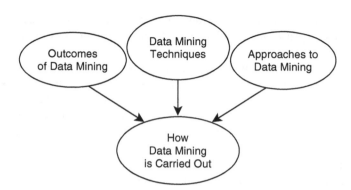

FIGURE B.29 Aspects of data mining.

Various types of data mining are used. By this I do not mean the actual techniques used to mine the data, but what the outcomes will be. Some of these outcomes, as discussed in [AGRA93], are outlined in this book. These outcomes have also been referred to as data mining tasks.

In one outcome of data mining, called *classification,* records are grouped into some meaningful subclasses. For example, suppose an automobile sales company has some information that all the people on its list who live in city X own cars worth more than $20K. They can then assume that even those who are not on their list, but live in city X, can afford to own cars costing more than $20K. This way the company classifies the people living in city X.

A second outcome of data mining is *sequence detection.* That is, by observing patterns in the data, sequences are determined. This is an example of sequence detection: "After John goes to the bank, he generally goes to the grocery store."

A third outcome of data mining is *data dependency analysis.* With this outcome, potentially interesting dependencies, relationships, or associations among the data items are detected. For example, "If John, James, and William have a meeting, then Robert will also be at that meeting." This type of mining appears to be of much interest to many.

A fourth outcome of mining is *deviation analysis.* For example, "John went to the bank on Saturday, but he did not go to the grocery store after that. Instead he went to a football game." With this type, anomalous instances and discrepancies are found.

As mentioned earlier, various techniques are used to obtain the outcomes of data mining. These techniques could be based on rough sets, fuzzy logic, inductive logic programming, or neural networks, among others; or they could simply be some statistical technique. Furthermore, different approaches have also been proposed to carry out data mining including top-down mining as well as bottom-up mining. Data mining outcomes, techniques, and approaches are illustrated in Figure B.29.

Numerous developments have been made in data mining within the past few years. Many of these focus on relational databases. The data are stored in relational databases and mined to extract useful information and patterns. Several research prototypes and commercial products include those developed at the International Business Machines Corporation (IBM) Almaden Research Center and at Simon Fraser

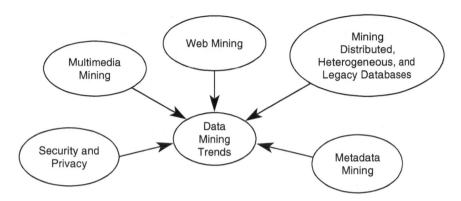

FIGURE B.30 Data mining trends.

University, Vancouver, B.C. The prototypes and products employ various data mining techniques including neural networks, rule-based reasoning, and statistical analysis. The various data mining tools in the form of prototypes and products are also discussed in this book.

B.13.4 Directions and Trends for Data Mining

Although several developments have been made, many challenges remain. For example, due to the large volumes of data, how can the algorithms determine which technique to select and what type of data mining to do? Furthermore, the data may be incomplete or inaccurate. At times, redundant or insufficient information may exist. It is also desirable to have data mining tools that can switch to multiple techniques and support multiple outcomes. Some of the current trends in data mining include the following and are illustrated in Figure B.30:

- Mining distributed, heterogeneous, and legacy databases
- Mining multimedia data
- Mining data on the World Wide Web (WWW)
- Security and privacy issues in data mining
- Metadata aspects of mining

In many cases, the databases are distributed and heterogeneous in nature. Furthermore, much of the data are in legacy databases. Mining techniques are needed to handle these distributed, heterogeneous, and legacy databases. Next, current data mining tools operate on structured data; however, large quantities of data still are unstructured. Data in the multimedia databases are often semistructured or unstructured. Data mining tools have to be developed for multimedia databases. The explosion of data and information on the WWW necessitates the development of tools to manage and mine the data so that only useful information is extracted. Therefore, developing mining tools for the WWW is an important area.

Privacy issues also are becoming critical for data mining [THUR96]. Users now have sophisticated tools to make inferences and deduce information to which they are not authorized. Therefore, although data mining tools help solve many problems in the real world, they also invade the privacy of individuals. Throughout my previous book [THUR97], I repeatedly stressed the importance of metadata for data management. Metadata also plays a key role in data mining [THUR98].

In addition to the trends in the preceding areas, several other challenges exist. These include handling dynamic data, sparse data, incomplete and uncertain data, as well as determining which data mining algorithm to use and on what data to operate. In addition, mining multiple languages is also a challenge. Researchers are addressing these challenges.

B.14 OBJECT TECHNOLOGY

B.14.1 OVERVIEW

Object technology (OT), or object-oriented technology (OOT), encompasses different technologies. These include object-oriented programming languages, object database management systems, object-oriented design and analysis, distributed object management, and components and frameworks. The underlying theme for all these types of object technologies is the object model. That is, the object model is the very essence of object technology. Any object system is based on some object model, whether it is a programming language or a database system. The interesting aspect of an object model is that everything in the real world can be modeled as an object.

The organization of this section follows: Section B.14.2 describes the essential properties of object data models (ODMs). Section B.14.2 summarizes all the other object technologies. These include object-oriented programming languages (OOPL), object-oriented database (OODB) systems, object-oriented design and analysis (OODA), distributed object management (DOM), and components and frameworks (C&F). An overview of the various object technologies is illustrated in Figure B.31. For a more detailed discussion of object technology, refer to [THUR00].

B.14.2 OBJECT DATA MODEL

Since the birth of object technology sometime during the 1970s, numerous object models have been proposed. In fact, some object models trace back to the language Simula in the 1960s. Initially, these models were to support programming languages such as Smalltalk. Later, these models were enhanced to support database systems and other complex systems. This section provides an overview of the essential features of object models. Many of the features presented in this text are common for object models developed for different types of systems such as programming languages, database systems, modeling and analysis, and distributed object management systems.

Although no standard object models exist, the Uniform Modeling Language (UML) proposed by the prominent object technologists (Rumbaugh, Booch, and Jacobson [FOWL97]) has gained increasing popularity and has almost become the standard. This discussion of the object model has been influenced by much of my

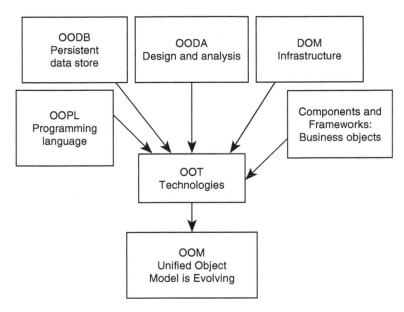

FIGURE B.31 Object technologies.

work in object database systems as well as the one proposed by Won Kim et al. [BANE87]. I call it an object-oriented data model.*

The key points in an object-oriented model are *encapsulation, inheritance,* and *polymorphism.* With an object-oriented data model, the database is viewed as a collection of objects [BANE87]. Each object has a unique identifier called the object-ID. Objects with similar properties are grouped into a class. For example, employee objects are grouped into EMP class whereas department objects are grouped into DEPT class, as shown in Figure B.32. A class has instance variables describing the properties. Instance variables of EMP are SS#, Ename, Salary, and D#, whereas the instance variables of DEPT are D#, Dname, and Mgr. The objects in a class are its instances. As illustrated in Figure B.32, EMP has three instances and DEPT has two instances.

A key concept in object-oriented data modeling is *encapsulation.* That is, an object has well-defined interfaces. The state of an object can only be accessed through interface procedures called methods. For example, EMP may have a method called Increase-Salary. The code for Increase-Salary is illustrated in Figure B.32. A message, for example, Increase-Salary(1, 10K), may be sent to the object with an object ID of 1. The current salary for the object is read and updated by 10K.

A second key concept in an object model is *inheritance,* where a subclass inherits properties from its parent class. This feature is illustrated in Figure B.33, where the

---

* Two types of object models have been proposed for databases. One is the object-oriented data model proposed for object-oriented databases and the other is the object-relational data model proposed for object-relational databases. I discuss the object-oriented data model in this section. Object-relational models are discussed in the section on object database management.

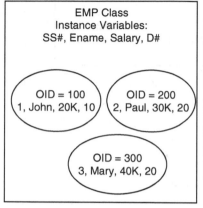
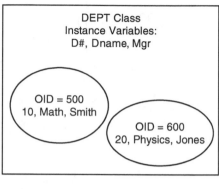

Increase-Salary (OID, Value)
Read-Salary (OID, amount)
Amount = Amount + Value
Write-Salary (OID, Amount)

FIGURE B.32 Objects and classes.

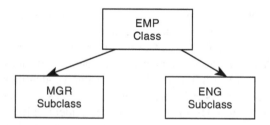

FIGURE B.33 Class–subclass hierarchy.

EMP class has MGR (manager) and ENG (engineer) as its subclasses. Other key concepts in an object model include polymorphism and aggregation.* These features are discussed in [BANE87]. Further information can also be obtained in [THUR97]. Note that a second type of inheritance is when the instances of a class inherit the properties of the class.

A third concept is *polymorphism*. This is the situation where one can pass different types of arguments for the same function. For example, to calculate the area, one can pass a sphere or a cylinder object. Operators can be overloaded also. That is, the add operation can be used to add two integers or real numbers.

Another concept is the *aggregate hierarchy,* also called the *composite object* or the *is-part-of hierarchy.* In this case, an object has component objects. For example, a book object has component section objects. A section object has component paragraph objects. Aggregate hierarchy is illustrated in Figure B.34.

---

* Inheritance is also known as the *is-a hierarchy.* Aggregation is also known as the *is-part-of hierarchy.*

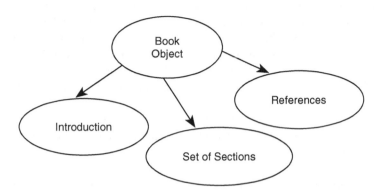

FIGURE B.34 Aggregate object.

Objects also have relationships between them. For example, an employee object has an association with the department object, which is the department he is working in. Also, the instance variables of an object could take integers, lists, arrays, or even other objects as values. All these concepts are discussed in the book by Cattell [CATT91]. The Object Data Management Group is also proposing standards for object data models [ODMG93].

B.14.3 OTHER OBJECT TECHNOLOGIES

Programming languages — Recall that OOPL essentially goes back to Simula in the 1960s, although it really became popular with the advent of Smalltalk by Xerox Palo Alto Research Center in the late 1970s. Smalltalk is a pure object-oriented programming language where everything is considered to be an object. Implementations of Smalltalk were under development throughout the 1980s. Around the mid-1980s, languages such as LISP and C were made object-oriented by extending them to support objects. One such popular extension is the C++ language. In the early to mid-1990s a lot of the programming was carried out in C++. Around the 1990s, Sun Microsystems wanted to develop a language for its embedded computing and appliance business that would not have all the problems associated with C++ such as pointers. The resulting language was first named Oak and then was eventually called Java. Java became immensely popular because of the Internet.

Database systems — I have discussed three types of object database systems [THUR00]. One is OODB systems, which make OOPL persistent. The second is extended-relational systems, which extend relational database systems with object layers. The third system is object-relational system where objects are nested within relations. The previous two sections addressed OOPLs and OODM. Around the same time (i.e., in the 1980s), there was a lot of interest in using object technology to design and analyze applications. Prior to that, various analysis techniques such as structured analysis and Jackson diagrams were used to analyze the application. At the same time, ER models were very popular for representing the entities of the application and the relationships between them.

Design and analysis — With the advent of OOT, interest increased in using objects to model and analyze applications. Various design and analysis methodologies were proposed. Notable among them was the method of Booch, Usecases by Jacobson, and Object Modeling Technique (OMT) by Rumbaugh et al. Because this subject elicited so much controversy, extremely contentious debate on this subject arose at the 1993 Object-Oriented Programming Systems, Languages, and Applications (OOPSLA) Conference. Surprisingly, within the next 2 years, it was announced that the three groups were merging and were producing a unified methodology. This unified methodology is called UML [FOWL97]. UML has essential features from the three approaches and is now more or less a standard for object modeling and analysis.

Distributed object management — DOM technology is becoming increasingly used to interconnect heterogeneous databases, systems, and applications. With this approach, the various systems and applications are encapsulated as objects and the objects communicate with each other through exchanging messages. An example of a DOM system that is used as middleware to connect heterogeneous database systems is based on the OMG CORBA. CORBA is a specification that enables heterogeneous applications, systems, and databases to interoperate with each other. As stated in [OMG95], CORBA has three major components. The first is the object model; the second is the ORB through which clients and servers communicate with each other, and the third is the Interface Definition Language (IDL), which specifies the interfaces for client–server communication.

Components and frameworks — This is one of the latest object technologies and has really taken off since the mid-1990s. When talking to various people and reading different texts, I have found that the terms *components* and *frameworks* have no standard definitions. An excellent survey of the field appeared in the *Communications of the ACM* magazine in October 1997 by Fayad and Schmidt [ACM97]. In a sense a framework can be considered to be a skeleton with classes and interconnections. One then instantiates this skeleton for various applications. Frameworks are under development for different application domains including financial and medical. Components, on the other hand, are classes, objects, and relationships among them that can be reused. Components can be built for different applications such as for financial, medical, and telecommunication purposes. These components are also called business objects.

B.15 SUMMARY

This appendix discusses various aspects of database systems and provides a lot of background information to understand the chapters in this book. I begin with a discussion of various data models, choosing relational and ER models because they are more relevant to what is addressed in this text. Then I provide an overview of various types of architectures for database systems, including functional and schema architectures. Next, I discuss database design aspects and database administration issues. This appendix also provides an overview of the various functions of database systems, including query processing, transaction management, storage management, metadata management, security, integrity, and fault tolerance.* A brief discussion of distributed databases and interoperability is followed by an examination of data warehousing, data mining, and finally object technology.

Many of the chapters in this publication discuss the varied data management and data mining system aspects related to multimedia information processing. These include query processing, storage management, metadata management, security, distribution, and interoperability.

B.16 REFERENCES

[ACM90] Special issue on federated databases, *ACM Comput. Surv.,* September 1990.

[ACM91] Special issue on next generation database systems, *Commun. ACM,* October 1991.

[ACM97] Special issue on components, *Commun. ACM,* October 1997.

[AFSB83] Air Force Summer Study Board Report on Multilevel Secure Database Systems, Dpt. of Defense Document, 1983.

[AGRA93] Agrawal, A. et al., Database Mining a Performance Perspective, IEEE Transactions on Knowledge and Data Engineering, December 1993.

[BANE87] Banerjee, J. et al., A data model for object-oriented applications, *ACM Trans. Office Inf. Syst.,* March 1987.

[BELL92] Bell D. and Grimson, J., *Distributed Database Systems,* Addison-Wesley, Reading, MA, 1992.

[BENS95] Bensley, E. et al., Evolvable Systems Initiative for Real-time Command and Control Systems, Proc. First IEEE Complex Systems Conference, Orlando, FL, November 1995.

[BERN87] Bernstein, P. et al., *Concurrency Control and Recovery in Database Systems,* Addison-Wesley, Reading, MA, 1987.

[BROD84] Brodie, M. et al., *On Conceptual Modeling: Perspectives from Artificial Intelligence, Databases, and Programming Languages,* Springer-Verlag, New York, 1984.

[BROD86] Brodie, M. and Mylopoulos, J., *On Knowledge Base Management Systems,* Springer-Verlag, New York, 1986.

[BROD88] Brodie, M. et al., *Readings in Artificial Intelligence and Databases,* Morgan Kaufmann, San Francisco, CA, 1988.

[BROD95] Brodie, M. and Stonebraker, M., *Migrating Legacy Databases,* Morgan Kaufmann, San Francisco, CA, 1995.

[CATT91] Cattel, R., *Object Data Management Systems,* Addison-Wesley, Reading, MA, 1991.

[CERI84] Ceri, S. and Pelagatti, G., *Distributed Databases, Principles and Systems,* McGraw-Hill, New York, 1984.

[CHEN76] Chen, P., The entity relationship model — Toward a unified view of data, *ACM Trans. Database Syst.,* March 1976.

[CHOR94] Chorafas, D., *Intelligent Multimedia Databases,* Prentice Hall, Englewood Cliffs, NJ, 1994.

[CODD70] Codd, E.F., A relational model of data for large shared data banks, *Commun. ACM,* May 1970.

* Various texts and articles have been published on database systems. Examples include [KORT86], [ULLM88], [DATE90], [THUR97], [THUR98], [THUR00], [CERI84], [FROS86], [DAS92], [LLOY87], [PRAB97], [BROD84], [BROD86], [BROD88], and [CHOR94].

[DAS92] Das, S., *Deductive Databases and Logic Programming*, Addison-Wesley, Reading, MA, 1992.

[DATE90] Date, C. J., *An Introduction to Database Management Systems*, Addison-Wesley, Reading, MA, 1990 (6th ed. published in 1995 by Addison-Wesley).

[DMH94] von Halle, B. and Kull, E., Eds., *Data Management Handbook*, Auerbach Publications, New York, 1994.

[DMH95] von Halle, B. and Kull, D., Eds., *Data Management Handbook Supplement*, Auerbach Publications, New York, 1995.

[DMH96] Thuraisingham, B., Ed., *Data Management Handbook Supplement*, Auerbach Publications, New York, 1996.

[DMH98] Thuraisingham, B., Ed., *Data Management Handbook Supplement*, Auerbach Publications, New York, 1998.

[DOD94] Proc. 1994 DoD Database Colloquium, San Diego, CA, August 1994.

[DOD95] Proc. 1994 DoD Database Colloquium, San Diego, CA, August 1995.

[ELMA85] Elmasri, R., The entity category relationship model, *Data Knowledge Eng. J.*, April 1985.

[FOWL97] Fowler, M. et al., *UML Distilled: Applying the Standard Object Modeling Language*, Addison-Wesley, Reading, MA, 1997.

[FROS86] Frost, R., *On Knowledge Base Management Systems*, Collins Publishers, United Kingdom, 1986.

[GRUP98] Grupe, F. and Owrang, M., Database mining tools, in *The Handbook of Data Management Supplement*, Thuraisingham, B., Ed., Auerbach Publications, New York, 1998.

[IEEE91] Special issue in heterogeneous database systems, *IEEE Comp.*, 1991.

[IFIP] Proc. IFIP Database Security Conferences, 1990–1994.

[INMO93] Inmon, W., *Building the Data Warehouse*, John Wiley & Sons, New York, 1993.

[KIM85] Kim, W. et al., *Query Processing in Database Systems*, Springer-Verlag, New York, 1985.

[KORT86] Korth, H. and Silberschatz, A., *Database System Concepts*, McGraw-Hill, New York, 1986.

[LLOY87] Lloyd, J., *Logic Programming*, Springer-Verlag, Heidelberg, Germany, 1987.

[LOOM95] Loomis, M., *Object Databases*, Addison-Wesley, Reading, MA, 1995.

[MAIE83] Maier, D., *Theory of Relational Databases*, Computer Science Press, Rockville, MD, 1983.

[META96] Proc. IEEE Metadata Conference, Silver Spring, MD, April 1996.

[MIT] http://web.mit.edu/TDQM/

[ODMG93] Object Database Standard: ODMB 93, Object Database Management Group, Morgan Kaufmann, San Francisco, CA, 1993.

[OMG95] *Common Object Request Broker Architecture and Specification*, OMG Publications, John Wiley & Sons, New York, 1995.

[OOPS94] OOPSLA 94 Workshop on CORBA, Portland, OR, 1994.

[ORFA94] Orfali, R. et al., *Essential Client–Server Survival Guide*, John Wiley & Sons, New York, 1994.

[ORFA96] Orfali, R. et al., *The Essential, Distributed Objects Survival Guide*, John Wiley & Sons, New York, 1994.

[PRAB97] Prabhakaran, B., *Multimedia Database Systems*, Kluwer Publications, Norwood, MA, 1997.

[SHET90] Sheth A. and J. Larson, Federated database systems, *ACM Comput. Surv.*, September 1990.

[SIMO95] Simoudis, E. et al., Recon Data Mining System, Technical Report, Lockheed Martin Corp., May 1995.

[SQL3] SQL3, American National Standards Institute, Draft, 1992 (a version also presented by J. Melton at the Department of Navy's DISWG NGCR meeting, Salt Lake City, UT, November 1994).

[THUR97] Thuraisingham, B., *Data Management Systems Evolution and Interoperation,* CRC Press, Boca Raton, FL, 1997.

[THUR98] Thuraisingham, B., *Data Mining: Technologies, Techniques, Tools, and Trends,* CRC Press, Boca Raton, FL, 1998

[THUR00] Thuraisingham, B., *Web Information Management and Electronic Commerce,* CRC Press, Boca Raton, FL, 2000.

[THUR01] Thuraisingham, B., *Managing and Mining Multimedia Databases,* CRC Press, Boca Raton, FL, 2001.

[TSIC82] Tsichritzis, D. and Lochovsky, F., *Data Models,* Prentice Hall, Englewood Cliffs, NJ, 1982.

[ULLM88] Ullman, J. D., *Principles of Database and Knowledge Base Management Systems,* Vol. I and II, Computer Science Press, Rockville, MD 1988.

[WIED92] Wiederhold, G., Mediators in the architecture of future information systems, *IEEE Comp.,* March 1992.

[YANG88] Yang, D. and T. Torey, A practical approach to transforming extended ER diagrams into the relational model, *Inform. Sci. J.,* April 1988.

Index

A

Acceptance tests, fault tolerance, 267
Access
  database security, 266
  gateways, 41–42
  remote database access (RDA) standard, 273
  storage management, 263–264
  web, 234
  Web database management, 41–42
  XML documents, 177
Access control model, 188, 189
ActiveX, 209
Adaptive Server, query processing techniques, 186
Administration of database, 260–261
Advanced concepts in XML, 4, 6, 7, 133–142
  data integration issues, 139–140
  future directions, 140–141, 142
  internationalization, 140, 141
  schemas, 137–138
  semantic issues, 133–134, 135
  Xlink and other constructs, 136–137
  XMLQL, 138–139
Agents, 2, 205
  DAML, 3
  digital library query processing, 19, 20
  e-commerce, 106
  information management applications,
    199–200
  semantic web, 144, 146, 148–149
  WWW
    information management technologies,
      80–85
    mining applications, 3
    Web crawlers as, 209
Agent service, distributed object management, 91
Aggregate hierarchy, 284, 285
Almaden Research Center data mining products,
  281
AltaVista Discovery, 206
American National Standards Institute, database
    system standardization, 241
Analysis of data, datavase administration, 261
Analytical processing, online (OLAP), 276
Annotations, 195
ANSI, database system standardization, 241
Applets, *see* Java

Application programming interfaces (APIs), 117
Applications, 3–4, 5, 6, 7
  data management systems, 246
  data management technologies, 249
Application server
  and data server, 43
  WWW tools, 207
Aquarelle project, 168
Architecture, 158, 159
  challenges and directions, 229
  database system standardization, 241
  data management applications, 191–193
  e-commerce, 99–103
  federated database, 271
  image processing system, 58
  semantic web, 214–216, 215–216, 220
  semistructured databases, 156, 157
  text retrieval, 53, 54
  video processing system, 62
  Web database management, 40–50
    access to database, 41–42
    communication, models of, 47–50
    federated computing, 50
    interoperability, 42, 44–45
    migration, 45–47
    three-tier computing, 42, 43
  XML applications, 184
Architecture-based interoperability, 272–273
Artificial intelligence, 72
Atomicity, consistency, isolation, and durability
    (ACID), transaction management, 262
Attributes, 127–128, 131, 257
Audio data, 2
  mining, 69
  multi-media DBMS, 68
  retrieval systems, 64–67
  semistructured databases, 30
Auditing, granularity of data for, 261
Authorization, database security, 266
Autonomous environment, federated databases,
  271, 272

B

Back-end tier, 42, 43
  multimedia computing, 75, 76
  XML databases, 192, 193

Banking, 40
Basic concepts in XML, 125–132
    components of document, 125–126, 127
    containers, elements, and attributes, 127–128
    data types, 129–130
    miscellaneous, 130–131
    namespaces, 128–129
Basic XML, 4, 6, 7
BEA Systems, 198, 207
BEA Tuxedo, 207
Bidirectional links, 118
Bioinformatics, 201
Broadcasting, 75
Brokering, 104, 105
Brokers, semantic web operation, 144, 147
Browsers, 205
    commercial products, 209
    e-commerce, 106
    text retrieval architecture, 53, 54
Browsing, WWW, 21–22
B-trees, 264
Building semantic web, 213–221, *see also*
        Semantic web construction
Business models, challenges and directions, 230
Business objects
    three-tier computing, 43
    XML databases, 191, 192, 193
Business process reengineering, 94
Business-to-business commerce, 97–98
    collaborative, 196–198
    federated, 100–101, 103
Business-to-consumer commerce, 97–98

C

C and C++, 285
Calculus, relational, 257
Call Level Interface (CLI), 274
Categories, entity-relationship data model, 257
Centralized architecture, 258
CGI, 13
Checkpointing, 188, 267
Classification (data mining), 280
Client-server architecture, *see also* Servers
    e-commerce, 99–100, 101, 102
    interoperability, 272–273
    semantic web, 215–216
Client-server databases, 272–274
    security, 40
    systems framework, 245
Client-tier, three-tier multimedia computing, 75,
        76
Collaboration/collaborative technologies, 2, 205,
        250
    challenges and directions, 230

commercial products, 209
data management technology overview, 243
DBMS functions, 261
distributed object management, 91
e-commerce, 106
    c-commerce, 196–198
    interoperability, 177
information management
    applications, 196–198
    technologies, 71–74
knowledge management, 78
multimedia data management for, 249
semantic web, 144
web crawlers, 209
WWW, 21
Comments, 125
Commerce One.Net, 180, 181, 198
Common Object Request Broker Architecture
        (CORBA), 12, 13, 44, 274, 286
Communication, models of, 47–50
Communications
    collaborative computing, 71
    multimedia information management, 75
    wireless, *see* Wireless information
Components
    document, 125–126, 127
    object technologies, 286
Composite article, 284
Computer-aided design (CAD), 242
Computer-aided manufacturing (CAM), 242
Computer-aided software engineering (CASE),
        257
Computer-based training (CBT), 86–87
Computer Corporation of America developments
        in database systems, 241
Concurrency control, 263, 265
Conference participation, collaborative computing
        applications, 71
Conferences
    database security, 38, 39
    data management, 203
    object-oriented programming, 286
    Web-mining, 32
    XML, 8
Constructs, 134
Consulting, e-commerce, 94
Consumer profiles, push model, 48
Consumers of multimedia data, 75
Containers, 127–128, 147
Content management, 52
CORBA (Common Object Request Broker
        Architecture), 12, 13, 44, 274, 286
Corporate information infrastructures
    collaborative computing, 73–74
    WWW, 14

D

DAML (DARPA Agents Markup Language), 3, 144, 148–149, 200
DAML + Ontology Interchange Language (OIL), 200
DARPA, 3, 17, 143
Data
  e-commerce client-server architecture, 99–103
  object databases, XML representation, 176
Data analysis, database administration, 261
Database computer-aided software engineering (CASE), 257
Database management
  agent functions, 82
  e-commerce functions, 105
  semistructured databases, 31
Database management, WWW, 25–52
  architectural aspects, 40–50
    access to database, 41–42
    communication, models of, 47–50
    federated computing, 50
    interoperability, 42, 44–45
    migration, 45–47
    three-tier computing, 42, 43
  databases, 26–32
    data representation and data modeling, 27
    semistructured, 30
    web database management functions, 27–29
  data mining, 30–40
    applications and directions, 37–38
    mining on web, 32–36
    security and privacy concerns, 38–40
    usage patterns, 36
  terminology, 25
  XML and, 50–52
Database management systems
  access without gateways, 42
  application server and data server, 43
  digital library, 19, 20
  functions of, 261–269
    fault tolerance, 267
    integrity of database, 265–266
    metadata management, 265
    query processing, 262
    security, 266–267
    storage management, 263–264
    transaction management, 262–263
  web database management, 25–26
Databases
  developments in, 240–244
  e-commerce, 106
  object-oriented, 285–286

semantic web, 149–152
web access, 234
Database systems and related technologies, 255–289
  administration of database, 260–261
  architectural issues, 158, 159
  client-server databases, 272–274
  database management system functions, 261–269
    fault tolerance, 267
    integrity of database, 265–266
    metadata management, 265
    query processing, 262
    security, 266–267
    storage management, 263–264
    transaction management, 262–263
  design of database, 259–260
  distributed databases, 267–269
  entity-relationship data models, 257
  federated databases, 270–271
  integration of heterogeneous databases, 269–270
  legacy database migration and applications, 274–275
  mining, 277–282
    definitions, 277–278
    directions and trends, 281–282
    technologies, 278–279
  object technology, 282–287
    object data model, 282–285
    other object technologies, 285–286
    technologies, 282, 283
  relational data model, 256–257
  semantic web, 144
  warehousing, 275–276
  WWW tools, 204–206
Data dependency analysis (data mining), 280
Data dictionaries, 183
Data Dictionary Systems, 241
Data distribution
  data management applications, 189
  semistructured databases, 164–165
Data filtering agent, 81, 82
Data integration issues, 134, 139–140
Data integrity, semistructured databases, 166–167
Data management, 6, 7
  applications, 183–194
    architectures, 191–193
    data distribution, 189
    data warehousing and mining, 190–191
    integration with ORBs, 193, 194
    interoperability and migration, 189–190
    metadata, 183–184, 185

object technology, 193
query processing, 186
security, integrity, and fault tolerance, 188,
    189
semistructured databases, 185
storage management, 187–188
transaction processing, 186
challenges and directions, 230
collaborative computing, 73
e-commerce applications, 176–177, 178
versus information management and
    knowledge management, 79–80
information management technologies, 71–74
metadata, 110, 111
semantic web, 216–217, 220
systems, development and trends, 239–253
    developments in database systems,
        240–244
    framework, building information systems
        from, 248–250
    framework, data management systems,
        245–248
    relationship between texts, 250–251, 252
    status, vision, and issues, 245
    support technologies and, 249–250
WWW, 203–212
    application server tools, 207
    breakthrough standards, tools, and services,
        210–212
    challenges and directions, 229–230
    database system tools, 204–206
    DOTNET, 211
    J2EE, 211–212
    knowledge management tools, 207–208
    metaData and XML tools, 208–209
    mining tools, 206–207
    miscellaneous information managent tools,
        209–210
    SOAP, 210
    UDDI, 211
    WSDL, 210–211
Data manipulation, semistructured databases, 162,
    163
Data mining, *see* Mining
Data modeling
    semantic web technologies, 144
    Web databases, 27
Data models, 256–257
    audio representation, 64, 65
    document representation, 53–54
    heterogeneous database integration, 269–270
    image processing system, 58
    semistructured databases, 3, 157–161
    video representation, 60
    W3C activities, 24

Data representation
    semistructured database, 30, 31, 159, 160
    Web databases, 27
Data requests, models of communication,
    47–49
Data retrieval agents, 81, 82, 83
Data server, and application server, 43
Data service, distributed object management, 91
Data sources, warehousing, 275, 276
Data structures, challenges and directions, 230
Data transactions, secure, 40
Data types, 30, 129–130
Data warehousing, *see* Warehousing
DB2 CXML, 186
Decision support, 205
    challenges and directions, 230
    data mining, 279
    e-commerce, 106
    information management applications, 199
    information management technologies, 78–80
    metadata, 110
    web tools, 209
Declarations, 125
Defense Advanced Research Projects Agency
    (DARPA), 3, 17, 143
Defense Information Infrastructure (DII), 14
Design
    collaborative computing, 71
    database, 259–260
Developments in database systems, 240–244
Deviation analysis (data mining), 280
Dictionaries, data, 183, 241
Digital Equipment Corporation, developments in
    database systems, 240
Digital libraries, *see also* Database management,
    WWW
    heterogeneous data integration, 44
    knowledge management, 198
    metadata management, 265
    updating, 29
    terminology, 25
Discretionary security, 166
Displays, three-tier computing, 43
Distance learning, 85–86
    information management technologies, 86–87
    web tools, 209
Distributed architecture, e-commerce, 99, 101
Distributed data, XML documents, 189
Distributed databases, 267–269
    data mining trends, 281
    management, 250
    metadata, 110, 115
Distributed Database Testbed System (DDTS),
    241
Distributed Multimedia Processor (DMP), 68

Distributed object management, 193, 286
  heterogeneous database interoperability, 249
  information management technologies, 91
Distributed processing, 250
  collaborative computing, 72
  data management systems, 246
  digital libraries, 19
  multimedia data management for
    collaboration, 249
  semistructured databases, 156, 159
Distributed processors, multimedia (MDP), 75
Distributed Relational Database Access (DRDA),
    274
Distributed work groups, collaborative computing,
    71
Distribution, e-commerce functions, 105
Document management, 2, 51
Document representation
  e-commerce applications, 175–176, 177
  semantic web, 217
  XML for, 27, 71, 118
Document sharing as knowledge management,
    79
Document structure
  components, 125–126, 127
  metadata, 183
Document type definitions (DTDs)
  in XML, 69–70
  web mining, 36
Domain-specific ontologies, 116, 117
Domain-specific technologies, 201
Domain-type definitions (DTDs), 117, 135–136
  data types, 130, 131
  metadata, 183, 184
  properties, 136
  XML schemas, 137–138
  W3C activities, 24
DOTNET, 51, 203, 204, 205, 211
DTDs, *see* Document-type definitions; Domain-
    type definitions
Dynamic data, data mining trends, 282

E

e.Analysis software, 206
Easy Miner software, 206
E-business
  building blocks, 95, 96
  challenges and directions, 229
  web mining tools, 206
E-business XML, *see* Electronic Business
    Extensible Markup Language
E-commerce, 2, 3, 6, 7, 93–107, 234
  agent functions, 82
  applications of XML, 3–4

architectures for, 99–103
challenges and directions, 231
data mining uses, 32
as decision support technology, 80
E-business and e-commerce, 93–97
eXcelon applications, 208–209
functions, 103–104
future directions, 90–91
information technologies for, 104–105
knowledge management tools, 78
models for, 97–99
multimedia computing, 75
ontologies, 116
push model, 48
security, 40
web mining applications, 37–38
XML and, 105–106, 107, 175–182
  Commerce One-Net, 181
  discussion of applications, 175–177, 178,
    179
  ebXML, 177–180
  evolution of, 181–182
  RosettaNet, 180
Editor, text retrieval architecture, 53, 54
EJBs (Enterprise Java Beans), 12, 15–16, 41–42
Electronic books, 54
Electronic Business Extensible Markup Language
    (ebXML), 51, 177–180, 198
  decision support technologies, 199
  query language and query optimization, 186
Electronic data interchange (EDI), 4, 209
Elements, 127–128, 131
E-mail
  as knowledge management, 78, 79
  web mining, usage patterns, 36
Encapsulation (object-oriented model), 283
Encryption, 39–40, 209
End material, 126, 127
Enterprise applications, 230
Enterprise Java Beans (EJBs), 12, 15–16, 41–42
Enterprise resource management, e-commerce,
    94
Entertainment
  e-business, 94
  multimedia information management, 75
  web mining applications, 37
Entity-relationship data models, 257
European Research Consortium for Informatics
    and Mathematics (ERCIM), 200
eXcelon, 205, 206, 208–209
Expert systems, knowledge management, 78
Extensibility, DTDs, 136
Extensible database, 258, 260
Extensible Markup Language, *see* XML
Extensible Style Language (XSL), 117, 118, 137

F

Fault management, DBMS functions, 261
Fault tolerance, 267
    data management applications, 188, 189
    mobile agents, 84
    XML applications, 184
Federated databases, 270–271
    e-commerce, 100–101, 103, 105
    terminology, 243, *see also* Heterogeneous
        databases
    Web database management, 50
Federated distributed processor, 270–271
File manager, semistructured database
        architecture, 156, 157
Filtering agent, 81, 82, 84, 85, 86
Financial information systems, 201
Firewalls, 28, 209
Flat files, e-commerce applications, 176, 177
Format, text data structure, 54
Framework
    object technologies, 286
    XML, 4–7
Front-end tier, XML databases, 191, 192, 193
Future directions, 140–141, 142, 229–234
    e-commerce, 231
    web data management, 229–230
    XML and semantic web, 232
Fuzzy logic, 280

G

Gateways, database access, 41
Gemstone Systems, 242
Genesis web mining tools, 206
Geographic Markup Language, 220
Global data models, semistructured databases,
        30
Global metadata, distributed databases, 269
Government agencies, digital libraries, 17–18
Grant and revoke statements, 266
Granularity of data for auditing, 261
Graphs, updating, 187

H

Hashing, 264
Healthcare, 94, 96
Helpdesk, 96
Heterogeneous databases
    data mining trends, 281
    developments in, 242–243
    digital libraries, 19, 20–21
    integrating, 19, 189–190, 269–270, *see also*
        Integration of databases

interoperability, 249, 270, *see also*
        Interoperability
    metadata, 110, 115
    migrating legacy databases and applications,
        274–275
    multi-media DBMS, 68
    systems framework, 245
    web data management, 28, 29
Hewlett Packard developments in database
        systems, 240
HiLis software, 206
Honeywell developments in database systems, 241
HTML (Hypertext Markup Language), 11, 53, 133,
        185, 195
    data representation for web databases, 27, 28
    indexing documents, 117
    Java and, 15
    from Oracle databases, 203, 205
    WebDB, 204, 205, 206
    indexing, 117
HTTP (Hypertext Transfer Protocol), 12, 13, 40
Human computer interaction, 72
Hypermedia, 111
    web data management, 28
    WWW, 13
Hypersemantic data models, 161, 162
Hypertext Markup Language, *see* HTML
Hypertext Transfer Protocol (HTTP), 12, 13, 40
IBM
    data mining products, 280–281
    developments in database systems, 240, 241
    Distributed Relational Database Access
        (DRDA), 274
    knowledge management products, 198
    query processing techniques, 186
    web database management products, 206

I

IBM CXML, 186
Images/image data
    databases, 2
    metadata, 110
    mining, 33, *see also* Mining
        audio data applications, 66–67
        taxonomy for, 61
    multi-media DBMS, 68
    retrieval systems, 58–59
    video, *see* Video data
Indexing
    challenges and directions, 229
    HTML documents, 117
    storage management, 263–264
    XML documents, 177, 188
Inductive logic, 278, 280

Information extraction, DBMS functions, 261
Information infrastructures, collaborative
    computing, 73–74
Information management, 6, 7
    versus data management and knowledge
        management, 79–80
    e-business building blocks, 95, 96
    e-commerce functions, 105
    metadata, 110, 111
    semantic web, 216–217, 220
Information management applications, 195–202
    agents, 199–200
    collaborative computing, 196–198
    decision support, 199
    knowledge management, 198
    multimedia, 195–196
    other information technologies, 201
    wireless computing, 200–201
Information management technologies, 71–92
    agents for web, 80–85
    collaboration and data management, 71–74
    data management versus, 71
    decision support, 78–80
    knowledge management, 75–78
    miscellaneous, 85–91
        directions, 90–91
        quality-of-service aspects, 89
        training and distance learning, 86–87
        visualization, 87–88
        wireless information management, 89–90
    multimedia data management, 74–75
    semantic web, 144
    supporting technologies, 71–92
    WWW, 203–212, *see also* Data management,
        WWW
    XML and, 91, 92
Information request, pull model, 84, 86
Information Resource Dictionary System (IRDS),
    241
Information retrieval systems, 2, 3, 6, 7, 53–70
    agents, 83, *see* Retrieval agents
    augmentation of, 55, 56
    audio, 64–67
    image, 58–59
    markup languages and SGML, 68–70
    multimedia data types, 67–68
    supporting technologies, 53–70
    text, 53–57
    video, 59–64
    XML and, 70
Information service, distributed object
    management, 91
Information sharing, web crawlers, 209
Information systems, building data management
    systems, 248–250

information technologies, e-commerce, 104–105
Informix
    developments in database systems, 240
    web database management products, 206
Infoworld, 203, 204
Infrastructure, web, 234
Ingres Corporation developments in database
    systems, 240
Ingres Project, 257
Inheritance (object-oriented model), 283–284
Integration manager, semistructured databases,
    156, 158
Integration of databases, 217–219
    heterogeneous, 19, 189–190, 269–270
        digital library, 20–21
        web data management, 28, 29
    semistructured, 31, 156, 158
    web, 44
Integration platform, web as, 234
Integration with ORBs, data management
    applications, 193, 194
Integrity, 265–266
    data management applications, 188, 189
    DBMS functions, 261
    web data management, 28, 29
Integrity manager, distributed (DIM), 269
Intelligence analysis, web mining tools, 206
Interactive data mining, 87–88
Interface Definition Language (IDL), 44, 193,
    286
International Federation for Information
    Processing (IFIP) conference on
    database security, 38
Internationalization, 140, 141
International Standards Organization (ISO), 11
    remote database access (RDA) standard, 273
    web mining standards, 36
    XML internationalization, 140
Internet, *see* World Wide Web
Interoperability, 205
    client-server architecture-based, 272–273
    database systems, 241
    data management applications, 189–190
    e-commerce, 101, 106, 177
    heterogeneous databases, 249, 270
    metadata and, 183–184
    semantic web, 150–151, 152, 217–219
    semistructured databases, 167
    web-based, 13
    Web database management, 42, 44–45
    web data management, 28, 29
    XML applications, 51
Intranets, knowledge management, 78
ISO, *see* International Standards Organization
Is-part-of-hierarchy, 284

J

Java, 11, 12, 13, 285
    applets as agents, 82, 83
    query processing techniques, 186
    XML applications, 51
Java 2 Enterprise Edition (J2EE), 51, 203, 205,
    211–212
Java Database Connectivity (JDBC), 16, 18, 41,
    204
JavaScript programming, 196
JDBC (Java Database Connectivity), 16, 18, 41,
    204
JINI, 12, 16
Journalism, multimedia information management,
    75
Junglee system, 33

K

KDD Nuggets, 206
Kensington Open Infrastructure for Enterprise
    Data Mining, 206
Keywords
    text retrieval, 53–54
    XML document indexing, 188
Knowbots, 209
Knowledge
    metadata and, 184
    resource description frameworks,
        134, 135
    XML schemas, 138
Knowledge desktop, 208
Knowledge Discovery in Databases Conference
    (1998), 39
Knowledge Discovery in Databases Conference
    (1999), 32
Knowledge management, 2, 234
    versus data management and information
        management, 79–80
    e-commerce, 106
    information management technologies, 75–78,
        198
    semantic web, 144, 220
Knowledge Management Platform, 207–208
Knowledge management tools, 205, 207–208
Knowledge service, distributed object
    management, 91

L

Lagunita report, 242
Languages
    multiple, data mining trends, 282
    XML internationalization, 140

Learning, 85–86, *see also* Training
    e-business, 94, 96
    knowledge management, 77, 78
Legacy databases
    data mining trends, 281
    integration with ORBs, 194
    metadata, 115
    migration, 45–47, 189–190, 274–275, *see also*
        Interoperability
    semantic web interoperability, 150
    systems framework, 245
    XML data integration issues, 139–140
Legal aspects, security and privacy issues, 39
Libraries, digital, *see* Database management,
    WWW; Digital libraries
Library data, text data structure, 54
Library of Congress digital libraries, 18
Links, 117, 118, 131, 134, 136–137
LISP, 285
Location of resources, 82
    agent functions, 80–81
    pull model, 84, 86
Locator agents, 83, 84, 85
Lockheed Martin Corporation data mining tools,
    278
Log files
    fault tolerance, 267
    transaction management, 263
Loose-coupling integration architecture, 156, 157
LORE project, 30, 167–168

M

Machine learning, 278, 279
Management
    data, *see* Data management
    database, *see* Database management
    e-commerce functions, 105
    semistructured databases, 31
Manager functions, e-commerce, 99
Maps
    semistructured databases, 31
    three-tier computing, 43
Marketing, 104, 105
Markup languages, retrieval systems, 68–70
Markup tags, XML, 118
Mass storage
    data management systems, 246
    digital libraries, 19
Mediation, 104, 105
Mediator approach to database migration,
    47, 48
Mermaid, 241
Message-oriented middleware (MOM), three-tier
    computing, 42

Metadata, 2, 3, 6, 7, 205
    challenges and directions, 230
    data management applications, 183–184, 185
    DBMS functions, 261
    distributed management, 189
    e-commerce functions, 105–106
    image, 59
    mining trends, 281
    semantic web, 144
    semistructured database architecture, 156, 157
    WWW, 22, 208–209
    XML schemas, 137, 138
Metadata, ontologies, and XML, 108–119
    background on metadata, 109–110, 111
    mining and metadata, 111–115
    ontologies, note in, 115–116, 117
    supporting technologies, 109–119
    for WWW, 111
    XML and, 117–119
Metadata management, 2, 265
    semistructured databases, 164
    web data management, 28, 29
Metadata manager
    distributed (DMM), 269
    text retrieval, 53, 54
Metalanguage, XML as, 27
Metamodels, semistructured databases, 30, 161,
        163
Microsoft
    ActiveX, 209
    developments in database systems, 240
    DOTNET, 211
    knowledge management tools, 207–208
    Open Database Connectivity (ODBC),
        273–274
    query processing techniques, 186
    Simple Object Access Protocol (SOAP), 51
    web database management products, 206
Microsoft OLE/COM, 44
Middle-tier server
    three-tier multimedia computing, 75, 76
    XML databases, 191, 192, 193
Migration, 274–275
    data management applications, 189–190
    metadata and, 183–184
    mobile agents, 84
    semantic web, 215
    semistructured databases, 167
    systems framework, 245
    Web database management, 45–47
    XML applications, 51
MINEit Software, 206
Mining, 205, 206, 277–282
    agent functions, 82
    audio data, 65–67, 66–67

challenges and directions, 229
data management
    applications, 190–191
    technology overview, 243, 244
DBMS functions, 261
as decision support tool, 78–79
definitions, 277–278
digital libraries, 19
directions and trends, 281–282
e-commerce, 100, 105
heterogeneous data integration, 44
images, 59
metadata, 110, 111–115
security, 266
technologies, 278–279
text, 55–57, 62
video, 60, 62, 63, 64, 63
visualization technologies, 87–88
Web data, 13, 28, 205, 206–207
Web database management, 30–40
    applications and directions, 37–38
    mining on web, 32–36
    security and privacy concerns, 38–40
    usage patterns, 36
    XML applications, 51, 184
Mobile agents, 82, 83, 84, 199–200
Mobile code, 83, 84
Modeling, data, see Data modeling; Data models
Model for semantic web, 144, 146
Money transfer transactions, 40
Monitoring agents, 84, 85
Monitoring of situations, agent for, 81, 82
Multibase, 241
Multilevel security, 166–167
Multimedia, 205, 234
    annotations, 195
    collaborative computing, 71, 72
    databases
        digital libraries, 19
        management, 250
        metadata, 115
        semistructured, 159, 160, 161, 163
        WWW, 21–22
    data management, 2
    data management technology overview, 244
    data models, 161, 163
    data types, retrieval systems, 67–68
    e-commerce, 106
    information management, 91
        applications, 195–196
        technologies, 74–75
    markup languages, 196
    mining, 33–34, 34, 281
    quality-of-service issues, 89
    semantic web, 144

semistructured databases, 30
systems framework, 245
technical developments, 242
web tools for information processing, 209
Multimedia distributed processors (MDP), 75

N

Namespaces, 128–129, 131
National Aeronautical and Space Administration
    digital libraries, 17
National Information Infrastructure (NII), 14
National Science Foundation (NSF), 17, 200
National Science Foundation (NSF) Lagunita
    Report, 242
Native XML Databases (NXDB), 185
Natural language processing, 201
Negotiations, 104, 105
Net Analysis, 205
Net Genesis products, 205, 206–207
Netscape browsers, 209
NetTracker software, 206
Network communications, multimedia information
    management, 75
Networking, 246, 250
Network protocol security, 40
Networks, collaborative computing, 72
Neural networks, 66–67, 278, 280

O

OASIS (Organization of the Advancement of
    Structured Information Standards),
    178–179, 186
Object Design Inc., 242
Object Management Group (OMG)
    challenges and directions, 229
    CORBA, 274, 286
    e-commerce services special interest group,
        101
    ORB-based tools, 44, 209
    web mining standards, 36
Object Modeling Technique (OMT), 286
Object models/object technology, 282–287
    CORBA, 274
    databases
        developments in, 241–242
        e-commerce applications, 176–177, 178
        metadata, 115
    data management applications, 193
    image processing system, 58
    management
        heterogeneous database interoperability,
            249
        XML applications, 184

migrating legacy databases and applications,
    274–275
object data model, 282–285
other object technologies, 285–286
semantic web, 215
semistructured databases 159, 160
    design of databases, 259
    XML document models, 161, 163
technologies, 282, 283
three-tier computing, 42, 43
Object-oriented programming languages, 285
Object-Oriented Programming Systems,
    Languages, and Applications
    (OOPSLA), 286
Object Query Language, Java applications, 16
Object-relational models, semistructured database,
    159, 160, 161, 163
Object request broker (ORB), 36, 209
    client-server database access, 274
    component integration, 44, 45
    e-commerce, 101, 104
    heterogeneous data source integration, 44
    infrastructure challenges and directions, 229
    integration, data management applications,
        193, 194
    interfaces, 44
    three-tier computing, 42, 43
ODBC (Open Database Connectivity), 16, 18,
    273–274
Office Document Architecture, 27, 28
Office information systems, 242
OLE/COM, integration of heterogeneous
    databases, 44
OMG, *see* Object Management Group
Object Management Group (OMG)
    challenges and directions, 229
    CORBA, 274, 286
    e-commerce services special interest group,
        101
    ORB-based tools, 44, 209
    web mining standards, 36
One.Net, 180, 181, 198
One-to-many links, 118
Online analytical processing (OLAP), 276
Online transaction processing (OLTP), 276
Ontologies, 2, 3, 6, 7, 115–116, 117, 234, *see also*
        Metadata, ontologies, and XML
    challenges and directions, 230
    metadata, 183, 184
    resource description frameworks, 134, 135,
        217
    semantic web, 144, 217
        interoperability, 150, 151
        role of, 148
    XML issues, 138, 141, 142

Ontology Interchange Language (OIL), 200
Ontos Inc., 242
Open Database Connectivity (ODBC), 16, 18,
         273–274
OPENXML, query processing techniques, 186
Oracle
    browser tools, 209
    developments in database systems, 240
    knowledge management products, 198
    web database system tools, 204, 205, 206
ORB, *see* Object request broker
Organizational behavior, collaborative computing
         and, 72
Organization of the Advancement of Structured
         Information Standards (OASIS),
         178–179, 186

P

Paragraph objects, 284
Parallel architectures, 242
Pattern detection
    audio data, 66–67
    image mining, 59, 60
    video, 62
Personalized services, push model, 48
Pointers, 117, 131, 134, 136, 137, 187
Policies and procedures, database administration,
         261
Political and legal aspects, security and privacy
         issues, 39
Polymorphism (object-oriented model), 283,
         284
Portals, XML for, 198
Prediction of trends, web mining, 36
Presentation layer, XML databases, 191, 192,
         193
Privacy, *see also* Security
    challenges and directions, 229
    data mining trends, 281–282
Private database mining, 37
Proactive agents, 81
Problem solving, collaborative computing, 71
Process control, technical developments, 242
Procurement, e-business, 94, 96
Programming languages, object-oriented, 285
Prolog, 125, 127
Protocols, security of, 40
Prototypes, 6, 7
Public databases, web mining applications, 37
Publishers, semantic web model, 144, 145
Pull model, 84, 86
Purchasing, 72, 104, 105
Push model, 47–49, 84, 85
Push-pull models, 47–49

Q

Quality of service, 85–86
    information management technologies, 89
    semistructured databases, 165
Queries/query processing, 2, 262, *see also* SQL
    audio, 64–65
    challenges and directions, 230
    data management applications, 186
    DBMS functions, 261
    digital library, 19, 20
    distributed (DQP), 189, 269
    heterogeneous databases
         Aquarelle project, 168
         integration, 269–270
    images, 59
    semantic web, 144
    semistructured data management, 3, 162, 163
    text retrieval, 53–54, 57
    transaction management, 164
    video data, 60, 63
    web data management, 27, 28, 184
    XML (XMLQL, Xquery), 28, 118, 138–139,
         162, 184, 186
Query languages
    heterogeneous database integration,
         269–270
    W3C activities, 24
Query manager, *see* Architecture

R

Radio, audio data, 65
RDA (Remote Database Access), 241, 273
RDF, *see* Resource description framework
Real estate, 94
Real-time processing
    e-commerce, 106
    information management and, 91
    multi-media, 68
    semistructured databases, 166
Real-time service, distributed object management,
         91
Recovery
    database integrity, 265
    transaction management, 263
Recovery methods, 188
Relational calculus, 257
Relational databases
    data model development, 30
    developments in database systems, 240,
         240–241
    e-commerce applications, 176, 177
    metadata, 115
    text data conversion to, 55–56

three-tier computing, 42
web mining, 34
Relational data model, 256–257
semistructured databases, XML document
models, 161, 163
text data structure, 54
Relational interfaces, mining, 33
Relations, generation from representations, 260
Relationships, text processing, 54
Remote Database Access (RDA), 241, 273
Remote Method Invocation (RMI), 12, 16
Representations, generation of relations from, 260
Requests, models of communication, 47–49
Resource description framework (RDF), 134, 135,
141, 142, 143, 183
decision support technologies, 199
metadata and, 184
migrating legacy databases, 190
semantic web, 145–148, 150–151, 152, 215,
217–219, 220
Resource location
agent functions, 80–81, 82, 83
web crawlers, 209
Responsive agents, 81
Result-SetXML Java class, query processing
techniques, 186
Retrieval, *see* Information retrieval
Retrieval agents, 81, 82, 83, 85
mobile agents as, 84
pull model, 84, 86
Retrieval algorithms, storage management, 264
RMI (Remote Method Invocation), 11, 16
Root element, 125–126, 127
RosettaNet, 180, 198
Rough sets, 278, 280

S

Sales, 104, 105
Sane Solutions web mining tools, 206
Scalability, challenges and directions, 229
Schemas, 131, 137–138, 141, 142
architectural issues, 258, 259
heterogeneous database integration, 269–270
metadata and, 184
SDD-I, 241
Search engines, web mining applications, 38
secure Java, 209
Secure mobile agents, 83
Secure transactions, 40
Security, 205, 266–267
challenges and directions, 229
database administration, 260–261
data management applications, 188, 189
data mining trends, 281

DBMS functions, 261
distributed management, 189
distributed object management, 91
e-commerce, 105, 106
encryption products, 209
information management and, 91
semistructured databases, 166–167
W3C activities, 24
Web data management, 28, 29
Web database mining, 38–40
XML applications, 184
XML documents, 51
Security manager, distributed (DSM), 269
Semantic data models, image processing system,
58
Semantics, 133–134, 135, 234
decision support technologies, 199
interoperability, 217
metadata, 183, 184
resource description frameworks, 134, 135
semantic web, 217
XML issues, 141
data integration, 140
evolution, 184
XML limitations, 118
Semantic web, 4, 6, 7, 143–153
agents and DAML program, 148–149
challenges and directions, 232
concepts, 144–145
as database, 149–152
ontologies, 148
RDF, 145–148
techniques, 143–44
web versus semantic web, 152, 153
XML, RDF, and interoperability, 150–151,
152
Semantic web construction, 213–221
data and information management, 216–217
evolution and architecture, 214–216
interoperability, XML, and RDF,
217–219
putting it together, 220–221
web services, 219
web versus semantic web, 213–214
Semistructured databases, 4, 6, 7, 155–169
architectures, 156, 157
data management applications, 185
data models, 157–161
developments in, 167–168
e-commerce applications, 176, 177
functions, 161–167
data distribution, 164–165
data integrity and security, 162, 163,
166–167
metadata management, 164

quality of service, 165
real-time processing, 166
storage management, 164
transaction management, 164
user interface, 166
interoperability and migration of, 167
mining, 33–34
warehousing, 190–191
WWW, 30
XML and, 167
Semistructured data management, 3
Sequence detection (data mining), 280
Serializability, transaction management, 263
Servers, *see also* Client-server architecture
access without gateways, 42
applications and data, 43
e-commerce, 104, 105, 106
security, 40
three-tier computing, 43, 75, 76
Services, e-business, 94
Servlets, as agents, 82
SetXML, query processing techniques, 186
Seurity tools, 205
SGML (Standard Generalized Markup Language),
11, 53, 133, 185, 195
data representation for web databases,
27, 28
retrieval systems, 68–70
Simple Object Access Protocol (SOAP), 51, 132,
179, 203, 204, 205, 210, 233
Situation monitoring agents, 81, 82, 84, 85
SMIL, 196
SOAP (Simple Object Access Protocol), 51, 132,
179, 203, 204, 205, 210, 233
Social agents, 81
Software
web application server tools, 207
web mining tools, 206
SPARC (Systems Planning and Resource
Committee), 241
Speech, audio data, 65
Speech processing, 201
SQL (Structured Query Language)
database system standardization, 241
Java applications, 16
Oracle utility, 206
relational data model, 257
semistructured multimedia database, 161
web database management, 25
XMLSQL, 162
SQL Access Group Call Level Interface (CLI),
274
SQL-based relational data miner, 34
Standard Generalized Markup Language, *see*
SGML

Standardization, database systems, 241
Standards, 6, 7
database system standardization, 241
Java applications, 16
W3C activities, 24
WWW, 11, 12, 13
data model, 24
web mining, 36
Statistical packages, 278–279
Storage, 2, 263–264
data management applications, 187–188
multimedia data management for
collaboration, 249
semantic web, 144
semistructured databases, 3, 164
web data management, 28, 28, 29
XML documents, 177
Storage manager, *see* Architecture
Structure
document, metadata, 183
object databases, XML representation,
176
Structured Query Language, *see* SQL
Supply chain management, e-business, 94
Supporting technologies, 2, 3, 6, 7, 249–250
data management systems, 246
e-commerce, 93–107, *see also* E-commerce
information management technologies, 71–92,
see also Information management
technologies
information retrieval systems, 53–70, *see also*
Information retrieval systems
metadata, ontologies, and XML, 109–119, *see
also* Metadata, ontologies, and XML
web database management, 25–52, *see also*
Database management, WWW
WWW, 15–23
digital libraries, 17–21
HTML, review of, 23
hypermedia systems, 21–22
Java, role of, 15–16, 17
Sybase
developments in database systems, 240
query processing techniques, 186
Syntax
interoperability, 217
resource description frameworks, 134, 135
semantic web heterogeneity, 217
XML, 142
XML evolution, 184
System Development Corporation (SDC), 241
System R, 241
System security officer (SSO), 260–261
Systems Planning and Resource Committee
(SPARC), 241

T

Tags, *see also* Domain-type definitions
    markup, 118
    semistructured database architecture, 156, 157
Taxonomy
    audio data, 64–65
    audio mining, 67
    image retrieval and mining, 59, 61
    text retrieval, 57
    video retrieval, 63, 64
Taxonomy for web mining, 32
Teaching, *see* Learning; Training
Team spirit, knowledge management, 76–77
Technologies, 2–3, 4, 6, 7, *see also* Supporting
        technologies
Telecommunications, 199–200
Teleconferencing, 250
Text data
    audio data integration with, 65
    data management system developments and
        trends, 250–251, 252
    extraction from video, 62
    mining
        integration for multimedia mining, 69
        multimedia, 34
        multi-media DBMS, 68
        retrieval systems, 53–57
        semistructured databases, 30, 31
Text retrieval, 2
Third-party agent, web mining applications, 38
Three-layer model, systems framework, 245–246
Three-level schema, database system
        standardization, 241
Three-schema architecture, 258, 259
Three-tier architecture
    e-commerce client-server, 100, 102
    multimedia computing, 75, 76
    semantic web, 215–216
    Web database management, 42, 43
    XML databases, 191, 192, 193
Tight-coupling architecture, 156, 157
Training, 85–86, 205
    challenges and directions, 230
    e-business and e-commerce, 96, 106
    information management technologies, 86–87,
        91
    knowledge management, 77, 78
Transaction processing and management, 2,
        262–263
    challenges and directions, 229, 230
    data management applications, 186
    DBMS functions, 261
    distributed, 189
    online (OLTP), 276

recovery, 263
semantic web, 144
semistructured databases, 164
web data management, 28, 29
XML applications, 184
Transmission Control Protocol and Internet
        Protocol (TCP/IP, 11
Trends, 1–2, 36
Trojan horses, 40
Trust, e-business, 99
Two-phase commit, 263
Two-tier client-server system, e-commerce, 99

U

Uniform Modeling Language (UML)
    data representation for web databases,
        27, 28
    object technology, 193, 282–283
Uniform resource identifiers (URIs), 129
Uniform resource locators (URLs), semistructured
        databases, 168
United Nations Center for Trade Facilitation and
        Electronic Business (UN/CEFACT),
        178–179
Universal Business Language (UBL), 179
Universal Description Discovery and Integration
        (UDDI), 203, 204, 205, 211, 233
Universities and schools, e-business building
        blocks, 95, 96
University of California Ingres project, 257
Update manager, *see* Architecture
Updating
    DBMS functions, 261
    transaction processing, 187
Usage patterns, web mining, 36, 37
Usecases, 286
User identification, database security, 266
User interface, semistructured databases, 166

V

Versant Object Technology, 242
Video data
    audio data management, 65
    databases, 2
    mining, 33, 34, 69
    multimedia, 34, 69
    multimedia DBMS, 68
    retrieval systems, 59–64
Virtual relational databases, web mining, 34
Visualization, 205
    e-commerce, 106
    heterogeneous database interoperability, 249
    information management, 87–88, 91

mining, 35, 279
multimedia data management for
    collaboration, 249
Visuals, three-tier computing, 43

W

Warehousing, 275–276
    database security, 266
    data management applications, 190–191
    data management technology overview, 243,
        244
    DBMS functions, 261
    heterogeneous data source integration, 44
    metadata, 110, 111
    text database, 56
    web data management, 28
    web mining, 34, 35
    XML applications, 184
Web, *see* World Wide Web
Web browsers, *see* Browsers
Web crawlers, 209
WebDB, 204, 205, 206, 206, 209
WebLogic software, 205, 207
Web Services Description Language (WSDL),
        179, 203, 204, 205, 210–211, 219
White spaces, 125
Wireless Application Protocol (WAP), 200, 201
Wireless information
    information management applications,
        200–201
    information management technologies, 89–90
Wireless Markup Language (WML), 200–201
Work flow systems, collaborative computing, 72
Work groups, collaborative computing, 71
Workshops, XML, 8
World Wide Web, 6, 7, 11–24
    access to databases, 234
    agents, 80–85
    browser/client, 205, *see also* Browsers
    collaborative computing, 73–74
    corporate information infrastructures, 14
    database management, *see also* Database
        management, WWW
        agent functions, 82
        supporting technologies, 25–52
    databases, 3, 6, 7
        metadata, 115, 265
        terminology, 25
    data and information management, 203–212,
        see also Data management, WWW
    challenges and directions, 229–230
    technology overview, 243, 244
    e-business, hosting services, 94
    evolution of, 12–14

knowledge management, 78, 79
metadata, 110, 111
mining trends, 281, *see* Mining
security protocols, 40
semantic web comparison, 152, 153, 213–214
semantic web services, 219
servers, 205, *see also* Client-server
    architecture; Servers
    access without gateways, 42
    three-tier computing, 43, 75, 76, *see also*
        Three-tier architecture
server tools, 205
standards, 11
supporting technologies, 11–24
    digital libraries, 17–21
    HTML, review of, 23
    hypermedia systems, 21–22
    Java, role of, 15–16, 17
trends, 1
usage tracking software, 206
Web pages, 4
    e-commerce client-server architecture,
        99–103
    as knowledge management, 79
    from Oracle databases, 203, 205
    WWW consortium and XML, 23–24
World Wide Web Consortium (W3C), 13
    data and information management white
        papers, 203
    query language and query optimization, 186
    SMIL specifications, 196
    web mining standards, 36
    and XML, 23–24, 27, 28
Wrappers, 185
WSDL (Web Services Description Language),
        179, 203, 204, 205, 210–211, 219

X

Xlink, 117, 134, 136–137, 187
XML
    challenges and directions, 232
    e-commerce, 105–106, 107
    information management technologies, 91, 92
    retrieval systems, 70
    and semantic web, 150–151, 152, 217–219, *see*
        also Advanced concepts in XML; Basic
        concepts in XML; Semantic web
    semistructured databases, 167, *see also*
        Semistructured databases
    Web database management, 50–52
XML applications, 3–4, 5, 6, 7, 246, 249
XML framework, 4–7
XML link language (Xlink), 117, 134, 136–137,
        187

XML pointer language (Xpointer), 117, 134, 136, 137, 187
XML Query Language (XMLQL), 118, 138–139
  development of, 186
  web database management, 28
XML standards for B-to-B exchange (XCC), 198

XML technologies, 2–3, 4, 6, 7, *see also* Supporting technologies
XML tools, WWW, 208–209
Xpath, 137
Xpointer, 117, 134, 136, 137, 187
Xquery, 118, 162
XSL (Extensible Style Language), 117, 118

9 780367 396244